CATAPHRACTS

For my brother, Sean, and my grandfather, Robert.
You are missed every day.

CATAPHRACTS

Knights of the Ancient Eastern Empires

Erich B Anderson

Pen & Sword
MILITARY

First published in Great Britain in 2016 by
PEN & SWORD MILITARY
an imprint of
Pen & Sword Books Ltd
47 Church Street
Barnsley
South Yorkshire
S70 2AS

ISBN 978-1-47383-798-0

Printed and bound in England By
CPI Group (UK) Ltd, Croydon, CR0 4YY.

Pen & Sword Books Ltd incorporates the Imprints of Pen & Sword Aviation,
Pen & Sword Family History, Pen & Sword Maritime, Pen & Sword Military,
Pen & Sword Discovery, Pen & Sword Politics, Pen & Sword Atlas, Pen & Sword
Archaeology, Wharncliffe Local History, Wharncliffe True Crime, Wharncliffe
Transport, Pen & Sword Select, Pen & Sword Military Classics, Leo Cooper, The
Praetorian Press, Claymore Press, Remember When, Seaforth Publishing and
Frontline Publishing.

For a complete list of Pen & Sword titles please contact
PEN & SWORD BOOKS LIMITED
47 Church Street, Barnsley, South Yorkshire, S70 2AS, England
E-mail: enquiries@pen-and-sword.co.uk
Website: www.pen-and-sword.co.uk

CONTENTS

ACKNOWLEDGEMENTS

First of all, I am extremely grateful to Philip Sidnell of Pen & Sword who has not only given me this opportunity to write my first history book, but has also been crucial to the editing process. Furthermore, I want to thank him and several other historians for their earlier work, who have all helped me greatly in telling the story of the cataphracts, including Mariusz Mielczarek, John W. Eadie, M. Michalak, Valerii P. Nikonorov, M.P. Speidel, Bezalel Bar-Kochva, Eric McGeer, and Timothy Dawson, among many others. I must also give my thanks to Dominic Allen for his superb work on the design for the book cover/jacket, and also to Matthew Jones for his excellent work on the production of the book.

I owe a great amount of gratitude to Northern Illinois University as well, particularly the faculty of the history and anthropology departments. Among these excellent professors, I especially need to thank Jason Hawke, Michael Kolb and Valerie Garver. They were pivotal to my early development as a historian and without their guidance I may not have become the published author that I am today.

Jasper Oorthuys of *Ancient Warfare* accepted my first magazine article proposal, which was titled 'The Seleucid Cataphract: Origins of Armored Cavalry.' This first freelance job not only initiated my career as a writer, but also writing the article made me realize that few people outside of the academic world were even aware of the existence of cataphracts. Therefore, the article helped to put me on the path of creating this book, so for that I owe an enormous debt of gratitude to him. Additionally, I am very grateful to Josho Brouwers, Dirk van Gorp, Edward Zapletal, Erin van der Pijl, Paul Lay, William Welsh, Tim Williamson, Alicea Francis, Lindsay Fulcher, Thomas Hauck, Neil Faulkner, Charlotte Crow, Dennis C. Forbes, J. Peter Phillips, Kyle Lockwood, Peter Konieczny and Jona Lendering. These editors have made it possible for me to pursue my dream career so I give them my deepest thanks.

And last, but certainly not least, I am extremely thankful for the amazing family and friends I am lucky to have in my life, especially my mother and father, Martina and Mark. Without their love and support I may not have gotten this far with my history writing and for that

I am beyond grateful. Furthermore, gratitude is due to Kim, Johnny and Rich. Special thanks must also be given to Shannon, Hillary, Jason, Dan, Joe, Rod, P.J. and Ben, among many others that would take too long to list. Becoming a writer is difficult, but their friendship and help have made it easier.

LIST OF ILLUSTRATIONS

1. Seleucid arms and armour captured by the Romans after their victory at Magnesia in 190 BC. Illustration by Mark Birge-Anderson.
2. Terracotta plaque of a Parthian cataphract hunting a lion, from Babylonia, 2nd century AD. British Museum, London.
3. Depiction of a fully armoured cataphract. Redrawn version of a crude graffito found at Dura Europos, 2nd–3rd century AD. Illustration by Mark Birge-Anderson.
4. A fragment of ancient Roman scale armour (*lorica squamata*). Museum of Somerset, Taunton, UK.
5. Sarmatian cataphracts flee from Roman cavalry during the Dacian wars (AD 101–106) from the reliefs on Trajan's Column, Rome, constructed in AD 113. Photo by Conrad Cichorius, 1896.
6. Sassanian cavalryman with a *kontos* attacking a fully armoured Parthian rider. Silver plate with gold coating. Azerbaijan Museum, Tabriz, Iran. Photo by Alborz Fallah.
7. Relief from Firzubad, Iran, depicting the victory in AD 224 of the Sassanian emperor, Ardashir I (r. 224–242), and his son, Prince Shapur. Illustration by Eugene Flandin, 1840.
8. Relief from Naqsh-i Rustam, Iran, depicting the Sassanian emperor, Bahram II (r. 274–293), in combat with a foe carrying a broken *kontos*.
9. Relief from Naqsh-i Rustam, Iran, showing a Sassanian emperor, Hormuzd II (r. 303–309), unhorsing an unknown opponent.
10. A relief of a Sassanian ruler armoured as a *clibanarius* from Taq-i Bustan, Iran. It depicts either Khosrow II (r. 590-628) or Peroz I (r. 459-484). Photograph by Javad Yousefi.
11. Drawing of a relief, which depicts laminated limb armour and a helmet with a metal facemask, from the Column of Arcadius, constructed in 5th century Constantinople.
12. Mosaic depicting a Late Roman armoured cavalryman mounted on an armoured horse. Photograph courtesy of Simon MacDowall.
13. Facemask for Roman cavalry, early 1st century AD, from Kalkriese. Museum und Park Kalkriese, Germany. Photograph by Carole Raddato.

INTRODUCTION

Over 2,000 years ago in the spring of 53 BC, Roman general Marcus Licinius Crassus led an enormous army across the Euphrates River in Mesopotamia. Crassus was the third member of the Triumvirate, the alliance of the three most powerful senators who ruled the Roman Republic, which included Pompey the Great and Julius Caesar. Even though he had acquired more wealth than any other plutocrat in the capital and achieved great renown for crushing the slave revolt of Spartacus, Crassus craved further glory in order to ultimately surpass his two rivals. In emulation of Alexander the Great, Crassus planned to accomplish his goal through the conquest of the East; primarily, against the warriors of the Parthian Empire, Rome's most powerful adversary along its vast borders. Therefore, he raised a considerable force of seven legions, 4,000 auxiliary light infantry, and 3,000 cavalry; altogether, a huge host that numbered between 42,000 and 44,000 men.[1]

Given the past encounters between the Romans and the armies of the east, Crassus and his numerous soldiers traversed the enemy territory with confidence; first from the successful campaign of Lucius Lucullus, along with those led by Pompeius Magnus, the two generals had practically turned the entire region into client kingdoms under Roman hegemony. And yet, regardless of their overwhelming belief in their own martial superiority, fear lingered amongst many of the Roman legionaries due to reports proclaiming the extreme lethality of the Parthians' soldiers and their tactics. According to Plutarch, an eyewitness account stated:

> 'When [the Parthians] pursued', they declared, 'there was no escaping them, and when they fled, there was no taking them; and strange missiles are the precursors of their appearance, which pierce through every obstacle before one sees who sent them; and their cataphracts were so provided that their weapons would cut through anything, and their armour give way to nothing'.[2]

The legionaries knew how deadly the Parthian horse-archers were with their deadly missiles, but it was the latter warriors mentioned in the report that caused far more terror within the Roman ranks; the mounted warriors called cataphracts. The Romans had known about such heavily armoured cavalrymen for over a century, ever since they first overcame the formidable warriors at the Battle of Magnesia in 190 BC. More recently, in 69 BC, Lucullus and his men had slain many of them at the Battle of Tigranocerta. However, the terrible thought of thousands of mounted warriors, in which both the riders and their steeds were fully encased in armour, rushing down upon them, wielding gigantic lances that could easily pierce straight through the most heavily armoured infantryman, was enough to cause dread in even some of the bravest legionaries.

Crassus and his legions pursued the Parthian army until the two forces finally confronted each other in the open desert near the town of Carrhae on 6 May. After the fear was allowed to swell within them for weeks over their inevitable clash with the cataphracts, the Roman legionaries were incredibly relieved to see that their enemy only numbered a paltry 1,000 cavalrymen, all of which appeared to be clothed merely in hides. The cataphracts in their bright armour were nowhere to be seen, a cause for hope to spread throughout the Roman ranks. However, the optimism was quickly dashed, as according to Plutarch:

> But when [the Parthians] were near the Romans and the signal was raised by their commander, first of all they filled the plain with the sound of a deep and terrifying roar. For the Parthians do not incite themselves to battle with horns or trumpets, but they have hollow drums of distended hide, covered with bronze bells, and on these they beat all at once in many quarters, and the instruments give forth a low and dismal tone, a blend of wild beast's roar and harsh thunder peal. They had rightly judged that, of all the senses, hearing is the one most apt to confound the soul, soonest rouses its emotions, and most effectively unseats the judgment.[3]

Then the terror within the hearts of the Roman soldiers increased considerably, for their worst nightmare was realized; the Parthian commander, Surena, had cunningly ordered the front ranks of his cavalry to cover themselves with animal skins and robes; his clever deception was soon revealed:

> When [the Parthians] had sufficiently terrified the Romans with their noise, they threw off the covering of their armour, and shone like lightning in their breastplates and helmets of polished Margianian steel, and with their horses covered with brass and steel trappings.[4]

The cataphracts were revealed in all of their magnificent, yet dreadful, glory, clad from head to toe in metal armour, upon steeds covered with metal as well. Yet the trickery of Surena was not over, for the Romans next witnessed in horror that another 9,000 horse-archers were concealed behind the recently unveiled cataphracts. The superb generalship of the Parthian commander became only more apparent as the battle raged on, since he showed the Romans how deadly and effective the heavily armoured lancers can be when used in conjunction with the highly mobile missile launchers. At the Battle of Carrhae, Surena, with his Parthian cataphracts and horse-archers, caused one of the most disastrous defeats the Romans ever endured (Described in detail in Chapter 3: The Parthian Cataphracts).

Who were these ancient cavalrymen that so closely resembled knights, yet existed centuries before the medieval warrior came to be? And where did the cataphracts come from? This book is the author's attempt to answer these questions using the numerous ancient accounts of these warriors, along with several extraordinary archaeological discoveries that have been made which support the existence of such a heavily armoured warrior who lived in the ancient world. Fortunately, there is also an extensive amount of research that has been done on the subject of ancient heavy cavalry and the cataphracts by many prominent experts, from early scholars such as William Woodthorpe Tarn, R.M. Rattenbury, M.I. Rostovtzeff and John W. Eadie, to more recent work by A.D.H. Bivar, Valerii P. Nikonorov and Mariusz Mielczarek. However, whereas the focus of most of their work has been the scholarly pursuit to discover the exact distinctions between the cataphracts and their variant types (mainly the difference between the terms *cataphracti*, *cataphractarii* and *clibanarii*), the goal of this book is to be more of a general history of all of the different types of cataphracts from their origins in the Ancient era to the Middle Ages. The elite infantrymen of Antiquity, specifically the Hellenistic hoplite and the Roman legionary, have received a considerable amount of attention from scholars throughout the twentieth and early twenty-first centuries, with a large amount of books written specifically about them. Likewise, few can dispute the popularity of armour-clad medieval knights, with more than their fair share of media devoted to them, from history books to historical fiction, fantasy novels and even in a considerable amount of cinematic films as well. On the other hand, the story of the cataphracts has rarely been told. Therefore, hopefully, this book will serve as an introduction to the cataphracts for general readers of the public who are fascinated with ancient military history, but who were unaware of, or knew little about, the existence of the extraordinary armoured horsemen.

Long before the knight dominated the European battlefields of the Middle Ages, the cataphracts struck both awe and terror across the ancient world. The word 'cataphract' is originally derived from the Greek term *kataphraktos* (pl. *kataphraktoi*), which literally means 'covered with armour'. However, the modern English name for the heavy cavalrymen is more similar to the Roman Latin variant of the term, which is *cataphractus* (pl. *cataphracti*). The most basic arms and armour of the earliest cataphracts included a metal helmet made of either bronze or iron, and a lamellar, mail or scale cuirass to protect the torso, along with further armour that nearly covered all of the limbs of the rider. The horses were provided with a metal facemask, chest armour and, for the mounts of the most important troops, a full body trapper of overlapping metal scales. To wear such extensive armour, as well as carry a heavily armoured rider, cataphracts required a heavy warhorse that was ideally 16 hands high or larger. The favoured weapon of the cataphracts was an enormous lance, predominately known as the *kontos* (pl. *kontoi*), which was typically 3.6 metres (12 feet) in length. A large spear-tip was secured at the killing end of the *kontos*, and a butt spike was attached to the back end of the pole in order to improve the overall balance of the long lance. One of the most impressive features of the cataphract was the lack of one specific, very important piece of equipment that many modern scholars considered to be a necessity for the medieval knight: the stirrup.[5] Until quite recently, many scholars who wrote about the cataphracts believed that ancient armoured horsemen without stirrups were not effective as heavy cavalry, which is entirely false. Even though cataphracts quickly adopted stirrups once they were introduced to them, and the revolutionary equestrian equipment did improve their overall performance in battle, the fact that the heavy cavalrymen primarily used lances in combat for centuries before the existence of stirrups, proves that the equipment was certainly a bonus but not entirely necessary.[6]

Without the added balance afforded by the use of stirrups, the ancient cataphracts could not fight with lances in the manner of the knights of the Middle Ages; i.e. with the lance held in the couched position, that is with the lance secured underneath the armpit. Therefore, cataphracts attacked with the *kontos* in one of three ways. The first method cataphracts used to wield their lances was overarm in order to stab downward onto their opponents. The most effective way to combat infantry was to hold the *kontos* in one hand along the horse's flank and keeping it parallel to the ground, while the other hand controlled the reins. With the lance held in this manner, the cataphracts often fought in a column order formation with a slightly broad front than usual (especially when compared to the narrow wedge formation) in order to gain a slight advantage over an infantry phalanx armed with *sarissae*, or long pikes. The last technique utilized by the cataphracts with their *kontoi* was primarily for melee with other cavalry units; the lance was held in both hands with the pole across the horse's neck and the spear point to the left of the beast's head. In this way, the *kontos* was levelled directly at an opposing mounted soldier. Furthermore, the rider could more fully utilize the momentum of the horse to maximize the impact of the blow as much as possible. When fighting against enemy cavalry, cataphract troops also changed their formation to one shaped as a wedge with a narrow front that increased with each successive rank behind it. The variant type of cataphract known as the *clibanarius* often fought with these techniques against other mounted warriors.[7]

Although the differences between the *cataphracti*, *cataphractarii* (sing. *cataphractarius*) and *clibanarii* (sing. *clibanarius*) are discussed in much greater detail in later chapters, it is important to know that all three terms were used to describe the heavily armoured horsemen of the Ancient era. In this book, I have tried as much as possible to use the same specific terms that the ancient writers used to label the cataphracts at the time that their accounts were written. However, in order to simplify the overall story of the ancient heavy cavalrymen, the modern English words 'cataphract' or 'cataphracts' are also used frequently throughout the manuscript as general terms for all of the different variations of armoured horsemen.

The development of the cataphract was a long process of over 1,000 years that first began among the semi-nomadic tribes of the Eurasian Steppes in the seventh century BC. Eventually, the heavily armoured warriors of the Parthian nobility influenced the Hellenistic Seleucid Empire to adopt similar troops, which became the first cataphracts. The Parthian Empire that succeeded the Seleucids in the east maintained the use of a core of cataphracts in their forces, as well as the Sassanian Persian Empire that arose after them and which more commonly fielded the soldiers that were frequently referred to as *clibanarii*. In the *Aethiopica* of the third century AD, Heliodorus provided a description of these formidable Persian warriors:

> *Before him was only the troop of cataphracts; it was his great confidence in these that emboldened him to venture battle. This phalanx*

xvi*Cataphracts*

*was always the Persians' strongest force, and was posted in the van
as an impenetrable wall. The fashion of their armament is the following. The men are selected for physical ruggedness. Each man wears a
helmet cleverly fashioned in one piece to fit closely over his face like a
mask. It is solid down to the neck except for eyeholes to see through.
The right hand carries a spear of uncommon length; the left is unen-
cumbered, to manage the reins. A scimitar hangs at his side. Not his
breast alone but his whole body is sheathed in armour. The armour
is fashioned of a number of separate plates of iron or bronze a span
square fitting over each other at each of the four sides and hooked or
sewn together beneath, the upper lapping over the lower, and the side
of each over the edge of the plate next in order. The effect is a shirt of
mail which fits easily over the whole body and each limb separately,
without hindering or straining movement. The armour is fitted with
sleeves and extends from the neck to the knees; only the inside of the
thighs are uncovered, to facilitate riding. This mail coat deflects any
stroke and prevents any wound. The greaves reach from the feet to
the knee, where they are attached to the coat. The horse is as well
protected as his rider. Greaves cover his legs, and a frontal fitted with
a spike protects his whole head. From his back a sheet of iron mail
hangs down either flank, loose enough not to impede his movements,
but at the same time affording him full protection. When the horse is
so accoutred and, as it were, molten in his armour, his rider mounts
him; because of his weight the rider cannot leap up, but is lifted by
others. When the time for battle comes, the rider loosens his reins,
fixes his spurs, and charges his adversaries, looking like an iron man
or a solidly wrought statue in motion. His spear extends directly
forward much further than the ordinary spear. It is supported by a
loop at the horse's neck and its butt is fixed by a noose to its croup.
So attached it yields to no shock, but assists the hand of the rider, who
merely directs the stroke. Propelled with such great force, the spear
penetrates deeply and pierces everything it encounters; frequently it
transfixes two opponents at a single stroke.[8]*

The Romans were slow to accept the effectiveness of the heavily
armoured cavalrymen, but after facing the cataphracts of the Seleucids,
Armenians, Parthians, and Sassanians, as well as the similarly protected heavy cavalry lancers of the Sarmatians, the empire started to
utilize several different types of cataphracts beginning in the second
century AD. By the end of the Western Roman Empire, *cataphracti,
cataphractarii* and *clibanarii* units had become an integral part of the

imperial army. The fierce competition between the two rival empires of Rome and Persia raised the pinnacle of both the armament and protection of their cataphract soldiers. Julian was so awed by the sight of the Roman cataphracts that in his fourth century AD work titled *Panegyric in Honour of the Emperor Constantinus*, he stated:

> *What emperor can one cite in the past who first planned and then reproduced so admirable a type of cavalry and such accoutrements? First you trained yourself to wear them, and then you taught others how to use such weapons so that none could withstand them. This is a subject on which many have ventured to speak, but they have failed to do it justice, so much so that those who heard their description, and later had the good fortune to see for themselves decided that their eyes must accept what their ears had refused to credit. Your cavalry was almost unlimited in numbers and they all sat their horses like statues, while their limbs were fitted with armour that followed closely the outline of the human form. It covers the arms from wrist to elbow and thence to the shoulder, while a coat of mail protects the shoulders, back and breast. The head and face are covered by a metal mask, which makes its wearer look like a glittering statue for not even the thighs and legs and the very ends of the feet lack this armour. It is attached to the cuirass by fine chain-armour like a web, so that no part of the body is visible and uncovered, for this woven covering protects the hands as well, and is so flexible that the wearers can bend even their fingers. All this I desire to represent in words as vividly as I can, but it is beyond my powers, and I can only ask those who wish to know more about this armour to see it with their own eyes, and not merely to listen to my description.[9]*

After the fall of the western half of the empire in 476 AD, the Eastern Romans, also known as the Byzantine Empire, and the Neo-Persians, called the Sassanians, continued to face each other with cataphracts and *clibanarii* until the latter empire was conquered in the Islamic expansion of the seventh century AD. After a brief decline in importance for a couple of centuries during the Arab ascendancy throughout the region, the Byzantine cataphracts underwent a rapid resurgence in the imperial forces during the tenth century AD. The emperor primarily responsible for the rebirth of the cataphract in the Byzantine army was Leo VI (r. 886–912 AD). The martial emperor provided a description of the properly armed and armoured cavalry troops in his work, the *Taktika*:

Each man should have the following armament. Full coats of mail reaching to their ankles, fastened with thongs and rings, along with their carrying cases. They should also have iron helmets, polished and always with small plumes on their crests. Each man should have a bow suited to his own strength and not above it, more indeed on the weaker side, and cases broad enough so that, when necessary, the strung bows can fit in them. They should also have spare bowstrings in their saddlebags, suitable quivers, too, with their covers, holding about thirty-to-forty arrows. Small files and awls in their baldrics. They should also have short cavalry lances with small thongs in the middle of the shaft and with pennons. In addition, they should have swords hanging from their shoulders, in the Roman manner, as well as daggers or large knives on their belts. All recruits who do not know how to shoot should have lances and full shields. It will be very useful if some can afford iron gauntlets, called cheiropsella. *They should have small tassels on the hindquarters of the horses as well as small pennons over the armour around their shoulders. For the more handsome the soldier is in his armament, the more confidence he gains in himself and the more fear he inspires in the foe. If possible, they should wear breastplates, polished and shiny, that are now called* klibania. *Also greaves, now called* podopsella, *and sometimes spurs. Also surcoats to put on when needed. All the Roman recruits, up to the age of forty, must definitely be required to carry bow and quiver, whether they be expert archers or just average. The fact that archery has been completely neglected and fallen into disuse among the Romans has caused a great deal of harm nowadays. They should possess two lances as to have a spare one at hand in case the first one misses. Inexperienced men should employ lighter bows. With enough time, even men who do not know how to shoot will manage to learn, for it is an essential skill. If possible, they should also have at least two javelins or throwing weapons so that, at the proper moment, they may readily hurl them against the enemy. That is how you shall arm the cavalryman.*[10]

Along with the arms and armour of the Byzantine cataphracts, the *Taktika* also contains a detailed description of the armour worn by their mounts, and the saddle equipment as well:

The horses, especially those of the officers and the other special troops, should have protective armour of iron or of padding, such as cow hide, over their heads and breasts. Their breasts and necks and, if possible, their abdomens will be covered by small pieces of what is called quilt-ing, hanging from the saddles. These have often preserved the horses as well as those riding on them from great dangers. In particular, the men stationed in the front line of battle should have these items. Let the saddles have large and thick cloths, and let there be strong bridles of good quality. Two iron stirrups should be attached to the saddles along with a lasso with thong, a hobble, a saddlebag large enough, when the situation so demands, to hold three or four days' rations. There should be four tassels on the haunch strap; likewise, one on the horse's brow and one under the chin. By all means, the cavalry sol-dier must have a double-sided axe, one side having the long form of a sword and the other the large and sharp form of the point of a spear. It should be hanging from the saddle in a leather case.[11]

Finally, there is also information regarding the clothing of the cataphracts:

The clothing of the soldiers, whether linen, wool, or other material, should be loose fitting so they may not be impeded as they ride along; it should cover their knees and give a neat appearance. They should have a loose, padded mantle with very broad sleeves so that in arming themselves and wearing the body armour with the bow if, perchance, it should rain or the dew cause the air to become quite humid, then by wearing these over their body armour and bow, they may both protect their armament and not be impeded when they want to make use of the bow or the lance. These padded mantles may also be necessary in another way on patrol or reconnaissance. When the body armour is covered by them its brightness will not be seen far off by the enemy and they will also provide protection against being hit by arrows. We also order that each squad should carry sickles and axes to meet their unavoidable needs.[12]

This description of the medieval Byzantine cataphract mentions sev-eral changes to the equipment of the heavy cavalrymen, such as the addition of the bow, arrows, and stirrups, which provides a glimpse of how much the arms and armour of the cataphracts evolved over the centuries.

A little over two hundred years before the complete collapse of the Byzantine Empire, the sack of the imperial capital city of Constantinople in 1204 AD devastated the Eastern Romans to such an extent that they were never able to fully recover. With decreased imperial territories and native manpower in the army, as well as far less overall wealth, the formidable, yet highly expensive, cataphracts rapidly fell out of use. With no more Eastern Roman cataphracts, the declining Byzantine Empire of the thirteenth century became the last state to refer to their heavily armoured riders, atop equally armoured mounts, as *kataphraktoi*, or cataphracts. Although this introduction is meant to be a brief summary of the cataphracts, the far more detailed tale of the legendary horsemen began well over 1,000 years earlier on the Eurasian Steppes, as described in the next chapter.

CHAPTER ONE

ORIGINS OF THE CATAPHRACTS

The development of heavy cavalry that ultimately led to the creation of the extremely armoured horseman known as the cataphract began when domesticated horses were ridden for the first time during the first half of the fourth millennium BC. Before that revolutionary point in time, wild horses across the vast Eurasian Steppes were originally hunted for meat, and then even after the initial stages of domestication began, the animals were still utilized predominately as a source of food.[1] It is uncertain exactly when and where horseback riding first occurred; however, archaeological evidence uncovered has suggested that the origin of the practice is located either in what is now modern-day northern Kazakhstan, or further west in the steppe region between the Don and the Dnieper rivers. Two stockbreeding cultures emerged in these areas: the Botai Tersek Culture (3700–3000 BC), who inhabited the first region, and the Srednyi-Stog Culture (4500–3500 BC) of the latter location. These two groups were the first ancient peoples to begin the process of the domestication of horses that gradually transformed the animals into mounts able to be ridden. While it is very likely that the earliest horseback riders belonged to one of these two cultures, it is not only unclear in which region the practice began, but there is also no substantial evidence that tells us exactly when it occurred either.[2] Some scholars suggest that the horse may have been ridden as early as 4000 BC.[3] But evidence of horseback riding, such as remains of horses' teeth which show signs of wear from a bit, and remnants of cheek pieces that were possibly used for bridles, did not become more prevalent in the archaeological record until 3500 BC.[4] Skeletal remains of possible domesticated horses discovered from this era provide a range of approximately 12.2 to 14.1 hh (hands high) for the size of the animals.[5]

The earliest mounts of the fourth millennium BC were predominately used to make the hunters of the vast plains incredibly more mobile and effective, though it did not take long before the tribal stockbreeders of the Steppes began to trade their valuable domesticated animals with the prosperous urban civilizations to the south.[6] By 2500 BC, domesticated horses had reached Mesopotamia and for the next 500 years, the animals spread throughout Syria, Palestine and Anatolia as well. In these regions where the wheel had already been in existence for centuries, the horse rapidly became a vital beast of burden, initially used to pull wagons and then other wheeled vehicles. In the first half of the second millennium BC, domesticated horses became such a prized commodity across the Middle East that kingdoms, which spanned from Iran to Egypt, established their own stockbreeding cultures to produce the best steeds possible. Over time, these new breeds gradually grew until the average size of the animals increased to between 14.1 and 15 hh.[7] It was also during this period that horse-driven chariot combat arose and rapidly became the pre-eminent type of warfare across the region. By the latter half of the second millennium BC, nearly all of the elite warriors of states such as Assyria, Babylon, Egypt and Mycenaean Greece fought as charioteers.[8]

Although wheeled vehicles were the most prevalent type of equine transportation utilized throughout the Middle East in the second millennium BC, riders mounted on horseback also existed at this time as well. The earliest solid evidence discovered of a rider on horseback is from the Mesopotamian cylinder seal of Abbakalla of Ur, a scribe of the Sumerian King Shu Sin (r. 2037–2029 BC).[9] However, mounted cavalry predominately consisted of individual messengers or scouts, instead of units of troops armed for combat.[10] On the other hand, in the Eurasian Steppe lands, where horseback riding occurred before the wheel, true mounted warfare developed instead of chariot-focused combat to the south. By 1500 BC, the equestrian skills of the tribal peoples of the steppes became so great that they could both ride and fire the deadly composite bow that had been recently invented in the region; thus, revolutionary warriors of unprecedented mobility and lethality were created. Then, the riding skills of the tribal cavalrymen increased even further around 1200 BC when improved, single-piece bits made of bronze began to replace the older versions comprised of merely bone or wood. With the new bits, steppe horsemen were able to gain further control over their mounts, and thus could much more confidently engage in mounted combat.[11]

Horseback riding was far more advanced on the steppes, yet equestrian equipment for riders in the Middle East also continued to develop throughout the second half of the second millennium BC. In Egypt around 1500 BC, an even greater bit than the single-piece bronze version was invented, known as the split, two-part bit. When the superior Egyptian type of bit finally reached the steppes north of the Caucasus Mountains in the ninth century BC, the equipment was largely adopted by the tribal cavalrymen throughout the region, even as far as Mongolia. The horse-archers of the Eurasian Steppes particularly prized the new, highly advanced bit for it gave them so much control over their mounts that they were able to perform what would later be referred to as the 'Parthian shot', in which the rider was able to flee and yet still turn around and fire his small, recurve bow at an enemy behind him.[12] As the steppe horsemen perfected their riding skills in the beginning of the first millennium BC, contemporary mounted cavalry units began to rise among the kingdoms of the Middle East. An image on a plaque from Ugarit in Syria of the twelfth century BC may be a depiction of a cavalry unit, which is possible evidence of the emergence of true cavalrymen within the Near Eastern kingdoms as early as the end of the second millennium BC.[13]

Regardless of the introduction of armed riders upon mounts into the armies of the Middle East, the chariot retained its dominant position in the militaries of the region even after the beginning of the first millennium BC. And just as the horseback riding ability of Near Eastern troops improved, so too did the soldiers' skills in chariotry, along with the technology involved in that type of combat as well. During this era, there were two main types of chariot troops: one light and the other heavy. The latter type of chariot warfare was especially popular in the armed forces of the Hittite Empire of Anatolia and consisted of a large, well-crafted vehicle capable of carrying two to three soldiers commonly armed with spears and shields. Over time, the equipment of the heavy chariot crews improved and began to include heavy armour for the shield-bearing spearmen on board the vehicle. At first, the armour primarily consisted of a bronze-scale cuirass, known as a *sariam* in the ancient Near Eastern language of the Mitanni, and a helmet called a *girpisu* in the same language. The sleeves of the scale cuirass only extended to the elbow and the scales covered the torso to the waist, but the cuirass was sometimes more like a coat with a length that reached the middle of the calf. The scales of the armour were not only laced to a fabric backing, but also to each other and made to overlap. Eventually, due to the fact that heavy chariot crewmen did not need to ride, or even necessarily walk while in combat, super heavy charioteer armour was also created, such as the Mycenaean Greek remains from the end of the 14th century BC called the Dendra Panoply. The extremely heavy armour consisted of large, thick sheets of bronze that were constructed to wrap around the warrior.[14]

Along with the development of armour for the crewmen of the heavy chariots, the warriors became a key part to the creation of the cataphracts for they were the first to start armouring their steeds as well. Horse barding was not frequently utilized at this time but, when it was worn, the armour was sometimes extensive enough to cover the chest and shoulders, as well as the back and flanks of the animal. The most common type of barding was called a *parashshamu* in Mitanni and was constructed with hair or thick felt, commonly augmented with further neck protection known as a *milu*, also made with one of those materials. The most heavily armoured horses that pulled chariots wore scale barding, also known as a *sariam*.[15] In as early as the reign of King Muwatalli II (r. 1295–1272 BC), the Hittites armoured chariot horses with scale armour that covered the neck, back and flanks of the steeds.[16] The development of armour for both the horses and the charioteers progressed throughout most of the ancient Near East at the end of the second millennium BC. Then, in the tenth century BC, the rapid resurgence of the Assyrian Empire in Mesopotamia resulted in the military dominance of one major superpower over the entire region. In the armies of the Neo-Assyrian Empire, not only did the development of the heavy chariots reach their apex, but also it was from within the ranks that the first true heavy cavalry units were created and flourished on the battlefield.

The Neo-Assyrian Empire

Early in the 2nd millennium BC, the Assyrian King Shamsi-Adad I (r. 1813–1781 BC) established his rule over the region in between the three founding cities of Ashur, Nineveh and Arbil, near the banks of the great Tigris River of Mesopotamia. In the following centuries, the kingdom survived through continual conflicts with neighbouring states along its borders, either by defence or with pre-emptive aggression to end potential threats. Therefore, the military was in a near-constant state of evolution, finding new ways to defeat their many enemies. Yet even with their powerful armies, the superior strength of their rivals, along with the periodic reigns of weak rulers, meant that the Assyrians remained a relatively minor power for much of the millennium when compared to states such as the Hittite Empire and the Kingdom of Egypt. In the fifteenth century BC, the power of the Assyrians reached such a low point that they were even forced to become a vassal state under the hegemony of the Kingdom of Mitanni. By the eleventh century, the Assyrians had long regained their independence, though after the death of King Tiglath-Pileser I in 1076 BC, they rapidly lost all of their territory until it only encompassed the Assyrian heartland founded by King Shamsi-Adad I, nearly 1,000 years earlier.[17] However, when King Adad-Nirari II rose to power in 911 BC, the ancient Middle East had greatly changed. The former superpowers of the last half of the second millennium BC, such as the Hittites, Egyptians, and Mitanni, had either completely collapsed or were in a much weaker state than before. Therefore, the new ruler was able to put his kingdom on track to become the greatest empire that had existed up to that point. For the next three centuries, the Neo-Assyrian emperors used their impressive military to its full potential, especially making revolutionary changes to the ways in which horses were used on the battlefield.

Like most of the other Near Eastern militaries of the period, the main arm of the Neo-Assyrian forces were its chariot contingents. In the reign of Emperor Ashurnasirpal II (r. 883–859 BC), the chariots utilized were strictly the lighter type, manned by two charioteers and pulled by two to three horses. However, by the reign of Emperor Ashurbanipal (r. 668–627 BC), the Assyrians had largely replaced the smaller vehicles for considerably heavier chariots pulled by four armoured steeds and able to carry four armed and armoured men. Although one crewman typically carried a bow, the rest of the crew wielded spears, shields and swords.[18] As the heavy chariots and their crews increased in size over the centuries, so too did the Assyrians' preference for that style of vehicle increase over the lighter, skirmishing type of chariot.

The main reason for the eventual supremacy of the heavy chariots over the lighter ones in the Assyrian army of the seventh century BC was due to the rise of true cavalry troops from among the ranks. In the beginning of the Neo-Assyrian era, mounted riders only replaced chariots that were used as scouts, but then cavalrymen began to fulfill all of the duties required for reconnaissance. By the reign of Emperor Tukulti-Ninurta II (r. 890–884 BC) at the earliest, the equestrian skills of the Assyrians had expanded to include skirmishing roles as well when the first known official cavalry units were created. These early light cavalry troops were rudimentary, however, for they were armed with bows and required another rider and mount to move beside them in order to hold the reins of both horses as they shot their arrows, as seen on the bas-relief sculptures in the palace of Ashurnasirpal II.[19] Furthermore, both riders sat upon their mounts improperly, more towards the back of the horse, similar to where Assyrian riders were accustomed to sit upon donkeys. Though a rearward seat is appropriate for riding a donkey due to the sharp spine along the rest of its back, the Assyrians were unaware at that point of how sitting near the rump of a horse could cause damage to the animal's kidneys. The novice horsemen did benefit from the introduction of a new leather and cloth saddle, however, which originated in the eastern part of Central Asia and reached the Assyrian Empire in the ninth century BC. The depictions of the early Assyrian cavalrymen also show the driver of the pair of horses armed with a spear in the other hand. These units remained primarily light cavalry, for both the riders and the mounts were unarmoured.[20]

One century later, Assyrian reliefs from the reign of Emperor Tiglath-Pileser III (r. 745–727 BC) contain depictions of the first armoured heavy cavalry. Not only were these warriors true horsemen, in that they controlled their own mounts without the support of a companion, but also they sat much further forward on their horses' backs. The heavy cavalrymen wore a helmet and a scale cuirass that extended to the waist but did not have sleeves. Although they primarily fought with a spear that may have been as long as 2.1 m (7 ft), the Assyrian horsemen were armed with swords as well.[21] After Ashurbanipal came to power in the seventh century BC, the heavy cavalrymen wore a lamellar cuirass and fought with both the lance and the bow. When in close combat, the lance was held by the rider overarm, in one hand, so that he could thrust the weapon down onto the enemy. The mounts of the horsemen were also slightly armoured with a barding made of thick fabric. It was at this point that the Assyrian cavalry had become so effective that it had finally surpassed the martial capabilities of the chariot units in the army.[22]

One of the main reasons for the ascendancy of cavalry within the Assyrian army was a lot of experience gained fighting against the predominately mounted troops of the Persians and Medes along the eastern borders of their empire. By the end of the eighth century BC, the territory of the Assyrian Empire had grown so much that its territory stretched from Egypt to Iran, which brought them into conflict with the horsemen of the eastern region around the Zagros Mountains, which had uneven terrain that was much more suited to cavalry than chariotry.[23] Yet even though Assyrian cavalrymen had improved greatly over the centuries, they were no match for the extremely lethal mounted warriors of the Scythians, a nomadic people that flooded into the region in the first half of the seventh century BC. Originally from the Eurasian Steppes, the Scythians showed the ancient Near Eastern world how much more deadly the plains horsemen could be than the cavalry of the southern urban states with militaries that had been dominated by the chariot for so many centuries.

The Scythians

By the end of the eighth century BC, an Iranian-speaking tribal group from the northern Pontic Steppe, known as the Cimmerians, crossed the Caucasus Mountains and moved south into the Near East. The Assyrians quickly came into conflict with the Cimmerians; however, the empire was unable to oust the invading horsemen from the region. Then in 679/78 BC, Assyrian Emperor Asarhaddon (r. 680–669 BC) crushed the forces of the Cimmerian King Teuspa, forcing the nomads to shift their focus towards the west against the Kingdom of Phrygia, whose territory spread from central to western Anatolia. Shortly after the Cimmerians invaded in 676 BC, Phrygia was conquered, but their push west did not stop there. For over thirty years the Kingdom of Lydia became the next main target of the nomadic warriors, but their attacks were not limited to just that Anatolian state, for they continued to do battle with the Assyrians as well. Ultimately, the rise of the Cimmerians in the ancient Near East was short-lived though. At the end of the seventh century BC, a new king ascended the throne in Lydia named Alyattes (r. 619/05–560 BC) who finally managed to put an end to the Cimmerians once and for all.[24] On the other hand, Alyattes did not act alone and it may be more correct to credit his ally for the destruction of the nomadic warriors; that ally was a related, yet far more dangerous, Iranian tribal group known as the Scythians.

Originally from the east of Central Asia, the Scythians crossed the Ural Mountains, the Volga River, and then moved into the northern region of the Caucasus around the same time that the Cimmerians invaded the Near East near the end of the eighth century BC. There, the nomadic invaders not only conquered the Maeotae, who were native to the region before the arrival of the Cimmerians, but they also subjugated the remainder of the latter group that did not make the journey south across the Caucasus Mountains with the majority of their tribesmen. Some of the Scythians remained in the area, establishing the Kuban and the northern Caucasus region into their new homeland. On the other hand, many of the mounted warriors decided to follow in the footsteps of the Cimmerians and make the trek south across the mountains. Once they were on the borders of the Assyrian Empire, the Scythians, led by their king, Ispakaia, immediately formed an alliance with the neighbouring Mannaeans who inhabited the land east of Lake Urmia. Even with their new ally, however, the first Scythians in the ancient Middle East could not withstand the might of the Assyrian army. Asarhaddon defeated King Ispakaia and the Assyrian emperor managed to establish an alliance with his successor to the Scythian throne, Bartatua. From then on, King Bartatua and his people supported the Assyrians in wars against their rivals; when the empire was in conflict with the Medes in 673 BC, the Scythians helped and were heavily rewarded for it with spoils of war.[25]

The Scythians came to the aid of the Assyrian Empire again around 644 BC when it was in dire straits. The Medes had not only invaded Assyria but were in the process of besieging the capital city of Nineveh when the new Scythian ruler, Bartatua's son Madyas, attacked with his forces. King Madyas and his nomadic horsemen won a great victory over the Medes that greatly weakened them and caused the Scythians to rise and become the greatest power in the region. With tribute flowing in from the conquered Median Kingdom, the Scythian ascendancy was not only due to increasing wealth, but also to great improvements in their military forces. The Scythians maintained their alliance with the Assyrians, and from that relationship the tribal warriors benefited significantly from what they gained in armour technology, specifically in the construction of scale type protection. The Scythians utilized no defensive armour, or very little, before this point so the adoption of the technology was revolutionary for the nomadic horsemen. Yet even though the Scythians had to be introduced to the invention by the Assyrians, the tribal warriors of the steppes were the first to realize the full potential of scale armour. Whereas the Assyrians only used scale to protect their torsos, the Scythians began to lace the overlapping rows of iron scales not just to their leather cuirasses, but also to their belts, thigh guards, leg pieces and then even to their shields and helmets. The scale helmet, though, was one of the later innovations made by the Scythians, along with a unique lamellar shield that was also developed. The shield sometimes had a half-moon shape, or it was oval or rectangular, and was commonly attached not only to the back, but also to both underarms of the cavalrymen, which allowed the warrior the free use of his hands while in combat. Scale armour was so prized by the Scythians that the mounts of the wealthiest horsemen were even given the protection to cover the chests of the animals.[26]

The Scythian method to construct scale armour began with sheets of metal that were cut with either shears or a type of pointed tool to make the scales. Depending on the area of the body that the scales were meant to cover, they were cut into different sizes. For places that required more flexibility, like the elbows and shoulders, smaller scales were made, whereas the more static regions of the body, such as the back or stomach, were covered with larger scales. Iron was typically utilized to make the scales, however, polished bronze was occasionally used in conjunction to create an impressive look with the combination of the two unique metals. Scale armour construction was an intensive process, for in order to make the larger pieces of armour, such as a cuirass with long sleeves, several hundred scales may have been required, though short-sleeved corselets were much more common among the Scythians of this period. Animal tendons or thin thongs made of leather were then used to attach the scales to a leather backing in rows one over the other so that either a third, or even up to one half, of each scale was covered by another one and made the armour resemble the scales of a fish. Furthermore, other scales also covered the vulnerable areas of the armour, where the scales were attached to the leather base. With the scales overlapping in that manner, as many as four layers of metal had to be penetrated in order to break through the armour.[27] The result was a highly protective, yet lightweight and flexible armour that was ideal for combat on horseback.

Before the Scythian horsemen adopted scale armour and began employing it over their bodies, and sometimes even their horses, the warriors were predominately light cavalry armed with bows. Therefore, the addition of substantial armour created new heavy cavalry troops from amongst the ranks. However, the light cavalrymen were still a vital part of the army. Typically, the Scythian battle tactics began with the horse-archers raining barrages of arrows down upon the enemy in an attempt to cause disorder in the hope of creating gaps in the opposing front lines. Then, once the front lines of the foe had been softened up enough, the heavy cavalrymen armed with lances were sent in to engage in shock combat and charge the vulnerable gaps. If the charge of the lancers was successful in breaking the enemy, leading to their rout, the Scythian light cavalry then pursued the retreating forces, easily picking them off with arrows into their backs.[28]

Yet the armoured lancers were a smaller, elite force within the overall military of the Scythians, as evidenced from the remains of numerous gravesites known as kurgans, which were barrow-mounds of deceased warriors that included their most important possessions. While nearly all of the warriors were buried with only a bow, arrows and one or two spears, the much rarer kurgans of kings and aristocratic cavalrymen contained swords, bows, quivers full of arrows, and sometimes dozens of spears and javelins, along with helmets, cuirasses and all sorts of armour. The scale armour found in the graves of the noblemen was sometimes very elaborate. Some of the scales had depictions of lion, elk and deer heads on them, while the most decorative were embellished with fine gold leaf.[29] Although the heavy cavalry-men were not as numerous as the lightly armoured horse-archers, or the poorest that fought as footmen within the Scythian army, the armoured lancers were still an essential contingent who used their greater financial resources in the constant pursuit of obtaining the best equipment available; predominately, this meant the search for both the highest quality and quantity of armour.

The Scythian supremacy in the Near East did not last long, how-ever, for only a few decades later, in either 624 or 616 BC, Cyaxares II (r. 624–584 BC), ruler of the Medes, succeeded in his elaborate plot of removing the Scythian king and all of his most powerful aristocratic supporters. To do so, the Median king pretended to generously provide the nomadic elites with copious amounts of alcohol at a grand feast and, once they were sufficiently inebriated, the Medes murdered every single one of them. With their leadership annihilated, most of the sur-viving Scythians returned to the northern Caucasus to live in the heart-land of their Scythian kin to the north, depriving the Assyrian Empire of its most important ally. Not all of the deadly horsemen fled from the region though. Some of the warriors switched sides and fought as mercenaries in the army of Cyaxares when he finally conquered the Assyrian Empire in 612 BC. Afterwards, the remaining Scythians in the Near East were responsible for instigating a war between the Kingdom of Lydia and the Medes from 590–585 BC, though they never came anywhere near to the position of power and influence they had in the region during the seventh century BC. Possibly for this reason, the last Scythians left the Near East to join the rest of their people after 585 BC.[30]

When the Scythians returned north, they brought with them their vast military experience from numerous campaigns in the Near East, along with their superior armour technology, and thus managed to subdue their kinsmen and seize control over the Kuban, which had remained the heartland of the nomadic tribe north of the Caucasus Mountains. However, violent outbreaks were frequent between the newcomers and previous inhabitants, forcing many of the Scythians to seek less volatile lands to the west. Therefore, the Scythians began to settle along the middle and lower reaches of the Dnieper River. The new lands not only provided the horsemen with highly fertile grass-lands, abundant with pastures for their herds, but also increased their material wealth, for they were able to subjugate the farming villages of the forest steppes to the north and dominate the luxurious Black Sea trade with the Bosporan and Greek urban centres to the south. Over time, the Scythians treasured the area to such an extent that nearly all of them settled there and by the end of the sixth century BC the northern Pontic steppe had become the new heartland of the Scythians. For the next 200 years, the Scythians expanded their territory until it included the lands along the Black Sea coast and the Kuban in the south to around where modern day Kiev is located in the north, and from the Don River in the east to the Danube in the west.[31]

As the territory of the Scythians changed from the sixth to the fourth century BC, the armour of the heavy cavalrymen also evolved over the period. One of the first and most significant developments was the complete replacement of the older, cast-bronze helmets for the helmets constructed with scale protection. Commonly referred to as the Kuban helmet due to the numerous remains of the style of headgear found in kurgans throughout the Kuban region of the northern Caucasus, the earlier bronze helmet provided much protection over the head and face with cheek protectors attached, however, it was much heavier as well. By the fifth century BC, the Kuban helmets were largely discarded in place of scale helmets. Modelled upon the popular, pointed leather hats or hoods often worn by the Scythians, known as Phrygian caps, the scales were simply laced into the leather that was then augmented with attached cheek protectors and a neck guard. Because of its lighter weight and how easy it was to construct when compared to the previous cast-bronze helmet, it did not take long before the headgear became one of the most popular helmets of the Scythians, even among the heavy cavalrymen. On the other hand, it was also in the fifth century BC that some of the wealthiest aristocratic warriors took advantage of their dominance of the trade with the Greek cities of the Black Sea coast to obtain superior helmets of Hellenistic craftsmanship. Over sixty Greek helmets made of bronze have been discovered in the kurgans of noblemen, nearly all of which were either in the Attic, Corinthian or Chalcidian style.[32]

At the time, some of the Scythian heavy cavalrymen began to replace another part of their armour with Greek pieces as well. Where the horsemen had previously utilized leather leg defences covered with scales, in the fifth century BC the most-heavily armoured warriors then adopted Hellenistic-style solid metal greaves worn over trousers of fabric. Over time the horsemen modified the Greek leg armour, however, in that the knee part was cut off and replaced with a separate domed guard that was better for cavalry use than the traditional, longer greaves meant primarily for infantry. Once again, the wealthiest warriors often wore embellished armour, for some of the greaves contained gilded decorations. One of the more elaborate examples discovered of a pair of greaves worn by the Scythians contains depictions of snakes along the sides and the heads of Gorgons on the knee-pieces.[33]

The last piece of armour that also underwent much development throughout the period was one of the most important defences to the heavy cavalryman, the shield. Whereas most Scythian warriors utilized a smaller, wicker shield, the heavily armoured horsemen carried much larger, wooden shields covered with iron scales. The common method of attaching the scales included sewing them together with wire first before lacing them to the wooden backing. As with most aspects of their panoply, the most prosperous aristocratic warriors utilized both the most defensive and elaborate shields. Many of the heavy cavalrymen carried shields with a single sheet metal facing over the wooden base instead of the scales. However, even if the shields with scale protection were used, most noblemen decorated the front with motifs using other metals. Two of these plates made of gold have been found in kurgans located in the Kuban, one in Kostromskaya Stanistsa with a depiction of deer and the other in Kelermes with the image of a panther.[34]

The most heavily armoured Scythian cavalrymen of the fourth century BC most likely would have worn a Hellenistic style helmet with a Scythian type of scale aventail attached that protected the back of the neck. They would have utilized a scale cuirass with long sleeves, which also extended past the waist to cover the thighs. Occasionally, a triangular plate was worn over the chest to augment the protection of the torso that was already provided by the scale corselet. Hellenistic-style greaves, yet modified for cavalry use, would have also been worn. Horse armour was rare among the Scythian heavy horsemen; however, the mounts of the most heavily armoured cavalrymen wore barding over the chest. The mounted warriors carried large, round shields and fought with lances and swords, as well as bows that were stored in the unique combined bowcase/quiver known as a *gorytos*. Although the bow was the primary weapon of most Scythian horsemen, the favoured weapon of the heavy cavalrymen was the lance, which was at least 3m (10ft) long. A golden plate uncovered in the Geremesov barrow contains a depiction of a Scythian warrior armed and armoured in a similar manner with much of this equipment.[35] With the Scythian heartland shifted to the west, much of the armour development of the heavy cavalry involved the adoption of western styles. However, to the east in Central Asia, there were other nomadic horsemen who also began to adopt Near Eastern armour technology, possibly as early as the sixth century BC.

The Massagetae, Choresmia and the Heavy Cavalry of the Steppes

Although most of the ancient accounts and archaeological evidence suggest that the Scythians were the first highly skilled horsemen of the Eurasian steppes to fully embrace extensive armour for both the rider and the mount of the heavy cavalry, it is highly probable that advanced armour technology spread to other areas of Central Asia as well via contact with the Scythians, which then led to other proto-cataphract type warriors. Foremost among those nomadic tribes so influenced were the Massagetae because their contact with the revolutionary technology was not just from the Scythians but also from interactions with the eastern Medes, who previously adopted armour due to their direct conflicts with the Assyrians. The Massagetae were related to the Scythians yet remained in the east, inhabiting the lands near the Aral Sea, mainly in the corridor between that body of water, the Syr Darya and the Caspian Sea. The territory of the nomadic tribe covered most of modern day southeastern to western Kazakhstan, which included the settled region of Choresmia. Some Massagetae tribesmen lived much more sedentary lives in the urban settlements of Choresmia with the resources necessary to create a metal working industry capable of producing large quantities of armour for heavy cavalrymen.[36]

In the later half of the sixth century BC, Spargapises became the new king of the Massagetae after the death of his father. However, the new ruler was too young to lead, thus his mother, Tomyris, ruled the tribe as a regent. Earlier, in 550 BC, a Persian prince had over-thrown his Mede father-in-law to create a considerably more powerful, united empire of both Persians and Medes which he ruled as Cyrus II (r. 550–530/529 BC). In the following decades, Cyrus the Great, as he was known, had expanded the territory of his new Achaemenid Empire until he reached the borders of the Massagetae lands in 530/529 BC and decided to exploit the vulnerability of the tribe as it underwent the change in leadership. As stated by Herodotus, Cyrus managed to abduct Spargapises through an elaborate ploy, which led to the young king's suicide. However, the furious Queen Tomyris quickly rallied her people and attacked the invaders. In the resulting battle, the Massagetae were victorious and the great king of the Persians was slain. The queen then exacted revenge for the death of her son by having Cyrus decapitated and placing his head in a wineskin filled with blood.[37]

Several scholars have suggested that the Massagetae had already fully embraced extensive armour for their heavy cavalry by the time of the invasion; Hubertus von Gall specifically has argued that it was the armoured mounts of the horsemen that gave the tribal warriors the advantage over the imperial forces, which led to their victory.[38] Even if the Massagetae had not yet adopted the practice of providing their steeds with barding, the horses of the nomadic warriors certainly wore armour by the fifth century for in the account of Herodotus, he stated in his description of the horsemen:

> *They make very extensive use of gold and bronze; they use bronze for the heads of their spears and arrows and for the blades of their sagareis, and gold to decorate their headgear, belts and chest-bands. The same goes for their horses too: they put bronze breastplates on their fronts.*[39]

The Massagetae were not the only Central Asian tribe to follow the trend set by the Scythians. Throughout the rest of the fifth century and into the fourth century, elite warriors in the surrounding regions and within the various related tribes increasingly wore more extensive armour until there were early proto-cataphract types of heavy cavalrymen among the Saka, the Dahae, in Bactria, and throughout most of Transoxania.[40]

The heavy cavalry of the nomadic tribesmen from Bactria and the surrounding region to beyond the Syr Darya River in the eastern part of modern day Uzbekistan greatly benefited from the larger size of their horses located there, when compared to other ancient breeds of the time. Due to their size, these animals were more physically able to wear barding and carry an armoured rider at the same time. The first breed originated in Bactria and Sogdiana, which is most of modern day Uzbekistan, Turkmenistan and all of Afghanistan, and the horses were so renowned that it gave the Bactrian capital city of Balkh the nickname of Bactra-Zariaspa, meaning 'Bactra of the Golden Horses'. The Bactrian horses may have been as tall as 15.2 hh and would have been the most similar in appearance to both of the modern day breeds, the Akhal Teke and the Turcoman. The other breed came from the Ferghana Valley of eastern Uzbekistan and may have been even taller at approximately 15.3 hh.[41]

The Scythian heavy cavalrymen were also a major influence on the ruling elite of the Sargat Culture who inhabited the region of the western part of the Siberian forest steppe. Although the vast majority of the Sargat people were native Finno-Ugric speakers, the aristocratic warriors were Iranian nomadic tribesmen related to the Saka, as well as the Scythians. The kurgans of wealthy noblemen belonging to the Sargat Culture contained abundant arms and armour, including iron scale cuirasses and helmets with scale neck guards attached, along with lances and long swords made of iron, and bows as well. In the first centuries after the culture arose in the fifth century BC, the type of bow utilized by the Sargat warriors was similar to the short, recurve bow used by the Scythians. Later, however, in the first millennium AD, the older bow was replaced with the asymmetrical composite bow of the Huns. The new bow was much more effective and was at least 120cm (47in) long.[42] The heavy cavalry tradition of highly armoured riders and mounts had spread throughout the Iranian-speaking elite of the Central Asian steppes, but the practice was not fully embraced at first by the great Persian Empire to the south, in the Middle East. Yet after their conflict with the Massagetae, the Persians were not done dealing with the nomadic tribesmen of the north and, through their increased contact, the imperial army became increasingly convinced of the usefulness of heavily armoured cavalry.

The Achaemenid Persian Empire

Although Cyrus the Great failed to subdue the Massagetae, by the end of his reign in 530/529 BC he had conquered Parthia, Hyrcania, Margiana, Choresmia, Sogdiana and Bactria, while also subduing the Saka. In 522 BC, the Saka revolted against their Persian oppressors so the new emperor, Darius I (r. 522–486 BC), led a campaign to put down the rebellion in 519 BC. After defeating the Saka and capturing their king, Skunkha, Darius placed one of his supporters on the throne. However, the Scythians also threatened the western borders of the empire; therefore, Darius shifted to focus his attention on them next. In 513/512 BC, the Persian army invaded the Pontic steppe only to find the fields burnt to the ground and the nomads nowhere to be seen. As Darius advanced further inland to find his enemy, the Scythians continued to retreat northward, setting fire to every edible resource in their wake, which left the Persians with almost nothing to forage. The farther the Achaemenid army travelled from its homeland, the more frequent were the attacks of the Scythians on the invaders, using guerrilla tactics to wither away their forces as they desperately tried to forage. Eventually, the Persians could no longer take the constant attacks and were forced to retreat from the Scythian lands with the remaining forces they still had left. From then on, Darius ceased his campaigns against the Saka, the Scythians and the other Iranian-speaking nomadic tribes; however, the Persian ruler had successfully put Sogdiana and Bactria, as well as many of the Saka warriors, firmly under his control, commanding them to supply horsemen for his armies.[43] Though most of these mounted warriors were horse-archers, some of the nomadic heavy cavalry also joined the Achaemenid forces as well.

In the beginning of the fifth century BC, Persian aggression was focused to the far west on the ancient Greek city-states, mainly Athens and Sparta. Ultimately, the elite units of the Persian army, mostly comprised of cavalry, were unable to overcome the deadly heavy infantry of the Greek phalanx. After losing the war and failing to conquer mainland Greece, the Achaemenid Persian Empire underwent a period of decline in which it was frequently embroiled in civil strife from within. Throughout the second half of the fifth century BC, foreign threats along the frontiers were minimal, yet infighting between the aristocracy, and even outright rebellion against the emperor, was nearly constant. In these decades of turmoil, the elite warriors of the nobility began to increase the armour worn by the heavy cavalry, much like their Scythian and Massagetae foes. Over time, lethal contingents of heavily armoured cavalry developed with much greater skills in shock tactics than any other Persian cavalry unit had before. While in battle, the Persian heavy horsemen were arrayed in a column formation rather than in a line and focused their charge at the centre of the opposing front line in the attempt to break and rout the enemy. This period of aristocratic and royal rivalries also led to many displays of single combat, often between a rebel contender for the throne against the emperor's primary general, or even against the Persian ruler himself. Similar to the jousts of the later European medieval world, the heavy cavalrymen dueled on horseback with light spears as their primary weapon. Ctesias of Cnidus, a physician employed at the royal court of the Persian emperor, documented these personal duels in his *Persika*.[44]

The Achaemenid Persian heavy cavalrymen that arose in the latter half of the fifth century BC fought with a spear made of cornel-wood known as a *palta* that was also occasionally used as a javelin as well. The Persian horsemen were also armed with daggers, maces, bows and quivers that often held as many as thirty arrows. The heads and torsos of the mounted warriors were covered with traditional bronze helmets and cuirasses respectively, however, the legs of the riders may have been protected with a more unique and innovative piece of equipment, an armoured saddle. Adopted in either the late fifth or fourth century, the distinctive saddle had armour attached to it that curved around the legs of the rider, especially over the thighs, but sometimes the protection encompassed the entire limb from the waist down to the foot. The ancient Parthian document called the *Vendidad*, or 'Anti-Demonic Law', provides a list of the arms and armour of the earlier Persian heavy cavalry that not only included horse armour, but also a piece of armour referred to as a 'thigh-protector', which may have been a reference to the armoured saddle. The barding worn by the mounts of the heavy cavalrymen included both a metal facemask over the head of the animal, along with a breastplate to protect the chest of the horse as well.[45]

A major reason that the newer, more heavily armoured Persian cavalrymen were so deadly was that many of them were mounted upon one of the largest, if not the largest, breed of warhorses in the ancient world, which was from the Nisaean plain in Media. The breed was particularly muscular, and thus perfectly suited for war with the more extensive armour of the cavalrymen because the horse could carry more weight than other breeds. The huge steeds could be as large as 16hh and white or black ones were the most prized by the Persians. The Nisaean horses were bred at a royal stud that supplied the emperor with the steeds.[46] According to Arrian, the stud had as many as 150,000 mares on site to breed more horses.[47] The exact location of the Nisaean plain is unknown; however, one possible site could be the Vale of Borigerd around 90 miles south of Ecbatana. Highly nutritious alfalfa that is exceptionally rich in protein, which was known as Median grass, grows in the area and may have once been the source of food for the huge ancient warhorses.[48] Even if some of the heavy cavalrymen were not able to ride Nisaean horses, the Persians also had a plentiful supply of the Bactrian, and possibly even the Ferghana, breeds ridden by the Saka and other nomadic tribesmen of the region of Bactria and the surrounding lands.[49]

In 401 BC, Prince Cyrus the Younger rebelled against his older brother, Emperor Artaxerxes II (r. 404–358 BC), with an army that included 600 elite heavy cavalry. These soldiers were armed and armoured similarly to the other aristocratic horsemen, except that these heavy cavalrymen specifically wore surcoats of crimson on top of Hellenistic-style cuirasses that consisted of solid metal breastplates. Even with his cuirassiers, Cyrus' attempt to seize the throne ended in failure, yet his rebellion resulted in a renewed conflict with the Greek city of Sparta. In the battles that followed, Xenophon witnessed the martial skills of the improved Persian heavy cavalry and was highly impressed with the mounted warriors. The ancient Greek writer was a cavalryman fighting for the Spartan King Agesilaus near Daskyleion in 396 BC when the Persian armoured horsemen caught the Greek cavalry off-guard and smashed into the front line that the frantic, Hellenistic mounted troops managed to form at the last minute. Xenophon watched as the Persian heavy cavalrymen charged in column formation and caused massive damage to the unprepared Greek horsemen.[50]

The Persian heavily armoured cavalrymen made such an impression upon Xenophon that in the years between 367 and 365 BC, he wrote two treatises, *The Cavalry Commander* and *On Horsemanship*, in which he advised the Greek heavy cavalrymen to not only attack in the column formation of their Persian counterparts, but also to adopt similar weaponry and heavy armour for both the rider and the mount.[51] In the latter book, the ancient Greek writer went into extensive detail in his description of what he believed the armour of the heavy cavalryman should include:

> To begin with the cuirass. This must always be made to fit the body; for if it fits well, the body supports its weight, but if it is very loose, the shoulders have to carry it all by themselves. As for too tight a cuirass, it is an encumbrance and not a piece of armour. Next, as the neck is one of the vital parts, I say that a covering should be made for it rising out of the cuirass itself to fit the neck. This will at once be an ornament; and if it is made as it should be, it will cover the rider's face when he pleases as far as the nose. For a helmet the Boeotian is the best, in my opinion, since it most completely protects all the parts that are above the cuirass, without preventing you from seeing. Let the cuirass be made so as not to hinder sitting nor stooping. Round the belly, the groin, and thereabouts, there should be flaps of such material and number as to protect these parts. Since the horseman is disabled if anything happens to his left arm, I consequently recommend the newly invented piece of armour called 'the hand'. It protects the shoulder, the arm, the elbow, and the part that holds the reins, and it can be extended or bent together; besides it covers the gap left by the cuirass under the armpit. The right arm must of course be raised whenever the rider wants to hurl his javelin or to strike a blow. The part of the cuirass that hinders this must therefore be removed, and in its place flaps put on at the joints, unfolding all together when the arm is raised and closing when it is lowered. For the arm itself, something worn like a greave seems to me better than to have it of a piece with the cuirass. The part of the arm that is bared

*when it is raised must be protected near the cuirass with calfskin or
bronze, else it will be left unguarded in its most vital part.*[52]

Xenophon also went on to describe the armour that should be worn by
the horses as well:

*The animal also should be armed with a frontlet, breastplate, and
thigh-pieces; the last serve at the same time to cover the thighs of the
rider. Above all, the horse's belly should be protected, as being the
most vital and the weakest part. It may be protected with the cloth.
The cloth must also be of such material and so sewn together as to
give the rider a safe seat and not to gall the horse's back.*[53]

When Xenophon speaks of 'thigh-pieces', he is referring to the
armoured saddle, which provided some protection for the rider's legs
but not entirely, as he states:

*But as the shins and feet would of course project below the thigh-
pieces, they too may be armed with top-boots of the leather which
shoes are made. These will at once protect shins and cover the feet.*[54]

Along with the extensive armour, Xenophon also recommended the
horsemen to be armed with a curved scimitar or sabre, instead of a
straight sword, and two *palta* since they could be used as javelins and
spears.

The extensive arm protection, called 'the hand' (*cheira*) by Xenophon,
was one of the last major additions to the armour of the Persian heavy
cavalryman. The decision to add the equipment was part of the cavalry
reforms made by the new Persian general, Datames, who was selected
to lead the campaign against Egypt in 372 BC. By that point, the war
with Sparta that Xenophon had participated in had long been over,
ending when the Persian fleet crushed the Spartans at the Battle of
Cnidus in 394 BC. In the decades following the reforms of Datames,
the empire was first plagued with another period of unrest and rebellion before their primary focus became the reconquest of Egypt in the
340s BC.[55] Although the Achaemenid Persians successfully conquered
Egypt in 343 BC, the empire faced the greatest threat it would ever
know less than ten years later when Alexander the Great, king of the
Macedonians, invaded.

In 334 BC, Alexander and his Hellenistic forces reached the
Granicus River but found their way opposed on the other side of the
waterway by an enormous Persian army of 20,000 cavalry in front of

another 20,000 heavy infantry comprised predominately of Greek mercenary hoplites. As Alexander often did in battle, he acted quickly and rapidly moved his army across the river in the hope that his speed would prevent the Persians from building up their courage. With only approximately 13,000 infantry, including 7,500 armoured pikemen, 5,500 light infantrymen, and over 4,200 cavalrymen, Alexander's army was greatly outnumbered.[56] Therefore, the first Macedonian soldiers to reach the opposite banks of the river were all cut down by the Persian horsemen. Yet once the king managed to make the crossing and joined the fray, he inspired his men to continue on, despite the brutal combat they would encounter on the other side. As more and more of the Hellenistic warriors assaulted the Persian cavalrymen, the crossing gradually became easier for the Macedonian army, though that was not the only reason Arrian gave for the tide shifting into Alexander's favour, as stated in the ancient writer's account of the battle within the *Anabasis of Alexander*:

> *Already, however, Alexander and his guards were getting the best of it, not only through their forcefulness and their discipline, but because they were fighting with stout cornel-wood lances against short javelins.*[57]

The Hellenistic cavalrymen wore less armour than their Persian counterparts, as did their mounts, for nearly all of their horses were completely unarmoured. Furthermore, the horses ridden by the Macedonian horsemen were tall compared to most other horses of the ancient world, but the steeds were still smaller than the mounts available to Persian cavalry with an average height of between 14½ and a little over 15hh. On the other hand, being armed with lance, as opposed to the shorter *palta* utilized by the Persian heavy cavalrymen, gave Alexander's mounted troops a significant reach advantage over their enemy. Known as a *xyston*, the lance of the Hellenistic cavalrymen had spearpoints at both ends so that the horsemen had a backup blade if the first spearhead broke off in combat. Unfortunately, the exact length of the *xyston* is still unknown for it is possible that it could have been as long as 4.6m (15ft), but it most likely would have been more around 3.6m (12ft) in length. Yet even if the Macedonian lances were the shorter length, they still outreached the smaller *palta* of the Persian cavalrymen.[58]

Once the momentum had shifted to the Macedonian side, the pressure continued to build for the Persians as they were gradually pushed back away from the river. The Persians struggled to contend with the long *xyston* lances, but they also began to suffer increasing casualties from the Hellenistic light infantry that had managed to force their way past the enemy front lines and move among the Persian cavalrymen to strike their vulnerable, unarmoured areas up close. Eventually the resolve of the Persian horsemen broke and they began to retreat from the Macedonian onslaught, leaving the Greek mercenary heavy infantry completely isolated. By this point, the Macedonian infantrymen had forded the river and attacked the front of the mercenary hoplites so Alexander broke off his pursuit of the routed Persian cavalrymen to simultaneously strike the rear or flank of the enemy Greek infantrymen. It did not take long before the surrounded mercenary hoplites were almost completely slaughtered. In the end, many Persian cavalrymen were slain and nearly 18,000 Greek mercenary infantrymen were massacred, while a further 2,000 were put into captivity in order to become slaves. On the other hand, the Macedonians lost only approximately 30 infantrymen and 85 cavalrymen.[59]

After his victory at the Battle of the Granicus, Alexander established his hold over all of Asia Minor as the Achaemenid Persian Emperor Darius III (r. 336–330 BC) gathered an enormous force to confront the invaders. By the summer of 333 BC, Alexander led his army out of Asia Minor and the two forces met on a thin stretch of plain between the mountains and the coast near the town of Issus. The ancient accounts have almost certainly exaggerated the size of the Persian army, which means that its exact number is still unknown; however, there is no doubt that Alexander was once again greatly outnumbered. The Macedonian army only consisted of around 5,300 cavalry and 26,000 heavy infantry, while the Persians certainly had over 50,000 soldiers and may have numbered as many as 100,000 men. The Persian centre consisted of over 60,000 Greek mercenary and Kardakes heavy infantry, whereas the majority of the cavalry was formed up on the right wing, including many of the most heavily armoured horsemen. To withstand the onslaught of the Persian heavy cavalrymen, Alexander gave his general, Parmenio, command of the Thessalian cavalry and some of the Thracian light cavalry, along with the horsemen of the allied Greek states, on the left wing. However, Alexander led his Companion cavalry, elite lancers, and the rest of his best horsemen from the right in order to make a devastating attack on the left flank of the Persian heavy infantry. As at the Battle of the Granicus, the Macedonian phalanx was formed up in the centre between the two cavalry wings.[60]

Alexander's strike against the Persian left flank was perfectly placed for the entire wing rapidly collapsed shortly after the attack. Yet

Darius' placement of the heaviest armoured cavalry on his right wing appeared to be a smart move as well, for their attack caused massive damage to Parmenio's cavalry. However, the dominance of the Persian heavy cavalry did not last long, for soon one of their best assets quickly became their greatest weakness, as stated by Quintus Curtius Rufus in his account of the battle in the *History of Alexander*.

> *But on the right the Persians were strongly attacking the Thessalian horsemen, and already one squadron had been ridden down by their very onset, when the Thessalians, smartly wheeling their horses about, slipped aside and returning to the fray, with great slaughter overthrew the barbarians, whom confidence in their victory had scattered and thrown into disorder. The horses and horsemen alike of the Persians, weighed down by the rows of armoured plates which covered them as far as the knees, were hard put to it to heave their column along; for it was one which depended above all on speed; for the Thessalians in wheeling their horses had far outstripped them.*[61]

Since the armoured riders atop armoured mounts of the Persian cavalry were not nearly as mobile as the Hellenistic horsemen, Parmenio and his men were able to outmanoeuvre them so the fight became brutal for both sides as they engaged in a fierce contest of hand-to-hand close combat.

While Alexander and his cavalrymen pursued the fleeing Darius who had retreated with the routed Persian left wing, and the horsemen under Parmenio were embroiled in a vicious stalemate with the enemy heavy cavalrymen, the Macedonian phalanx in the centre was on the verge of collapse. As the right side of the Macedonian heavy infantry was swept up by the momentum of Alexander's spectacular charge, and thus eagerly advanced forward, the left side was held back by the deadly assault of the Persian heavy horsemen; therefore, a gap had formed in the Macedonian front lines that the Greek mercenaries of the Persian army quickly moved in to exploit. However, just before the Greek hoplites managed to break through the Macedonian phalanx and rout them, Alexander and the Companion cavalry returned to assault the flank of the heavy infantry fighting for the Persians. As a result, the rest of the Persian infantry were routed instead, leaving the heavy cavalrymen of the right wing still fighting the Thessalians as the only Persian force left on the field.[62] Terrified of being cut off from the rest of their army, the Persian heavy horsemen panicked and fled as well, yet their extensive armour would once again become a major hindrance, as stated by Arrian:

> *The Persian horses, with their riders heavily armed, suffered much in the retreat, while the riders who hurried in terror and disorder by narrow roads in a crowded horde were trampled to death by one another as much as by the pursuing enemy.*[63]

After saving his infantry and securing victory, Alexander and the Macedonians continued to chase Darius but it was to no avail. Regardless of that minor setback, the Macedonian king had won another major victory against the greatest empire of the ancient world. The Persian heavy cavalry did manage to display their true worth on the right wing along the coastal plain; however, the Battle of Issus ultimately proved the superiority of the Macedonian strategy, tactics and soldiers over the Persian army while under the command of Alexander the Great.

Heavily defeated on two occasions, yet not broken, Darius moved to Babylon and then managed to raise an even larger force by conscripting as many available men into his army as possible from the huge amount of territory he still controlled. Among these various warriors of the east were several units of heavily armoured Massagetae horsemen and Bactrian heavy cavalry under the command of Bessus, the satrap of Bactria. This entire contingent wore extensive armour on both the riders and the mounts and some of the Massagetae carried shields for even more protection. These heavy cavalrymen also possibly benefitted greatly from the development of a new and improved saddle that helped the rider keep his seat with the extra weight of the increased armour. Since it would be several more centuries until the invention of stirrups, such improvements in saddle technology were pivotal to the evolution of ancient heavy cavalry, and especially for the early cataphracts who arose a little over 100 years later. However, unlike the Hellenistic heavy horsemen who almost all wielded the large *xyston* lance, some of the Massagetae and Bactrian heavy cavalrymen carried lances, but many carried shorter spears and javelins like the Persian armoured cavalry, while others fought predominately with the bow. Darius desperately needed a victory or he was at serious risk of losing everything so he did whatever he could to arm as many of his cavalrymen as possible with longer lances and swords like the Macedonians, and with further protection similar to the extensive armour of the Massagetae and Bactrian contingent.[64] In his *Universal History*, Diodorus Siculus states that:

> *Darius had already assembled his forces from all directions and made everything ready for the battle. He had fashioned swords and lances much longer than his earlier types because it was thought that Alexander had had a great advantage in this respect.*[65]

Quintus Curtius Rufus agreed with that assessment for he said:

> *But although the army was almost half again as large as it had been in Cilicia, many lacked arms. These were being procured with the greatest zeal; the cavalry and their horses had coverings of interconnected iron plates; to those to whom before he had given nothing but javelins, shields and swords were added.*[66]

The Persian emperor even tried to increase the number of his cavalry:

> *And herds of horses to be broken were distributed to the infantrymen, in order that the cavalry might be more numerous than before.*[67]

After improving and increasing the heavy cavalry, Darius hoped that they could finally overcome the more-lightly armoured Hellenistic horsemen who had so far proven to be far more effective at charging the enemy with their greater overall shock tactics.

As Darius was preoccupied with his preparations for the next major encounter, Alexander went on to conquer Syria and then Egypt. In 331 BC, the Macedonian king advanced further into Persian territory and confronted Darius' army on a wide-open field near Gaugamela that was ideal ground for the emperor's huge numbers of cavalry and scythed chariots. The Persian front line was comprised of scythed chariots and nearly every cavalryman in the army, along with an elite infantry contingent of both Persians and Greek mercenaries in the middle to support the numerous horsemen. Most of the heavily armoured Bactrian and Massagetae cavalrymen were stationed in the front lines but Darius made sure to hold a unit of Bactrian horsemen in reserve to be a part of his own personal guard. The majority of the heavy cavalrymen were placed on the left wing to face Alexander and the Companion horsemen that usually fought with him on the Macedonian right wing. In front of the main line on this wing were posted 2,000 Massagetae and 1,000 Bactrian armoured horsemen with scythed chariots alongside them to their right. Behind them in the main line were another 8,000 Bactrian cavalrymen, supported by several thousand more horsemen, including 1,000 Dahae (which was another Iranian-speaking tribal group related to the Scythians); although many of these other horsemen fought as light cavalry, possibly covering the extreme left flank of this wing. To the right of the Bactrians, continuing the main line to join the left wing with the centre, were more cavalry, with infantry units interspersed to support them.[68]

Because Darius expected Alexander's main cavalry charge to hit the left side of his forces, there were fewer of the most heavily armoured horsemen on the right wing. On the other hand, the Persian emperor did make sure to place armoured Cappadocian and Armenian heavy cavalrymen in the front line of that wing, along with more scythed chariots. Thousands of light cavalry were stationed behind the heavy horsemen, like they were on the left wing, and among these numerous mounted troops were warriors from another tribe related to the Scythians, known as the Parni (and later as Parthians), along with many Saka as well. Altogether, Darius had more soldiers at his disposal than at the Battle of Issus, with an army that may have numbered over 100,000 men. Alexander was able to increase his forces as well to 7,000 cavalry and 40,000 light and heavy infantry, yet he was still more outnumbered than he had ever been before in battle. As the Persian emperor assumed he would, Alexander attacked from the right wing with his Companion cavalrymen, who numbered about 2,000 men, behind him. Likewise, Parmenio once again commanded 2,000 Thessalian cavalrymen and the rest of the left wing, while the Macedonian heavy infantry was stationed in the centre.[69]

The Battle of Gaugamela began when Alexander first charged toward the middle of the Persian army, but then quickly veered to the right, heading diagonally for the flank of the Persian left wing. Moving in this manner helped to prevent the significantly larger Persian heavy cavalry contingent from overwhelming the Macedonian right flank; on the other hand, the further that Alexander and the right wing moved away from the middle of his army, there was much greater risk of a detrimental gap opening that would make the right flank of the Macedonian pikemen extremely vulnerable to Persian cavalry charges. In reaction to Alexander's movements, the Persian heavy cavalry moved further to the left so that they could still outflank the Macedonian horsemen. Bessus, commanding the heavily armoured Massagetae and Bactrian mounted troops, then attempted to seize the initiative by moving past the rest of the Persian left wing in order to fully envelope the Hellenistic cavalrymen. A cavalry squadron led by Menidas first tried to counter the Bactrians but were quickly forced to withdraw from the much larger force. Before long, the Bactrians, along with many of the Massagetae, halted their leftward movement to engage the Paeonian light cavalry and Menidas' squadron again as well.[70] Arrian described the result of the combat between the opposing cavalry contingents:

> *Alexander's men fell in greater numbers, overwhelmed with the number of the Persians, and also because the [Massagetae] were better protected by defensive armour, both riders and horses alike.*[71]

The heavily armoured mounted tribal warriors were prevailing against their much more lightly armoured opponents; however, it could be argued that their success also had much to do with their greater numbers.

With the momentum in his favour, Darius then sent in his scythed chariots to assault the enemy front lines, yet the Macedonian light infantry quickly dealt with the vehicles. After assaulting the charioteers with a barrage of javelins and other missiles, the Agrianes and other light infantrymen in the Macedonian army rushed towards the chariots, surrounded them and then tore the drivers from the vehicles to slay them on the ground. Those few vehicles that managed to get past the light infantry passed through gaps that formed among the Companion cavalry and were then attacked and killed by the Macedonian infantry held in reserve. The charioteers that advanced against the Macedonian phalanx in the centre were slain in a similar manner, though the scythed vehicles had much more success against Parmenio's left wing. The chariots first successfully broke through the light infantry and then routed them, before engaging the rest of the Macedonian left wing as the numerous Persian cavalrymen were well on their way to almost enveloping the Thessalians on the far left flank.[72]

On the far right flank of the Macedonian forces, Alexander continued to send more squadrons of cavalry against the heavy cavalrymen of the Persian left wing until the Hellenistic horsemen actually managed to gradually overcome the superior numbers of the opposing cavalry contingent. As this was happening, Alexander finally saw the gap he had been waiting for opening up between the left wing cavalry that had followed his mounted troops and the rest of the Persian army. The Macedonian king at the head of his cavalry wedge formation exploited the gap to the fullest with a deadly charge that devastated the Persian forces, as the Hellenistic pikemen simultaneously charged the enemy front as well. As Darius watched the Macedonian cavalry wedge drive deeper into the ranks of his army, the emperor soon lost all hope and abandoned his men. The Persian forces in the centre were the first to witness the flight of the emperor so it quickly disintegrated and followed their ruler in retreat. Furthermore, the Macedonian horsemen of the right wing still fighting the Massagetae heavy cavalrymen defeated their adversaries when the tribal chieftain was slain.[73]

Not all of the Macedonian army faired so well in the Battle of Gaugamela. While Alexander was cutting his way through the Persian ranks, Indian and Persian cavalrymen had charged into the gap formed in the front lines of the Hellenistic forces, just as Alexander had done to their own army. However, instead of attempting to rout the Macedonian phalanx by assaulting it from the flanks or rear, the Persian horsemen penetrated the Hellenistic lines where they were the thinnest until they reached the baggage, and then massacred anyone in sight before a contingent of rearguard infantrymen managed to drive them off. Likewise, the Macedonian left-wing cavalry were still engaged in fierce combat with the numerous Persian horsemen, so Alexander decided to come to their aid instead of pursuing Darius. Yet as he approached, Median, Indian and Parthian cavalrymen of the Persian right wing had already resolved to flee with the rest of their army, and thus rode straight into Alexander and his Companions in their attempt to escape. The resulting clash was brutal because the auxiliary and subject warriors of the Persians were fighting for their very survival and, therefore, managed to kill about sixty of the Macedonian cavalrymen. Ultimately, some of the fleeing horsemen managed to break through the Royal Squadron and escape, yet victory belonged to Alexander in this engagement just as it had in the overall battle.[74]

As at Issus, the most successful Persian warriors at the Battle of Gaugamela were the most heavily armoured cavalry contingents. Darius attempted to use this advantage to the fullest by equipping as many riders and mounts as possible with armour, as well as giving them lances more comparable to the deadly Macedonian *xyston*, though neither the Persian emperor nor any of his commanders could equal the military brilliance of Alexander and his highly effective use of shock tactics. In addition, the vast majority of the Persian infantry was no match for the Macedonian pikemen. The east was primarily dominated by cavalry warfare, and continued to be even after the conquests of Alexander; therefore, the response of the eastern horsemen to the Hellenistic heavy infantrymen in their formidable phalanx formation was the further development of heavily armoured cavalry that ultimately led to the creation of the first cataphracts by one of Alexander's successors.

Macedonian Empires

After three battles, Alexander had effectively conquered the Achaemenid Persian Empire. Darius was murdered shortly after the Battle of Gaugamela and although Alexander faced fierce resistance as he continued to advance further east, none of the remnants of the Persian army, nor any of the various tribal warriors of Central Asia related to Scythians, were able to defeat or repel the invasions of the Macedonian king. By the end of his conquests, Alexander ruled an empire that stretched from Macedonia and Egypt in the west to as far as India in the east. Though the vast, fledgling empire came to an abrupt end shortly after the death of Alexander the Great in 323 BC, his generals, later called the Diadochoi or 'Successors', promptly carved up the conquered territories and went to war with each other until the most powerful among them established their own stable kingdoms. In 312 BC, one of the most successful of these Diadochoi managed to gain control of Babylonia and then most of the eastern territories. By 306 BC, he named himself King Seleucus I Nicator (r. 306–281 BC) and became the ruler of an empire (now known as the Seleucid Empire) whose borders encircled most of the lands once dominated by the former Achaemenid Persian Empire.

The Parthians

One of the regions ruled by the newly created Seleucid Empire was Parthia, which had been increased in size to include the adjacent region of Hyrcania as well. Throughout much of the first half of the third century BC, the larger province of Parthia was at first governed, but then effectively ruled, by a Persian named Andragoras who rebelled against Antiochus II (r. 261–246 BC) near the end of the Seleucid emperor's reign. After the rebellion had begun, the Parni, a member of the Dahae confederacy who occupied the lands southeast of the Caspian Sea that bordered the rebel province, elected a new ruler in 247 BC, King Arsaces (r. 247–211 BC). Under his leadership, the Parni invaded Parthia in 238 BC and Andragoras was killed. From then on, the Parni ruled the Kingdom of Parthia and became known as the Parthians. The Seleucids made attempts to expel the Parthians and reclaim their lost territory but they were all unsuccessful. Yet the eastern campaigns of the Seleucid army against the Parthians turned out to be very fruitful, because it was from those experiences that the idea arose to create the first units of cataphracts.

CHAPTER TWO

THE FIRST CATAPHRACTS

The Seleucid Empire

Shortly after King Arsaces conquered Parthia and seized it from the
Seleucid Empire, the rebel governor of Bactria, Diodotus II, named
himself the new king of his province around 235 BC. The Bactrian ruler
then also entered into a peaceful agreement with the Parthian king,
because both men knew they would soon face the wrath of the Seleucid
emperor.[1] The two new kings did not have to wait long, for later in the
year King Seleucus II (r. 246–225 BC) launched a campaign in the east
to reclaim his lost territory. Unfortunately for the Hellenistic ruler, his
attempts to reclaim Parthia and Bactria ended in failure and he was
forced to return in order to deal with a turbulent Babylon. A couple of
decades later, Seleucus' son, Antiochus III (r. 223–187 BC), was ready to
succeed where his father had failed. After stabilizing the western half
of the empire, Antiochus the Great made extensive preparations for an
eastern campaign. His aim was to either completely retake land or at
least force the eastern rulers to submit and become client kings as well
as give tribute to their acknowledged overlord. In 209 BC, the Seleucid
emperor carried out a campaign against the fledgling kingdom of
Parthia with a large army of around 15,000 heavy infantry, 6,000 cavalry and over 12,000 peltasts and other light infantry.[2]

Before Antiochus began his eastern expedition, King Arsaces
was succeeded by his son, Arsaces II (r. 211–185 BC), whose soldiers
attempted to slow or halt the Seleucid invaders by first preventing
them from gaining access to all of the wells or other sources of fresh
water in their path, and then by sending men to raid and harry the
Hellenistic forces as they marched. None of these actions stopped the
Seleucid army from advancing further into Parthia. Antiochus continued to overcome further resistance, then successfully besieged more
than one fortified settlement and captured several towns before he and
the Parthian king agreed to meet and make peace terms. In the agreement, Arsaces was allowed to keep his kingdom as long as he became
a vassal and paid tribute to the Seleucid emperor. Additionally,
the Parthians lost the important city of Hekatompylos, along with
much of the former region of Hyrcania, to the Seleucids.[3]

With Parthia made into a client kingdom, Antiochus moved on to deal with Bactria next. Yet before he reached the former province of the empire, the new rebel ruler of the Greco-Bactrian kingdom, Euthydemos, confronted the Seleucid army at the Arios River on the border. The Bactrian forces consisted primarily of cavalry that may have numbered as many as 10,000 men; thus, Antiochus proceeded with his horsemen, especially his 2,000-strong royal guardsmen, supported by many light infantry peltasts. Even though they were outnumbered, the Seleucid cavalrymen achieved victory against the Bactrian horsemen, forcing Euthydemos to retreat back to his capital city of Bactra. After a lengthy siege of two years, along with further violent encounters, Antiochus eventually gave in and expressed his desire to make peace with the Greco-Bactrian king. Similar to the terms made with Arsaces, Euthydemos was allowed to retain his kingship in exchange for a pledge of loyalty and the payment of a large tribute. Antiochus also confirmed his control over the regions of Margiana and Aria.[4] Parthia and Bactria were the primary targets of Antiochus' eastern expedition and, although he did not fully recover the lost territories, he forced their rulers into a state of vassalage, which was enough to satisfy the Seleucid emperor. Antiochus was then free to return to the west in order to settle unfinished business with a rival Hellenistic kingdom ruled by the Ptolemies in Egypt.

Earlier in his reign, several years before he left for his campaigns in the east, Antiochus had been defeated by Ptolemy IV Philopator (r. 221–204 BC) at the Battle of Raphia in 217 BC. The news that a rebellion had broken out in Egypt reached Antiochus in 206 BC, which was one of the reasons that the Seleucid emperor wished to end the siege of Bactra.[5] In 204 BC, the death of Ptolemy only fueled Antiochus' desire to seek revenge against the rival kingdom while it was weak and vulnerable. As he prepared in the years before his ultimate confrontation with the Ptolemaic Kingdom, Antiochus the Great created a new type of mounted warrior inspired by his combat experiences in the east, which later became known as the cataphract.

Although the Parthians and Bactrians that Antiochus faced in his eastern campaigns certainly utilized heavily armoured cavalry like their predecessors, it is unknown whether one or both regions had begun fielding riders and steeds armoured to the extent of the new Seleucid cataphracts. Whether Antiochus simply copied Parthian or Bactrian troops or innovated by developing the idea further, the new cavalry that would fight the Ptolemaic Egyptians at the Battle of Panion were definitely the first to be called cataphracts.

The events leading up to the confrontation at Panion resulted from Antiochus' moves to reclaim the region of Coile-Syria from the Ptolemies in 202 BC. The Seleucid emperor began his campaign with the seizure of the city of Damascus, which was accomplished in the first year. By 201 BC, Antiochus had not only captured Gaza, but he had also taken much of the land in between the two cities, which gave him control over Palestine, a large part of Coile-Syria. However, by the end of that year, the Aetolian mercenary commander of the Ptolemaic army, Skopas, managed to recruit a large number of mercenaries, which he combined with the native Ptolemaic forces. Then, early in 200 BC, Skopas launched a campaign to retake Palestine during winter in the hopes of catching the Seleucids off guard. The ploy worked; the region was soon back in Ptolemaic hands because the Seleucid army was still away in its winter quarters. In response, Antiochus quickly gathered the largest army he could muster and then marched south from Damascus until he met the Ptolemaic forces near Panion later in the summer.[6]

Within the ancient written records, there is one description of the Battle of Panion in Book XVI of the *Histories* written by Polybius. However, the account is not a full description of the events but rather a criticism of the report written by Zeno of Rhodes that described the conflict.[7] Yet the information that the critique of Zeno's account has provided, combined with the study of the local topography where the battle most likely took place from scholars such as Bezalel Bar-Kochva, is sufficient to construct a rough outline of the major events that occurred during the battle. The Seleucid army, comprised of as many as 60,000 soldiers, reached the site of the battlefield first. As the Seleucids travelled the route to Gaza, Antiochus halted the southward march of his forces to the south of Mount Hermon, near the town of Panion. After making a camp for the baggage, most likely located adjacent to the settlement, the army divided into two groups so that it could occupy the entire field to the southwest of the town because the Banias River cut through the level ground. One contingent, consisting of some of the infantrymen, cavalrymen and elephants, remained on the rougher terrain of the same side of the river as Panion in order to guard the camp. It was in this southern arena that Antiochus' son, Antiochus the Elder, took an elevated position atop the hill of Tel-Fakhr. Meanwhile, the majority of the army crossed the Banias River so that it could occupy the more level ground of the Banias Plateau on the north side of the waterway.[8]

In the northern arena, King Antiochus the Great commanded most of the Seleucid phalanx and the elephant line in front of the infantrymen located in the centre, while he sent his right-wing cavalry to take control of the hill of Tel-Hamra to the north, 'among which were the cataphracts, under the sole command of the younger of the king's sons Antiochus'.[9] Polybius used the Greek words *kataphraktoi hippoi* to describe the new cataphract troops, which is the first time the term has appeared in the historical record. While in his account of the earlier Battle of Raphia, the ancient writer uses the term *hippoi* for all of the cavalrymen in the Seleucid army, the fact that Polybius added the word *kataphraktoi* to describe a specific unit of cavalrymen at the Battle of Panion suggests that the heavy horsemen were covered with more extensive armour than was ever worn before by the Seleucid cavalry.[10] Opposing the Seleucid troops north of the river were the main body of the Ptolemaic phalanx, along with every elephant in their army because the Egyptian kingdom had fewer of the huge warbeasts than their eastern Hellenistic rival.[11] Like Antiochus, Skopas led from the centre and sent the majority of the Aetolian mercenary cavalry to the left wing in order to face the horsemen of Antiochus the Younger, which included the unique unit of cataphracts. The Aetolian horsemen were considered the best cavalry of Greece at the time, thus Skopas hoped they would be able to overcome their more heavily armoured opponents.[12] In the southern area, on the other side of the Banias River, the Aetolian mercenary infantrymen, supported by further Ptolemaic cavalrymen, were placed there in order to attempt to break through the Seleucid lines defending the route to Panion and try to seize the Seleucid army camp that contained the valuables of the baggage train.[13]

The combat commenced to the north when the Indian elephants of the Seleucids engaged the Ptolemaic African elephants and drove them off, allowing the Seleucid phalanx to slam into the front lines of the Ptolemaic infantry. Meanwhile, Polybius also states:

> *Antiochus the Younger and the cataphracts charged down from the high ground and put to flight and pursued the cavalry under Ptolemy, son of Aeropus, who was in command of the Aetolians in the plain on the left wing.*[14]

After the cataphracts managed to drive off the formidable Aetolian horsemen, the young prince then led his cavalry in a charge against the rear of the Ptolemaic phalanx as they were fighting the Seleucid infantrymen. The Ptolemaic forces had much more success in the southern arena for they managed to rout both the Seleucid cavalry and infantry, yet the wall of elephants stationed as a rearguard behind the Seleucid troops then successfully blocked the Ptolemaic advance. Unable to break through the elephants and capture the Seleucid camp in the southern arena, the Ptolemaic army was ultimately defeated, for their main phalanx was surrounded and crushed on the northern side of the river. Skopas was able to escape with 10,000 of his men, mostly Aetolian infantry from the southern arena, and reach the refuge of Sidon. However, King Antiochus was not far behind and soon put the city under siege, until it was taken by the summer of 199 BC and Skopas was forced to surrender.[15] Antiochus had won a spectacular victory at Panion that more than made up for his humiliating defeat at Raphia nearly twenty years before. The emperor's new creation, the cataphracts, were the main component contributing to the Seleucid success, which would not be forgotten by Antiochus who used the unit in much the same manner in his next major battle a decade later.

By 198 BC, Antiochus the Great had conquered all of Syria, but the conflict was not yet over with Ptolemaic Egypt, because the fighting merely shifted to Asia Minor and Thrace to the north. The Seleucid Empire eventually defeated the Kingdom of Egypt but their actions in the northern territories soon threatened the expanding Roman Empire that just recently had begun to take a major interest in the region.[16] Rome publicly desired to protect its Greek allies who felt endangered by the encroaching actions of Antiochus near their borders, but it is also safe to assume that the imperial aspirations of both the Seleucids and the Romans meant that an eventual war was unavoidable. As both sides prepared for their inevitable clash, it became clear that the Seleucid Empire was far superior in terms of cavalry; a fact that was exploited in attempts to intimidate the Romans, as stated in the account of Livy:

> *The ambassador of Antiochus was heard before the Aetolians. He, a boaster like most who are maintained by a king's power, filled seas and lands with an empty sound of words: an uncountable number of cavalry was crossing the Hellespont into Europe, partly equipped with breastplates – these they call the* cataphracti *– partly those who use arrows from horseback, and as a result of which there is no protection against them, since they aimed quite accurately backwards while fleeing on their horses.*[17]

The cataphracts were a major part of the threatening propaganda used by the Seleucids because their heavy metal armour made them look nearly invincible on the battlefield and they had already proven their worth against the Aetolian cavalry that was renowned throughout the ancient world. The fact that they were a new creation of the Seleucids probably only added to the fear they invoked before they were actually seen in person, for such heavily equipped horsemen were a rarity in the west. However, according to Plutarch, the Roman's responded in typically arrogant fashion to the threat of the new cataphracts and the rest of the enormous Seleucid army:

> *When King Antiochus was coming upon Greece with great forces, and all men trembled at the report of his numbers and equipage, he [Flaminius, the Roman consul] told the Achaeans this story: 'Once I dined with a friend at Chalcis, and when I wondered at the variety of dishes, my host said, "All these are pork, only in dressing and sauces they differ". And therefore be not you amazed at the king's forces, when you hear talk of cataphracts and men-at-arms and choice foot-men and horse-archers, for all these are but Syrians [Seleucids], with some little difference in their weapons'.[18]*

Although obviously propaganda, these quotes do not portray the fear and doubt that was probably felt by many on both sides for each empire had already proved to be extremely dangerous to their enemies. What is important to note regarding the cataphracts in both of these statements though, is that the latest addition to the Seleucid cavalry was quickly seen as one of the most lethal units in the imperial army. *The History of Rome* of Livy was also the first time that the cataphracts were written about in Latin, therefore, the Roman historian changed the Greek words *kataphraktoi hippoi* into the Latinized spelling of *cataphracti* in order to describe the revolutionary unit of horsemen to his Roman readers.

After Antiochus failed to invade Greece in 190 BC, he retreated with his army back to Asia Minor. The Roman response was quick for they sent an army under the command of the renowned general, Scipio Africanus, and his brother Lucius Scipio, which reached the Seleucid forces at Magnesia. Both armies were roughly the same size, especially regarding the infantry of each side, at around 50,000 men each; however, the Seleucid army certainly had a significant advantage in the number of cavalry with around 12,000 horsemen compared to around 3,000 cavalrymen in the Roman army. The centre and the left wing of the Roman army was comprised of heavy infantry legionaries with their left flank protected by the ancient course of the Phyrgios River, while nearly all of their cavalry was placed on the right wing. The Seleucid forces that opposed them were arrayed with the heavy infantry pikemen in the middle, which were supported by cavalry and light infantry on either side of them.[19] Among the cavalry, there were 6,000 cataphract troops that were divided evenly between each wing, as stated by Livy:

> On the right side of the phalanx, he placed five hundred Gallograecian horsemen. To these he joined three thousand horsemen clad in complete armour, whom they call cataphracti.[20]

And in his description of the left wing:

> Then, three thousand cataphracts; then, one thousand other horsemen, being a royal cohort, equipped with lighter coverings for themselves and their horses, but, in other respects, not unlike [the cataphracts].[21]

As his son did at Panion, Antiochus led the cataphracts and the rest of the cavalry stationed on the right wing.

While the infantry centres of both armies collided, the battle was decided by the actions of the cavalry of each side. First off, the cataphracts and the right-wing cavalry led by Antiochus charged into the Roman legionaries stationed on the left with such force that they not only broke through the frontlines, but also then completely routed the Roman infantry contingent. Most likely due to his Roman pride, Livy downplayed the collapse of the Roman legion in question, yet still made it known that Antiochus and the cataphracts were very successful in the attack as he recounted the significant event:

> For Antiochus, who commanded the right wing, having observed that the enemy, through confidence in the river, had placed no reserve there, except four troops of horse, and that these, keeping close to the infantry, left an open space on the bank of the river, made a charge on them, with a body of auxiliaries and cataphracts. He not only attacked them in front, but having surrounded the wing in the direction of the river, pressed them in flank also; until the routed cavalry first, and then the infantry that were next to them, fled with precipitation to the camp.[22]

Although Livy mentions cavalry, it is important to note that the vast majority of the Roman left wing that the cataphracts overcame was comprised of legionaries. In *The Syrian Wars*, Appian reinforced Livy's account, for he also stated that 'Antiochus, on the right, broke through the Roman line of battle, dismembered it, and pursued a long distance'.[23] This feat alone was particularly impressive for at this point in history, Roman legionaries were definitely considered some of the best, if not *the* best, infantry troops in the world; a legion defeated by a frontal assault in that manner was a rarity for the time. However, Antiochus followed up that brilliant action by attacking the Roman camp, which was guarded by Thracian and Macedonian allies of Rome, instead of striking the legionaries of the centre in the rear or the flanks. If he had done that, victory could have easily belonged to the Seleucids at that moment, but instead Antiochus and his cavalry were tied up in their combat with the camp garrison and the remainder of the routed legionaries who managed to rally and come to the aid of their allies at the fortified camp.[24]

At the same time that Antiochus led his charge on the right wing, the chariots he had placed in front of his left wing simultaneously advanced towards the Roman right wing, predominately composed of cavalry forces. Yet the light infantry stationed among the horsemen of the Roman army launched such a devastating barrage of javelins and arrows that the Seleucid charioteers were unable to withstand it, and thus they were forced to retreat with their vehicles back into their own lines. Chaos ensued, for the cataphracts were preparing to make their assault right as the chariots came rushing back towards them, which caused the armoured horsemen to completely lose their momentum. This allowed the cavalry on the Roman right flank to fully exploit the confusion on the Seleucid side and quickly overcome the lumbering heavy cavalrymen stuck in their tracks.[25] Livy recounted the disastrous sequence of events for the Seleucids, emphasizing the amount of armour worn by the cataphracts as a major contributing factor to the defeat of the Seleucid left wing:

> But that futile affair was soon the cause of real loss. For the auxiliaries in reserve, which were posted next, being terrified at the turn and disorder of the chariots, betook themselves to flight, leaving all exposed as far as the post of the cataphracts; to whom when the Roman cavalry, after dispersing the reserves, approached, they did not sustain their first onset. Some fled, and others, being delayed by the weight of their coverings and armour, were put to the sword. The whole left wing then gave way, and the auxiliaries, posted between the cavalry and the phalanx, being thrown into confusion, the terror spread even to the centre.[26]

In his account of the battle, Appian also stated that the heavy weight of the cataphract armour prevented them from successfully reacting to the unexpected retreat of the Seleucid chariots:

The horses being wounded in great numbers charged with their char-
iots upon their own ranks. The dromedaries were thrown into disor-
der first, as they were next in line to the chariots, and after them the
cataphracts who could not easily dodge the scythes on account of the
weight of their armour.[27]

Appian continued to stress how much their extensive armour nega-
tively affected the cataphracts:

[The Roman cavalry] made so heavy a charge that they put to flight
not only those, but the adjoining squadrons and the cataphracts, who
were already thrown into disorder by the chariots. The greater part
of these, unable to turn and fly quickly, on account of the weight of
their armour, were captured or killed.[28]

After crushing the cataphracts, and the rest of the Seleucid forces of the
left wing, the horsemen of the Roman army did what Antiochus failed
to do to achieve victory by slamming into the flank of the Seleucid phalanx. Yet, miraculously, the Seleucid pikemen held firm and withstood
the onslaught from the legionaries in the front and the Roman cavalry
attacking the flank. However, Antiochus had placed a small reserve of
elephants to protect the rear of the army, which was then the target of
severe missile fire from the archers and javelineers within the Roman
ranks. It did not take long for the barrage to cause the huge beasts
to panic and then rampage into their own infantry troops in front of
them, causing the Seleucid phalanx to collapse. The routed Seleucid
infantrymen fled to their camp, which was stoutly defended first by
the reserves and then by the flood of retreating men who poured into
the encampment, allowing many of the pikemen to escape the slaughter; although thousands of the Seleucid troops were slain on the field.
The Romans had won the battle.[29]

Magnesia was only the second major battle that the new Seleucid
cataphracts had participated in and for the first time their major weakness was fully exposed. Although nearly invulnerable due to their
extensive armour, those same defences could also be their Achilles'
heel, for it drastically limited their mobility, normally one of the greatest assets of cavalry troops. From battles such as Magnesia, and in
future conflicts, the later kingdoms and empires that utilized cataphracts had to learn that for the elite heavy cavalrymen to be the most
effective, they must be supported by light infantry and/or cavalry in
order to protect their flanks, or even more importantly, to drive off
attacks whenever the armoured horsemen were immobile. On the

other hand, the cataphracts' spectacular charge that caused the rare collapse of a Roman legion also reinforced how deadly the new heavy cavalry troops could be when used properly on the battlefield with shock tactics.

As the first cataphracts ever created, the least is known about the Seleucid version of the heavy cavalry warriors. The most complete depiction of the arms and armour of the Seleucid cataphract is located on the Balustrade Reliefs of the temple of Athena Polias Nikephoros at Pergamum. One of the most impressive features shown among the armament is a metal mask with an incredibly detailed face, including a sculpted beard that was attached to the helmet of the rider. The rest of the cataphract armour included a Hellenistic-style cuirass with traditional *pinions* and *pteruges* (strips hanging from the shoulders and lower edge respectively) attached, as well as laminated armour that covered the entire arm (*manica*) that was made of articulated metal or rawhide hoops that overlapped down the limb and were often riveted to inner straps.[30] An almost complete set of cataphract armour featuring physical remains of iron *manica*, like those depicted on the Pergamum frieze, have been found during excavations carried out by the French at the site of Ai Khanoum, an ancient Hellenistic city located in modern day Afghanistan. Similar laminated armour that covered the arms probably also protected the legs as well, along with Hellenistic-style greaves. A figurine of a warrior from Syria, now located in the Louvre, has also been discovered and is depicted wearing similar armour to the images on the reliefs at Pergamum. The figure is shown wearing a Hellenistic-style cuirass as well, most likely made of leather, with *pteruges*, and the arms of the heavily armoured soldier were covered with *manica*. Last but not least, the helmet of the Syrian figurine has the same metal face mask with the intricate sculpted beard. However, the armour of the cataphract slightly changed in the later years of the Seleucid Empire by the reign of Antiochus IV Epiphanes (r. 175–164 BC), in that the type of cuirass had been exchanged to mainly become a Roman type of mail coat instead of the previous Hellenistic corselet.[31]

The primary weapon wielded by the mounted warrior may have first been the lighter *xyston*-style lance but later it predominately became the *kontos* (heavy lance) that was most likely similar in length, at around 3.6 m (12 ft.), but may have been thicker and weighed more. The horse of the Seleucid cataphract also wore a metal facemask, but for the steed it was most likely constructed of bronze and ornamented with a feather crest. It is also clear that the heavy warhorse was provided with lamellar armour to protect the chest;[32]

however, it is likely that the armour was even more extensive for the cataphract than what is depicted on the reliefs at Pergamum.[33] The further protection was probably either a half-trapper or even a full body trapper worn by the horse, made of metal scales that overlapped upon a fabric backing, which fastened over the chest of the beast. The half-trapper only covered the shoulders and chest of the mount, while the full trapper provided armour for nearly the entire body; remains of horse trapper armour of the fuller type has been found at sites such as Dura Europos. Another possible addition to the cataphract equipment was an armoured saddle that provided a defence for the thighs of the riders, influenced by earlier Achaemenid models. A fragment dated to either the 4th or 3rd century BC from a terracotta relief flask found at the site of Khumbuz-Tepe, located in southern Khwarezm, contains a depiction of this unique heavy cavalry equipment.[34]

It is probable that the Seleucid cataphracts were predominately recruited from among the Iranian population of the empire, not the ruling Macedonian/Greek people.[35] Not only did the Iranian peoples have a much stronger background in cavalry warfare than the Hellenistic westerners, but they had also faced cataphract-type soldiers in combat on many more occasions, and their ancestors may have even fought as the elite heavy cavalry troops before the conquest of Alexander the Great that resulted in the creation of the Seleucid Empire. On the other hand, it is curious to note that when Livy described the cavalry units at the Battle of Magnesia in 190 BC, he clearly identifies the origins of many of them, but does not do so in his description of the cataphracts. Similarly, when the cataphracts are mentioned in the accounts of Polybius, he also does not use an ethnic term to describe them, which he often does for many other contingents of warriors. Therefore, it may also be possible that the cataphract units were comprised of regulars, primarily of Macedonian origin, that were recruited from the military colonies, not foreign allies or mercenaries.[36] Yet regardless of their origin, the cataphracts were most likely provided with armour in the style of the region the soldier fought in; in the east, the armour would have been predominately lamellar and scale armour types, while plate armour cuirasses were more common in the west.[37]

After the Battle of Magnesia, the Seleucids continued to utilize cataphract troops, yet due to their expensive cost to maintain in the field, there numbers were reduced. As a result of their defeat to the Romans, the empire lost important territory, specifically Asia Minor, as well as a significant portion of its army, and was, therefore, greatly weakened.

With fewer available men and decreased resources, the amount of cataphracts in the Seleucid army may have been reduced by thousands of soldiers. However, the empire was still powerful and the new emperor, Antiochos IV, attempted to prove that with a grand display of his military might. In 166 BC, the emperor held a festival at the city of Daphne in Syria with games and a majestic parade of all his best troops in their finest armour. In the account of Polybius, the cataphracts made an appearance in the procession:

> *Next came the cataphract cavalry, both men and horses acquiring that name from the nature of their panoply; they numbered 1,500. All the above men had purple surcoats, in many cases embroidered with gold and heraldic designs.*[38]

It is possible that the number of cataphracts was cut drastically from the 6,000 soldiers at Magnesia down to 1,500 men at Daphne, though there is also a chance that the heavy cavalrymen at the parade were only the base unit, while the overall numbers of the cataphracts were increased during times of war.[39]

The cataphracts continued to fade within the Seleucid army as the empire declined throughout the later half of the second century and into the first century BC. After the Romans seized much of the western territories of the empire, the Parthians then conquered substantial Seleucid lands in the east. The empire fractured into several different kingdoms after the death of Antiochus IV in 164 BC, allowing the Iranian tribal kingdom to easily conquer each former Seleucid region individually. From 160 to 140 BC, the ruler of the Parthians, Mithridates I (r. 165–132 BC), managed to seize most of the eastern regions, including Media, Persis, Elymais, Characene, Assyria, Babylonia and Gedrosia, transforming his kingdom into a full-fledged empire. The Seleucids first attempted to retake their lost territories in a failed campaign led by King Demetrius II (r. 146–138 BC) in 138 BC, and then again in 129 BC by his brother, Antiochus VII Sidates (r. 138–129 BC). After some initial success, however, Antiochus VII ultimately failed to overcome the Parthians.[40] By the first century BC, the once-formidable Seleucid empire was so weak that its land was reduced to the royal city of Antioch and part of Syria. In 96 BC, King Antiochus VIII Grypus (r. 125–96 BC) was murdered, which plunged the fragile kingdom into a state of anarchy that it would never recover from. Once the powerful king of Armenia, Tigranes the Great (r. 95–55 BC), was made aware of the chaotic situation in the Seleucid lands, he quickly exploited the situation and took control of the dying kingdom in 83 BC.[41] Even though the Seleucids underwent a minor resurgence a little over a decade later and regained their autonomy, Roman general Pompey the Great annexed Syria in 63 BC, thus the Seleucid Empire finally ended. Yet even though the Hellenistic state had collapsed, the Seleucids had certainly made their mark on the militaries of the ancient world with the creation of the cataphracts. When Asclepiodotus wrote his military treatise, *Tactica*, in the first century BC, the ancient writer made sure to include the new heavy cavalrymen in his work:

> Now the cavalry, which fights at close quarters, uses a very heavy equipment, fully protecting both horses and men with defensive armour, and employing, like the hoplites, long spears.[42]

The Kingdom of Armenia

When the kingdom of Urartu, a state contemporary with the Assyrians and the Hittites located in the Armenian Highlands from Upper Mesopotamia in the south to the Caucasus in the north, collapsed circa 590 BC, the Armenians rapidly took the ancient kingdom's place. However, the newcomers were soon subjugated by the Achaemenid Persian empire later in the sixth century BC and Armenia was turned into a province. As subjects of the empire, the Armenians were called up to serve in the armies of the Persians, such as the heavy cavalrymen that fought at the Battle of Gaugamela in 331 BC. Armenia was also a very important source of horses for the Persian Empire because they bred Nisaean steeds of the same quality as those that came from Media. After Alexander the Great conquered the Achaemenids, the satrap of Armenia, Ervand II (r. 331–325 BC), established the sovereign rule of the new kingdom of Armenia. However, the kingdom soon became a vassal of the Seleucid empire in 312 BC, and was periodically forced to pay tribute to its Hellenistic overlord. Yet when the Seleucids were greatly weakened after their defeat at the Battle of Magnesia in 190 BC, the kingdom rose in prominence under its new king, Artashes (r. 188–159 BC).[43]

The growing might of the kingdom of Armenia allowed it to seize land from the vastly expanded territory of the Parthian empire, as well as other surrounding regions, under the new king, Tigranes the Great. In 88 BC, the powerful Armenian king allied himself with King Mithridates VI of Pontus (r. 120–63 BC) and the two kings achieved victory over a Roman army commanded by Manlius Maltinus and Aquilius. This was the same Tigranes who five years later took control over the incredibly weak Seleucid kingdom. By 69 BC, Tigranes the Great had become one of the most powerful rulers in Western Asia.⁴⁴ The Armenians had a long tradition of utilizing heavily armoured cavalry dating back to even before the Battle of Gaugamela, yet it was not until the reign of Tigranes that cataphracts had become a substantial force within the army. In fact, cataphracts had spread from their origin in the Seleucid empire to become a major type of warrior fielded in armies throughout the region. In the description of the Caucasian Albanians in his *Geography*, Strabo stated, 'Still they fight both on foot and on horseback, both in light armour and as cataphracts, like the Armenians'.⁴⁵ Furthermore, according to a fragment of Arrian's *Parthica*, the kingdom of Edessa also had cataphracts.⁴⁶ However, another showdown between cataphract troops and the Roman Empire was long overdue, so it was only a matter of time before the legionaries would confront the elite heavy cavalrymen of the Armenians to once again see how effective they really were.

After his victory over King Mithridates and securing his control over the region of Pontus, Roman general Lucius Licinius Lucullus invaded the Kingdom of Armenia in 69 BC, which had harboured the defeated Pontic ruler. Lucullus advanced into Armenia with two legions and only 500 cavalry, equalling around 20,000 men in total.⁴⁷ Not only were the Romans aware of the fact that they were vastly outnumbered, especially in terms of horsemen when compared to the numerous cavalrymen of the Armenians, but they had also heard the tales of the formidable cataphracts, and thus, according to Plutarch, the men 'were most afraid of their armoured cavalry'.⁴⁸ Even so, regardless of their fear, the Romans bravely confronted the first 2,000 horsemen sent against them by the Armenian King Tigranes in the hope of halting the invasion, and managed to overcome the more numerous cavalry force of the defenders. With no more Armenian troops in the way to prevent their progress, Lucullus led his army to the capital, Tigranocerta, and besieged the city. In response, Tigranes raised an enormous army to face the Romans and end the siege.⁴⁹ According to Plutarch, the Armenian king 'was in command of 20,000 bowmen and slingers, and 55,000 horsemen, of whom 17,000 were cataphracts'.⁵⁰ Although without a doubt these numbers are greatly exaggerated, it is certain that Lucullus had many fewer men than his enemy, for in reality the Armenian army may have numbered as many as 60,000 men.⁵¹

Once Tigranes and his army reached the Romans outside of Tigranocerta, Plutarch recorded that:

> *His multitude formed in battle array, the king himself occupying the centre, and assigning the left wing to the king of the Adiabeni, the*

right to the king of the Medes. In front of this wing also the greater part of the cataphracts were drawn up.[52]

After viewing the troop formations of the Armenian army, Lucullus made his plan of attack, which focused specifically on the enemy cataphracts:

> But when he saw that the cataphracts, on whom the greatest reliance was placed, were stationed at the foot of a considerable hill which was crowned by a broad and level space, and that the approach to this was a matter of only four stadia, and neither rough nor steep, he ordered his Thracian and Gallic horsemen to attack the enemy in the flank, and to parry their long spears with their own short swords. (Now the sole resource of the cataphracts is their long lance [kontos], and they have none other whatsoever, either in defending themselves or attacking their enemies, owing to the weight and rigidity of their armour; in this they are, as it were, immured.) Then he himself, with two cohorts, hastened eagerly towards the hill, his soldiers following with all their might, because they saw him ahead of them in armour, enduring all the fatigue of a foot-soldier, and pressing his way along. Arrived at the top, and standing in the most conspicuous spot, he cried with a loud voice, 'The day is ours, the day is ours, my fellow soldiers!' With these words, he led his men against the cataphracts, ordering them not to hurl their javelins yet, but taking each his own man, to smite the enemy's legs and thighs, which are the only parts of these cataphracts left exposed. However, there was no need of this mode of fighting, for the enemy did not await the Romans, but, with loud cries and in most disgraceful flight, they hurled themselves and their horses, with all their weight, upon the ranks of their own infantry, before it had so much as begun to fight, and so all those tens of thousands were defeated without the infliction of a wound or the sight of blood.[53]

The Battle of Tigranocerta once again proved that without the support of light cavalry or infantry, the heavily armoured horsemen were extremely vulnerable to attacks in their flanks, which Lucullus exploited brilliantly to achieve victory. But even though the numbers of troops are always ridiculously exaggerated, it is important to note that when the battle is mentioned in the accounts of later Roman writers, the cataphracts are always emphasized while many other specific types of troops are never mentioned, such as in the works of Eutropius:

> *Lucullus, therefore, still pursuing his routed enemy, entered even the kingdom of Tigranes, who ruled over both the Armenias. Tigranocerta, the most noble city of Armenia, he succeeded in taking; the king himself, who advanced against him with 600,000 [cataphracts], and a hundred thousand archers and other troops, he so completely defeated with a force of only 18,000, that he annihilated a great part of the Armenians.[54]*

Festus' account is another example:

> *Lucius Lucullus pursued to Armenia Mithridates, who had been deprived of the rule of Pontus. The same man, with 18,000 Romans, conquered Tigranes, the Armenians' king, with 7,000 [cataphracts] and 2,000 archers.[55]*

The consistent mentioning of the cataphracts in the Roman accounts may show that even though successful Roman generals had learned how to overcome the formidable armoured cavalry, Roman warriors still had great respect for the elite eastern horsemen.

Although the exact arms and armour of the early Armenian cataphracts are unknown, it is possible to propose some theories mostly based upon the small amount of information given in Plutarch's account of Tigranocerta. Like the Seleucid cataphracts, the Armenian type of the heavy cavalrymen predominately wielded the *kontos*, and few, if any at all, carried secondary weaponry, such as swords. Both the Seleucid and Armenian cataphracts were trained in shock tactics, charging at enemy lines with their lances in either a wedge or column formation in the attempt to break the opposing ranks. Aside from that, the early cataphracts did not have another purpose in the armies of the two states. The Armenian cataphracts were also heavily armoured; however, unlike the Seleucid versions, the Armenian mounted warriors possibly wore less armour on their legs since that was the only vulnerable area of the riders and steeds; they certainly did not utilize the armoured saddle that may have been used by the Achaemenids and the Seleucids, for their thighs were left exposed. It also may be safe to assume that the Armenians probably wore more eastern styles of armour, particularly scale and lamellar, instead of the Hellenistic plate armour preferred in the west.

Even after his impressive victory at Tigranocerta, Lucullus was unable to fully subdue the Armenians; which may have had a lot to do with the fact that King Mithridates had returned to Pontus and began to successfully free his kingdom from Roman oppression. By 66 BC, the Roman Senate lost faith in the general, and thus he was recalled on charges of prolonging the war deliberately for his own personal benefit. Forced to return to Rome, yet not allowed to celebrate his earned triumph, Lucullus was prohibited from entering the city as he and his supporters fought for his rights in the courts. Eventually, the general won and acquired the legal permission to hold his triumph, and according to Plutarch, the defeated cataphracts had a prominent role in the parade:

> In the procession, a few of the cataphracts and ten of the scythe-bearing chariots moved along, together with sixty of the king's friends and generals.[56]

Meanwhile, back in the east, Pompey the Great was the Roman general selected to take Lucullus' place. The new commander was not only able to defeat Mithridates once and for all, but Pompey also secured Rome's control over the region and resettled the east; this included eradicating the remnants of the Seleucid kingdom and transforming Syria into a Roman province. The territory added to the empire, and the client kingdoms created in the region, put Rome's sphere of influence directly on the borders of the Parthian empire that had stretched to include all of the lands east of the Euphrates River in Mesopotamia. But Pompey did not attack the Parthians, nor did he conquer Armenia either, and instead attempted to kill two birds with one stone by trying to convince the Parthian king, Phraates III (r. 70–57 BC), to do his dirty work for him and invade the kingdom of Armenia.[57]

CHAPTER THREE

THE PARTHIAN CATAPHRACTS

The Parthian Empire

Pompey the Great's plan ultimately failed, for it turned out that neither the Parthian empire nor the Romans were able to completely remove the formidable Armenian king, Tigranes, from power. However, neither side cared any longer about the kingdom of Armenia because their primary focus was quickly turned towards each other at the end of the first half of the first century BC. This is the point where Rome's wealthiest plutocrat, Marcus Licinius Crassus, entered the scene, for he was appointed the governor of the province of Syria in 55 BC. As described in the introduction, Crassus, in his extreme lust for plunder and glory, used his new province as a base to raise an enormous army in order to conquer Rome's wealthiest and most powerful rival, the Parthian empire. The Roman general even had the opportunity to augment his already huge host with 10,000 cataphracts offered by the new Armenian king, Artavasdes II (r. 54–34 BC) if Crassus invaded Parthia from Armenia in the north. However, Crassus had already secured several fortifications in western Mesopotamia the previous year and so he decided to stick with his initial invasion route instead, thus declining the Armenian king's offer of the elite heavy cavalrymen.[1]

After the Parthian cataphracts revealed the bright shine of their glorious armour from beneath their animal hide coverings at the beginning of the Battle of Carrhae in 53 BC, Plutarch recorded that the combat commenced first with the actions of 1,000 heavily armoured horsemen, followed by the attack of 9,000 horse-archer light cavalry:

> And at first [the cataphracts] purposed to charge upon the Romans
> with their long spears, and throw their front ranks into confusion;
> but when they saw the depth of their formation, where shield was
> locked with shield, and the firmness and composure of the men, they
> drew back, and while seeming to break their ranks and disperse, they
> surrounded the hollow square in which their enemy stood before he
> was aware of the manoeuvre. And when Crassus ordered his light-
> armed troops to make a charge, they did not advance far, but encoun-
> tering a multitude of arrows, abandoned their undertaking and ran

*back for shelter among the men-at-arms, among whom they caused
the beginning of disorder and fear, for these now saw the velocity
and force of the arrows, which fractured armour, and tore their way
through every covering alike, whether hard or soft.*[2]

Once his first plan of sending the light infantry outside of the infantry square to disrupt the horse-archers failed, Crassus then decided to keep his legionaries in the defensive formation until the Parthians ran out of arrows. The Roman general knew that the Parthian cataphracts could not break through the dense ranks of his legionaries, but at the same time his men could not withstand for long the near-constant barrage of arrows that rained down upon them and managed to penetrate their large shields and heavy armour. Crassus assumed it would only be a matter of time until the Parthians ran out of their supply of the missiles; he would soon find out that he was horribly wrong.

To their great dismay, Crassus and his men soon discovered that the Parthians seemingly had enough arrows to fire at the Roman army for the entire rest of the day. Not only did the Parthian commander, Surena, make sure that there was a more than ample supply of the missiles, but he also came up with the ingenious idea of loading numerous camels with quivers full of arrows that were placed so close to the front lines that the horse-archers rapidly reloaded their ammunition with ease, before quickly moving on to continue to fire their dense volleys into the Roman ranks. Once Crassus fully realized the predicament he was in, the Roman commander knew that he must somehow break the encirclement of the Parthian forces around his army. Therefore, he ordered his son, Publius Crassus, to lead his Gallic 1,000 horsemen, along with 500 archers, 8 legionary cohorts and 300 additional cavalrymen, outside of the defensive square formation to assault the Parthians in the hope of giving the rest of his army a short reprieve from the constant barrage of arrows. As Publius and his men advanced, the Parthian cavalrymen that faced them broke and fled before the two sides came into contact. The Romans pursued.[3]

Publius and his men chased the Parthian horse-archers until the 1,000-strong contingent of cataphracts stood before them. Supported by their elite heavy cavalrymen, the horse-archers turned and faced the oncoming Romans with their bows in hand, thus the combat continued:

*But the Parthians merely placed their cataphracts to face the
Romans, and with the rest of their horse rode about scouring the*

field, and thus stirring up the sand, they raised such a dust that
the Romans could neither see nor speak to one another, and being
driven in upon one another in one close body, they were thus hit
and killed, dying, not by a quick and easy death, but with miser-
able pains and convulsions; for writhing upon the darts in their
bodies, they broke them in their wounds, and when they would
by force pluck out the barbed points, they caught the nerves and
veins, so that they tore and tortured themselves. Many of them
died thus, and those that survived were disabled for any service,
and when Publius exhorted them to charge the cataphracts, they
showed him their hands nailed to their shields, and their feet stuck
to the ground, so that they could neither fly nor fight. He charged
in himself boldly, however, with his horse, and came to close quar-
ters with them, but was very unequal, whether as to the offensive
or defensive part; for with his weak and little javelins, he struck
against targets that were of tough raw hides and iron, whereas the
lightly-clad bodies of his Gallic horsemen were exposed to the heavy
lances [kontoi] *of the enemy. For upon these he mostly depended,*
and with them he wrought wonders, for they would catch hold of
the kontoi, *and close upon the enemy, and so pull them from their*
horses, where they could scarce stir by reason of the heaviness of
their armour, and many of the Gauls quitting their own horses,
would creep under those of the enemy, and stick them in the belly;
which, growing unruly with the pain, trampled upon their riders
and upon the enemy promiscuously.[4]

Despite the bravery of the Gauls, courage was not enough to overcome
the extensive armour of the cataphracts who slew many of the auxiliary horsemen before the wounded Publius was able to make the order
for his men to retreat to the relative safety of a small hill nearby. After
carrying the injured and leading the horses to the mound of earth, the
legionaries surrounded the rest of their surviving comrades with their
shields locked; however, according to Cassius Dio, the defensive circular formation of the Roman infantrymen was not effective against the
tactics of the Parthian horse-archers and cataphracts:

For if [the legionaries] decided to lock shields for the purpose of avoid-
ing the arrows by the closeness of their array, the [cataphracts] were
upon them with a rush, striking down some, and at least scattering
the others; and if they extended their ranks to avoid this, they would
be struck with the arrows. Hereupon many died from fright at the

very charge of the [cataphracts], and many perished hemmed in by the horsemen. Others were knocked over by the lances or were carried off transfixed.[5]

Seeing that their defeat was inevitable, Publius and his officers took their own lives before the rest of the surviving men surrendered. Out of a force that originally numbered nearly 5,500 soldiers, there was less than 500 Romans left alive that the Parthians could take as captives.[6]

Meanwhile, the Parthian missile onslaught on the rest of the Roman army under the command of the elder Crassus decreased enough for the general to be able to move his forces to slightly higher ground close by, giving the Romans a little advantage over the Parthian cavalry and the short reprieve the legionaries desperately needed. Yet the relief did not last long for the Romans. Shortly after, Crassus and his men were horrified to see the severed head of Publius at the end of an upraised cataphract lance.[7] Though there was no time for even the father, or the rest of the Romans, to grieve over the loss of the contingent and its young commander, for the dreadful sight was quickly followed by another fierce Parthian attack that included the warriors who had returned after slaughtering Publius' men:

Then, as the enemy got to work, their light cavalry rode round on the flanks of the Romans and shot them with arrows, while the cataphracts in front, plying their kontoi, *kept driving them together into a narrow space, except those who, to escape death from the arrows, made bold to rush desperately upon their foes. These did little damage, but met with a speedy death from great and fatal wounds, since the* kontos *which the Parthians thrust was heavy with steel, and often had impetus enough to pierce through two men at once.[8]*

The carnage, pain and death experienced by the Romans as they desperately tried to protect themselves from the arrow volleys and cataphract lances lasted for the rest of the day until nightfall. Then, the Parthians withdrew, allowing the surviving Romans to escape in the darkness.[9]

Almost 20,000 Roman troops may have survived the disastrous day's fighting at Carrhae, but that number also included the wounded who certainly did not live past the night, for they were left behind by the rest of the fleeing Roman army. Furthermore, thousands more Roman troops perished on the long retreat back to Syria as the Parthians did not give up the pursuit. In the end, less than 10,000 Romans reached the safety of their province, while 10,000 men were taken captive and over 20,000 soldiers were slain, including Crassus and his son.[10] Although the Parthian victory at Carrhae should mostly be attributed to the continuous hail of arrows shot by the highly mobile horse-archers, the cataphracts also played a key role in the Parthians' success as well, utilizing their deadly shock tactics. Not only did the elite heavy cavalrymen kill almost all of the contingent led by Publius in their savage mêlée encounter, but the deadly charges of the cataphracts also devastated the Roman lines in the later stages of the battle. Additionally, even when they did not strike the Roman ranks, the threat of their charges caused the legionaries to condense, giving the horse-archers much easier targets to hit. More than any other battle that took place before, Carrhae showed how deadly cataphracts could be when used in conjunction with light cavalry and under the command of a brilliant general.

Even though it is possible that the Parthians may have been the first to use cataphracts, which inspired the Seleucid King Antiochus the Great to adopt the elite heavy cavalrymen, there is no solid evidence of Parthian cataphracts until the first century BC. However, it is certain that the Parthians fielded cataphracts from around the time of the Battle of Carrhae until the collapse of their empire centuries later. As the Parthian state changed and evolved over time, so too did the arms and armour of the Parthian version of the elite heavily armoured horsemen. All of the Parthian cataphracts wore either lamellar, mail or scale cuirasses constructed with iron and untanned leather. The Hellenistic-style cuirass of the Seleucid cataphracts was not adopted by any of the more nomadic peoples of the east, including the Parthians and their cataphract troops, for scale armour was often the preferred option. The terracotta tile from Babylonia in the second century AD and the statues at Staraya Nisa (along with actual remains of scale armour also found at that site) that depict the Parthian cataphracts in scale armour provide much evidence of the popularity of that type of armour among the elite heavy cavalrymen. In addition, although it is uncertain as to whether the graffito at Dura Europos depicts a Parthian cataphract, or another type of cataphract, the heavily armoured warrior is also wearing scale armour.

The Parthian cataphracts wore iron or bronze helmets, mostly conical in shape, that were sometimes ornamented with a small plume of dyed or natural horsehair. Unlike the Seleucid cataphracts, the

Parthian type did not wear a facemask, but occasionally an aventail, or another type of neck guard, constructed of mail, scale or lamellar armour, was attached to the helmet. Similar to the Seleucid version, the Parthian cataphracts commonly utilized laminated limb armour (*manica*) that extended all the way down the arm from the shoulders to the knuckles of the warrior. Sometimes the protection of the elite heavy cavalrymen even included gauntlets constructed of small metal plates or mail to cover the hands. Even though not all of the cataphracts were equipped with such extensive armour, most wore at least some sort of vambraces, rerebraces and other types of arm guards. The leg armour was often laminated as well, but the protection over the thighs was occasionally lamellar armour instead. Most of the Parthian cataphracts used laminated armour to cover the mail armour worn over their feet. The limb joints and other vulnerable parts of the body were protected with mail that was usually worn beneath the other layers of armour. Cloaks or small fabric tabards were sometimes worn over the armour of the cataphracts and were commonly made of silk brocade or a similar type of luxurious textile for the wealthier Parthian warriors.[11]

The armour for the mounts of the Parthian cataphracts included a metal facemask and chest protection. Further protection might have been worn in the form of the half-trapper or the full body trapper, which consisted of scale armour that was at times reinforced with alternating steel and bronze rows of metal plates for not only further protection but also for the more impressive appearance it provided; yet not all of the cataphracts utilized such heavy armour for their steeds. Like the Seleucid cataphracts, the Parthian heavy cavalrymen primarily fought with the *kontos* (heavy lance) that was mostly 3.6 metres (12 feet) in length.[12] In the accounts of Cassius Dio, the *kontoi* of the Parthians were so long 'that some of the pikes of the barbarians were bent and others were broken' as they were used in battle against the Romans.[13] Since it was so difficult to fight with such a large weapon, along with needing to control the reins as well, the shield was not a part of the cataphract equipment, as Cassius Dio also states 'Parthians make no use of a shield, but their forces consist of mounted archers and lancers, mostly armoured as cataphracts'.[14] Parthian cataphracts were also armed with long swords, daggers, axes or maces. According to Plutarch, one of the key sites for the manufacture of cataphract equipment, specifically the heavy armour, was located at Margiana. Archaeological excavations carried out at Merv, which revealed evidence of metallurgy, adds credence to his statement.[15]

The army of the Parthian empire consisted of a small royal contingent that strongly relied upon the forces of prominent nobles and satraps for larger campaigns. Therefore, not only did the Parthian kings utilize cataphract troops, but so too did the great suzerains have the heavily armoured cavalrymen in their retinues as well. The most powerful aristocratic families who were wealthy enough to own large tracts of land farmed by peasants, such as the Suren, Karen and Gew, were able to field the largest amounts of the expensive soldiers; besides, of course, the Parthian king himself. Yet even in the service of an affluent noble, the cost of the heavy armour and arms of the cataphract was so high that it meant that only the rich could fight as cataphracts.[16]

After Crassus' failed invasion of Parthia, the imperial cavalrymen of the east carried out minor raids for plunder throughout Roman territory, though they returned to their lands east of the Euphrates River in the summer of 50 BC. The Parthian Empire did not carry out true retaliation until ten years later when the Roman general, Quintus Labienus, defected to the service of the Parthian prince, Pacorus, and the two of them invaded the province of Syria in 40 BC. The Parthian army then divided into two forces; Pacorus led one to conquer the lands along the Mediterranean coast, while Labienus and his contingent advanced north into Asia Minor. Before long, most of the eastern territory of the Roman Empire belonged to the Parthians.[17]

A major reason that the Parthians under Pacorus and Labienus continued to have so much success against Rome was that the western empire was embroiled in civil wars, which all in some way involved the most powerful Roman of the age, Gaius Julius Caesar. After the death of the great general in 44 BC, one of his chief lieutenants, Mark Antony, made an alliance with Caesar's adopted son and heir, Gaius Octavian, who was later known as Caesar Augustus. The two of them then went after Caesar's assassins with much success, but even as allies the two men remained highly competitive rivals. Once the assassins were defeated, Octavian effectively ruled the west while Antony took command over the eastern territories. In the beginning of 39 BC, Antony felt confident enough with his position that he could send his best commander, Publius Ventidius, on a campaign to expel the troops of the Parthian Empire. Ventidius moved to attack Labienus in Anatolia first. The enormous army under the Roman general included eleven legions, along with a large amount of slingers. The latter were specifically recruited on the direct orders of Ventidius who hoped that the ranged infantrymen would be able to repel the Parthian horse-archers with their unique bullets made of lead. Unbeknownst to the Romans, the Parthian invasion forces of Pacorus and Labienus predominately consisted of cataphracts instead of the numerous horse-archers that were at the Battle of Carrhae.[18]

Ventidius and his men reached Labienus' forces so quickly that the Roman defector found himself under attack before he even knew that Ventidius had landed in Anatolia. Caught completely off-guard and heavily outnumbered, Labienus fled back to Syria to gather reinforcements. In the meantime, Ventidius swiftly reclaimed Cilicia, and then remained there to focus on stabilizing the administrations of the eastern provinces.[19] When the two commanders moved out to face each other again, they met at the battle of the Cilician Gates. Ventidius stationed his men on a hill to give his army, mostly made up of infantrymen, a slight advantage over the cataphracts and the rest of the cavalrymen fighting for the Parthians. Labienus and his Parthian troops attempted to draw the Romans out from behind their barricades several times but the legionaries refused to budge. Due to the success they had already gained over the Romans in their invasion of the empire, the Parthian cataphracts and horse-archers most likely believed the forces under Ventidius were cowards, therefore they charged up the hill to assault the legionaries protected by their minor fortifications. Once the Parthian cavalrymen ascended the slope, the Roman legionaries then rushed out to meet them in a fierce attack. The suddenness of the assault surprised the Parthian horsemen to such an extent that the front lines broke and then collided with the mounted troops behind them who were still advancing forward up the hill. The legionaries rapidly exploited the chaotic state of the enemy cavalry by manoeuvring up close to the slow-moving cataphracts to target the few vulnerable areas of their extensive heavy armour. It did not take long before the entire Parthian army was routed and in full retreat.[20]

After the defeat at the Cilician Gates, Labienus retreated with the Parthian troops to Syria, while the Romans were in pursuit. Aware of the approaching Romans, a Parthian army in northern Syria advanced further north and confronted the oncoming Romans on the border of Cilicia and Syria at the Gates of the Amanus. The Battle of the Amanus Pass began when Ventidius' chief lieutenant, Pompaedius Silo, with a small contingent of cavalry, managed to lure the Parthians away from their defensive position. The retreating Roman cavalry led the Parthian horsemen straight into an ambush where their flank was viciously assaulted with a barrage of lead bullets fired by the numerous slingers of the Roman army. The hail of leaden missiles was even effective against the heavy armour of the Parthian cataphracts. Ventidius was then able to move the majority of his forces to a strongly defensible position on higher ground. As at the Cilician Gates, the Parthian cavalrymen decided to take the offensive and charge up the hill with a large number of cataphracts. The ascending slope once again led to the Parthians' downfall for once they had advanced up it, the slingers first halted the forward movement of the Parthian cavalry with their numerous missiles, but then as the heavily armoured horsemen slowed down, the legionaries surged forward to face them. For the second time in a row, the Parthian cataphracts were completely crushed after attempting to charge a Roman army in an elevated position.[21]

Labienus was soon found and murdered shortly after the Roman victory at the Amanus Pass. In the later part of 39 BC, Prince Pacorus led the rest of the Parthian forces out of Syria, leaving the province free for Ventidius to retake. By the end of the year, the Roman general had reclaimed both Syria and Palestine as well before sending his soldiers to winter quarters. In the spring of 38 BC, Pacorus returned to Syria with another Parthian army. The Parthian forces travelled through Cyrrhestica and advanced until they reached the Roman camp near Mount Gindarus.[22] In the last two battles Ventidius fought against the Parthians, he faced a different enemy commander. Then yet again at the Battle of Mount Gindarus, it was the first time that Pacorus attacked Ventidius' army and made the huge mistake of leading his cavalrymen uphill to assault the fortified Roman camp. Cassius Dio recorded how the Roman heavy infantry, supported by many slingers, overcame the cataphracts once more:

> *In this way he met Pacorus in Syria Cyrrhestica and conquered him. For when he had not prevented them from crossing the river and had not attacked them at once after they had got across, they imputed sloth and weakness to the Romans and therefore marched against their camp, although it was on high ground, expecting to take it without resistance. But when a sally was suddenly made, the assailants, being cavalry, were driven back down the slope without difficulty; and although at the foot they defended themselves valiantly, the majority of them being cataphracts, yet they were confused by the unexpectedness of the onslaught and by stumbling over one another and were defeated by the heavy-armed men and especially by the slingers; for these struck them from a distance with their powerful missiles and so were exceedingly difficult for them to withstand.*[23]

As the armoured legionaries fought the Parthian heavy cavalrymen, Pacorus and his personal guard were killed in the combat. When the

Parthian troops then found out that their leader was dead, some of them courageously sacrificed their lives in the attempt to reclaim his body from the Romans, although the news ultimately led most of the Parthian army to retreat.[24]

For the third time, Ventidius utilized elevated and fortified terrain, along with ranged infantrymen, to completely negate the effectiveness of the elite Parthian cataphracts, and for the third time in a row the Roman general achieved victory over the armies of the great eastern rival of the Roman Empire. The spectacular Parthian victory at Carrhae redeemed the cataphracts after their overall disappointing performances at Magnesia and Tigranocerta, yet the battles of the Cilician Gates, Amanus and Gindarus showed that higher ground and slingers armed with lead bullets were also highly effective against the heavily armoured horsemen as well. Furthermore, these battles once again reinforced the fact that the cataphracts were most effective when used in conjunction with numerous light cavalry or infantry; and if they were the most numerous type of warrior in an army, the heavy cavalrymen could be extremely vulnerable when stationary, especially without the support of these additional troops.

After he won against Prince Pacorus and sent the Parthian army back to the east, Ventidius did not take any further actions against the Parthian Empire because he did not have permission to do so from his superior, Mark Antony. Yet the victorious Roman general became a hero to the Roman people and in their eyes he had redeemed the disaster at Carrhae. As the effective master of the eastern Roman Empire, Antony made sure that no invasions of the Parthian Empire were carried out until he could personally lead the campaign himself. Antony believed he was the true heir of Julius Caesar, even though the will of the recently deceased great man said that position belonged to his rival, Octavian. Therefore, Antony planned to use the conquest of the Parthian Empire as a way to prove that he was as good a general as the remarkable Julius Caesar. Before his death, Caesar himself had planned to invade the Parthian Empire and although he died before he was able to carry out the action, Antony inherited the intelligence and paperwork gathered by the brilliant general.[25]

At the end of 38 BC, Phraates IV (r. 37–2 BC) became the emperor of Parthia and, once in power, his first act was to have his father murdered. The new ruler then consolidated his control by killing several half-brothers and exiling his other brother, along with many among the nobility, which even included many of the aristocratic warriors who fought for Parthia against the Romans led by Ventidius. One of these exiled warriors, named

Monaeses, met with Mark Antony and promised to be his guide through Parthian territory. The following year, Antony quickly prepared for his massive campaign, hoping to exploit the instability of the Parthian Empire after the dramatic change in government. In his preparations, Antony also made an alliance with King Artavasdes II in order to gain some of his elite Armenian cavalry to combat the many Parthian horsemen. At the end of April or the beginning of May in 36 BC, the hopeful successor to Caesar's military genius headed for the east with an enormous army that may have numbered as many as 100,000 men, which included approximately 16 legions. Antony first led the Roman army north to the kingdom of Armenia where Artavasdes joined his forces with 7,000 infantrymen and 6,000 armoured heavy cavalry. The Armenian king also convinced Antony to attack first the kingdom of Media Atropatene, which was an ally of the Parthian Empire, because much of the Median army was supposedly away in Parthian territory at the time.[26]

The huge Roman baggage train of at least 300 wagons, loaded with tons of equipment, such as large siege engines, plus the numerous animals required to pull all of the vehicles, moved way too slowly for Antony so he decided to move ahead with the infantry and cavalry. The Roman general then led his forces to Praaspa, the capital of Media Atropatene, and put the city under siege. In the meantime, the allied kings of Parthia and Media Atropatene avoided Antony's forces that surrounded the capital and instead struck the ponderous baggage train while it was far from the rest of the army. After killing the Roman commander, Oppius Statianus, and routing the rest of the Roman forces that guarded the baggage train, the allied army burned all of the siege equipment and seized the rest as valuable plunder. To make matters worse, King Artavasdes abandoned the Romans. By the time news of the attack had reached Antony and he was able to respond, 10,000 of his men were already slain.[27] In the account of Cassius Dio, however, a large contingent of slingers were able to intercept some of the Parthian and Mede forces shortly afterwards:

> *When he met them a little later, he routed them, for as his slingers were numerous and could shoot farther than the archers, they inflicted severe injury upon all, even upon the cataphracts; yet he did not kill any considerable number of the enemy, because the barbarians could ride fast.*[28]

The Romans were most likely still intimidated by the impressive armour of the cataphracts even after Ventidius' great success against them; thus, the Roman writer was probably more than happy to emphasize how effective slingers were against them and specifically highlight one of the weaknesses of the formidable enemy cavalrymen once again.

Antony returned to Praaspa, but without the siege engines, the city was nearly impossible to take. Quickly running out of food and with the Parthian horse-archers constantly harrying the legionaries with hit-and-run attacks, especially against the foraging parties, Antony finally gave up. Even though the Parthians refused to fight a pitched battle with Antony, their tactics of rapid assaults were killing many of the Roman troops. Therefore, the Roman general decided to retreat at the beginning of winter before the weather conditions made the situation much worse. Antony led his men through the hill country to the north to avoid the same fate as Crassus in the open fields to the south; however, the terrain did not prevent the Parthians from continuing their attacks on the Romans as they tried to escape. By the time the Romans had finally reached the safety of Armenia, a total of around 24,000 men had perished in the campaign.[29]

Yet Antony and his men felt betrayed by the Armenian king for his desertion, so they did not stay long and quickly continued their journey to the Roman province of Syria, losing another 8,000 men to the harsh winter conditions. The Roman general spent the next year rebuilding his army and returned to Armenia in 34 BC. Antony and his forces then quickly captured Artavasdes and effectively conquered the kingdom, which intimidated the Median king to such an extent that he signed a treaty with the Roman general against the Parthian Empire. He may not have come anywhere near to conquering the Parthians, but when Antony eventually celebrated his triumph, the Armenian king was forced to participate in the procession before he was executed.[30] The hostile situation between the Romans and the Parthians was not resolved until several years later in 27 BC, for after Octavian defeated Antony and became Caesar Augustus (r. 27 BC–14 AD), the first emperor of the Roman Empire, the new ruler made peace with his great eastern rival. The official border was agreed upon by the two powerful states and Augustus even managed to regain the lost legionary standards from the Parthians in 20 BC.[31] Yet the cataphracts of the Parthians had successfully made their mark on the Romans, which would last for centuries to come. The terrifying mounted troops encased in metal had struck so much fear into the Roman people that it was reflected in their literature, for in the poem of 'Chaste and Faithful Galla' in *The Elegies* of Propertius, it was the cataphracts and the archers of the enemy that Galla feared would turn her into a widow while her husband was away fighting against the Parthian Empire:

> *[Galla] in the meantime will pine away at each idle rumour, for fear your courage will cost you dear, or the arrows of Medes enjoy your death, or the cataphract on a golden horse, or some bit of you be brought back in an urn to be wept over.*[32]

Throughout the first century AD, the ancient accounts do not mention any other major conflicts between the Parthian Empire and its mighty western rival where the cataphracts played a key role in the combat. However, in the last half of the century, the Parthians managed to gain control of the kingdom of Armenia when the brother of the Parthian emperor, Vologases I (r. 51–78), became its new ruler.[33] The Parthians continued their dominance over Armenia in 109 AD when Emperor Osroes I (r. 109–129) made sure his nephew, Exedares, was the next ruler of the kingdom. Since the Parthians then ruled over the two greatest eastern states, they became too great of a threat to the Romans, thus Emperor Trajan (r. 98–117) organized the largest eastern campaign against the Parthian Empire and their deadly cataphracts since the one led by Mark Antony.[34]

In the spring of 114, Trajan and the Roman army left Syria and headed towards the Kingdom of Armenia. By the end of the year, Trajan had seized the Armenian king, had him executed and made Armenia into a Roman province. After spending the winter in Armenia, Trajan led his forces into Mesopotamia. To take the region, the Roman emperor divided his army into two; one was led by his general, Lusius Quietus, and approached from the east, while the other half of the army was commanded by Trajan himself, which he led into Mesopotamia from the west. The two forces broke through all resistance they faced and reunited at the end of 115. On 21 February 116, Trajan sent a letter to the Roman Senate proclaiming his successful annexation of Armenia and Mesopotamia. The Roman army then spent the winter in Syria, yet returned to Mesopotamia in 116. After continuing to establish his hold over the region, Trajan led his men to capture Seleucia first and then the Romans seized the Parthian capital of Ctesiphon without facing any resistance because Emperor Osroes had already fled from the city. The Romans had advanced into his territory with an army much larger than he could muster at that moment, therefore the Parthian emperor made a tactical retreat to the protection of the Zagros Mountains. Once Ctesiphon was taken, Trajan considered himself the conqueror of the Parthian Empire and had 'Parthicus' officially added to his name.[35]

Emperor Trajan then decided to make a short trip down the Tigris River to the Persian Gulf. But when he returned shortly after, the Roman emperor found out that the Parthians had taken back much of the newly claimed Roman territory in Armenia and Mesopotamia, or instigated rebellions to destabilize the regions. The Roman emperor failed to properly garrison the new provinces he had made, thus the gains were quickly lost. To end the revolts, Trajan once again divided his forces, yet this time into three large contingents. Although the Parthians crushed one of the three armies, the other two Roman forces managed to reclaim much of the territory, including key cities like Nisibis, Edessa and Seleucia. The Roman armies then reunited and defeated the Parthians outside of Ctesiphon. Trajan followed up this victory by placing the son of Osroes, Parthamaspates, on the throne as a client king of Parthia, subservient to the Romans; the Roman emperor then made a similar arrangement with the Parthian who had seized the throne of Armenia. Ultimately, Trajan had finally fully realized how vast the eastern lands were that the Parthians held sway over while he carried out his eastern campaign; therefore, the Roman ruler lost all hope of ever fully taking control over the Parthian Empire and felt that putting a vassal on the throne was sufficient.[36]

Trajan may have put client kings on the thrones of Parthia and Armenia but areas of Mesopotamia were still under revolt when severe weather forced the Roman emperor to return to Syria. Furthermore, a massive Jewish rebellion erupted, which took a considerable amount of effort on the part of the emperor and his soldiers to put down. By the time he felt ready to return to Mesopotamia in 117 to re-establish his dominance over the region, Trajan was afflicted with a stroke, making him unable to carry out the campaign. Therefore, the emperor placed his future successor, Hadrian (r. 117–138), in command of the eastern forces of the Roman army. On the journey back to the west, the elderly Trajan became ill and died. As the new emperor, Hadrian's eastern policy was completely different than the one carried out by his predecessor. Although a few client kings in the region may have remained loyal to Rome, Hadrian effectively relinquished all control over the lands east of the Euphrates River, which practically negated everything that Trajan had accomplished. Before long, the only kingdoms that the Romans retained their hegemonic control over were Armenia and Edessa.[37]

In the beginning of Hadrian's reign, the border between the Parthian Empire and the Roman Empire returned to its traditional place along the Euphrates River; though while the boundary between the two great empires stayed the same, a major change was made to the Roman military during this period. The first unit of Roman cataphracts, known as *ala I Gallorum et Pannoniorum catafractata*, may have been created while Trajan was on his eastern campaign. On the other hand, it is more likely that the unit was introduced as a reform instituted by Emperor Hadrian.[38] Centuries after the Romans had faced cataphracts for the first time at the Battle of Magnesia against the Seleucid Empire in 190 BC, the predominately infantry-minded western empire finally realized the great worth of the horsemen and began to utilize the heavily armoured cavalrymen as a part of the extensive imperial military. One of the reasons for the Romans change of heart regarding cataphracts may have been from their encounters with the elite heavy horsemen of the Parthians during Trajan's eastern campaign. Even if Trajan's campaign against the Parthians was not specifically responsible for the emperor's adoption of a Roman version of the cataphracts, in later Roman history when cataphracts had become commonplace within the military, Roman writers understood that interactions with the Parthian cataphracts were a major factor in inspiring their predecessors to adopt this type of troops. For instance, when the later Roman writer Nazarius reflected on the conflict with the Parthian Empire in the second century AD, he stated:

> *When Antoninus, an outstanding Emperor in peacetime and not without energy and capacity in war, made trial of the Parthians in combat, after he had seen their cataphracts he lapsed so completely into fear that on his own he sent the King a letter promoting peace. And when the overly proud king had spurned it, the barbarian's insolence was vanquished indeed, but it was made clear that there is so much potential power in that type of armour that he who was to be overcome felt confident and he who was to conquer was afraid.[39]*

After the peace established in the beginning of the reign of Hadrian, the Parthians and the Romans did not come into major conflict again until the Parthian Emperor Vologases IV (r. 147–191) invaded Armenia in 162. A major reason that the Romans had enjoyed so much success against the Parthian Empire in Trajan's earlier invasion was that the eastern empire was embroiled in civil wars over control of the throne. While eastern Parthia was controlled by Vologases III (r. 105–147), Osroes I ruled the western territories of the Parthian Empire, yet the ruler of the west was weakened after fighting the Roman army under Trajan. Therefore, Vologases was able to seize control of most of the Parthian

Empire after the death of Osroes, and then the new ruler attempted to exploit the change in power in the Roman Empire after Emperor Antoninus Pius (r. 138–161) passed away. Once he quickly took control of the Kingdom of Armenia, Vologases followed the practice of many of his predecessors by placing a Parthian family member on the seized throne. Vologases also crushed a small Roman army led by a foolishly ambitious legate and then invaded the Roman province of Syria, which drove one of Rome's two emperors, Lucius Verus (r. 161–169), to command the first major eastern campaign since the one led by Trajan.[40]

Even though Verus travelled to the east with the army, the true command of the Roman forces belonged to his generals. In 163 AD, one of these generals, Statius Priscus, seized the Kingdom of Armenia and placed a pro-Roman client king on the throne. The next year, the chief Roman general of the campaign, Avidius Cassius, invaded Mesopotamia. Key cities in the region, such as Nisibis, Dura Europos and Edessa were taken, and the Roman forces defeated the Parthians on several occasions, including battles fought at Sura and Dura Europos. Near the end of 165, the Romans gained the important city of Seleucia without facing much resistance and then moved on to storm Ctesiphon. With these last two treasures won, the Roman generals had managed to reclaim all of the territory that Trajan had previously conquered. However, the victory over the Parthian Empire was bittersweet for a devastating plague ravaged not only the Roman soldiers, but also spread throughout the Parthian territories. The Romans returned to the west victorious, though they were forced to leave prematurely, and even worse, they brought the disease back to the Mediterranean world with them.[41]

The Romans returned to the east in 166 to consolidate their control over territory in Mesopotamia and invade the region of Media in the Parthian Empire. By the end of this next short campaign, the Romans once again overcame the Parthians and had extended the border of the empire to include western Mesopotamia, with the boundary of the province of Syria moved to as far as Dura Europos.[42] The Roman victories over the Parthians were certainly far from complete, yet the invasions had weakened the eastern empire. The decline of the Parthian Empire was exacerbated even further decades later when the Roman army successfully invaded in 197 AD, seized Ctesiphon once again, and burned the Parthian royal palace.[43] Even so, the Romans were forced to leave the total conquest of the Parthian Empire for another time, so it was not until civil war erupted between two Parthian princes, Artabanus V and Vologases VI, that the new Roman emperor, Caracalla

(r. 198–217) decided to strike while his great eastern rival was unstable and weak. Upon the death of his father in 211, Caracalla became the sole ruler of the empire and quickly began to prepare for his eastern campaign. The Roman emperor first increased his hold over the kingdom of Edessa by imprisoning its king. This was followed up by a similar attempt made in the kingdom of Armenia that failed to subdue the Armenian people. While the Armenians violently resisted the Romans, Caracalla prepared to invade the Parthian Empire. However, as time passed, the Roman ruler considered the situation in Armenia a higher priority; thus, he sent his general, Theocritus, to deal with the opposition. In 215, the Roman army advanced to Armenia, but once it reached the kingdom, Armenian forces managed to crush the Romans.[44]

Meanwhile, the conflict between the new emperor, Vologases VI (r. 208–228 AD), and his brother, Artabanus V (r. 208–224 AD), continued within the Parthian Empire. By 216, Artabanus had taken control over most of the empire, while Vologases retained his hold over the city of Seleucia and the surrounding territory. After Caracalla managed to cause much further damage at Ctesiphon and throughout Media (possibly due to a cruel, yet clever, ruse carried out by the Roman emperor), Artabanus remained in a superior position over his brother. The Parthian ruler then raised an army and advanced into the Roman controlled part of Mesopotamia. Caracalla was assassinated by one of his own guards in 217, so when the Romans confronted the Parthian invasion force it was under the command of the new emperor, Macrinus (r. 217–218). The ruler who took Caracalla's place desired a peaceful resolution, but Artabanus adamantly refused peace terms unless he was given back all of the Parthian lands that were taken by the Romans east of the Eurphrates River. Macrinus would rather fight than give up Roman territory, so the two armies met at the Battle of Nisibis.[45]

Like most Parthian armies, the forces under Artabanus consisted mostly of cavalrymen and archers. On the other hand, the Parthian army at Nisibis was unique in that it contained a contingent of a rare cataphract-type of warriors who were mounted not upon horses, but rather camels instead. In his *History of the Roman Empire*, Herodian first mentions the distinctive troops in the events leading up to the battle:

> *Artabanus was marching toward the Romans with a huge army, including a strong cavalry contingent and a powerful unit of archers and those cataphracts who hurl spears from camels.*[46]

The camel cataphracts fought with either spears or lances, and both riders and mounts wore extensive armour like the traditional cataphracts who rode horses. Along with the legionaries, the Roman army also included contingents of light infantry and Mauretanian cavalrymen. The fighting between the two ancient superpowers was brutal and lasted for three long days.[47] Herodian recorded how deadly the Parthian warriors, including the camel cataphracts, were on the first day of the fighting, yet he also described how the Romans eventually managed to gain the upper hand:

> *The barbarians inflicted many wounds upon the Romans from above, and did considerable damage by the showers of arrows and the long spears of the cataphract camel riders. But when the fighting came to close quarters, the Romans easily defeated the barbarians; for when the swarms of Parthian cavalry and hordes of camel riders were mauling them, the Romans pretended to retreat and then they threw down caltrops and other keen-pointed iron devices. Covered by the sand, these were invisible to the horsemen and the camel riders and were fatal to the animals. The horses, and particularly the tender-footed camels, stepped on these devices and, falling, threw their riders. As long as they are mounted on horses and camels, the barbarians in those regions fight bravely, but if they dismount or are thrown, they are very easily captured; they cannot stand up to hand-to-hand fighting. And, if they find it necessary to flee or pursue, the long robes which hang loosely about their feet trip them up.[48]*

However, with the coming of night and no clear victor to the battle, the two armies retreated to their camps to rest for the night.[49]

The second day of the fighting ended in a stalemate as well. The third day of the battle, however, decided the outcome when the Parthians changed their tactics to try and fully envelope the numerically inferior Roman force. In response to the encircling attempts of the Parthian soldiers, the Romans extended their own lines to compensate for the extended Parthian front. However, the Parthians were able to exploit the weakened thinner lines of the Romans and achieve a great victory. Knowing he had lost the battle, Emperor Macrinus retreated and, soon after, his men fled to the Roman camp as well. Although the Parthians won the Battle of Nisibis, it was a Pyrrhic victory for Artabanus; the losses were heavy for both sides. Since the Parthian emperor desired peace almost as much as Macrinus, Artabanus accepted only a substantial payment in return for a cessation of hostilities, as opposed to the territory he previously demanded.[50]

Although Emperor Macrinus was quickly defeated, executed and replaced by one of his rivals, Elagabalus (r. 218–222), in 218 , the Roman Empire continued to persist for centuries following its defeat at Nisibis. The Parthian Empire, on the other hand, became even weaker after its conflict with Rome and continued on its steady decline. Revolts from within the empire continued to plague Artabanus so he could not sit back and enjoy his success over the Romans. In 220, the leader of the Persians, Ardashir, managed to break free from Parthian rule and exploit the weakness of the empire to extend his control over more and more land. By 224, Artabanus met Ardashir on the field of battle and lost more than his life; the Parthian Empire collapsed shortly after his fall. In place of the Parthians, a resurgent Persian state arose known as the Sassanian Empire.[51] As the new supreme empire of the east, the armies of the Sassanians had some of the greatest warriors of the ancient world. Like its Parthian predecessor, the elite heavy cavalry of the Sassanian Empire were also cataphracts.

CHAPTER FOUR

CATAPHRACTS OF THE MINOR KINGDOMS

The Sarmatians

The semi-unified group of Iranian-speaking tribes known as the Sarmatians originally inhabited the lands east of the Pontic Scythians, in between the Don River and the Ustyurt Plateau of modern day western Kazakhstan. However, in the fourth century BC, the nomadic tribes shifted westward to occupy the territories previously held by the Scythians. Over the centuries, powerful Sarmatian tribes continued to migrate to western lands and eventually came into contact with the territories under the dominion of the Roman Republic. By the first century BC, the Roman Empire was repelling Sarmatian invaders.[1] Like their Scythian predecessors, the Sarmatian mounted warriors fought in particularly heavy armour for their time. Then, in the first century AD, the heavy cavalrymen of the nomadic tribesmen became much more formidable when they adopted the *kontos* (heavy lance). Even though the Sarmatian heavy cavalrymen were certainly skilled lancers on the battlefield, not all scholars believe that the mounted warriors were true cataphracts.[2] Different experts have different theories as to what exactly defined a cataphract, though the obvious argument to be made for the Sarmatian horsemen to not be considered cataphracts is that they were commonly not completely armoured, especially when it came to their mounts. Although the wealthiest Sarmatian warriors were able to provide their horses with at least some horse armour, most of the nomadic mounted troops wore a helmet, cuirass and very little other protection. Regardless of this, the Sarmatians were incredibly effective lancers who most likely were a major influence on the Roman heavy cavalry and their later *cataphractarii*. For that reason, it is important to include the Sarmatians to fully explain the history and evolution of the ancient cataphracts.

The scale cuirass was the most popular type of armour among the Sarmatian horsemen. Discoveries from archaeological excavations suggest that the wealthiest nobles wore cuirasses with iron and bronze scales as early as the sixth century BC, though the vast majority of the cavalry were equipped with much less. Many were only able to afford a few metal plates attached to their leather cuirasses over the chest.[3] Most of the earliest Sarmatian cavalrymen in the written records wore relatively light armour made primarily from raw ox hides and consisting of a corselet and a helmet, as in Strabo's account in 107 BC.[4] However, by the first century AD, the armour of the mounted horsemen typically became much heavier and was increasingly constructed with larger metal scales and then eventually plates. The Sarmatian scale cuirass of this period extended to the middle of the thigh but had sleeves that did not pass the elbow. Since the wearers of the scale cuirasses predominately fought on horseback, slits were cut along both sides of the armour from the thighs up to the belt in order to make it easier to ride; the leather belt also helped, for it took some of the weight of the armour off the shoulders of the rider. By the third century AD, the adoption of plates led to an increase of laminar style armour (comprised of horizontal bands or rows of overlapping metal plates), a sign of the influence that the Alans and other tribes of Central Asia had over the Sarmatians.[5]

The experimentation of the Sarmatian heavy cavalrymen with metal strips also led to a unique type of armour made with bands that covered the torso. The pedestal of Trajan's Column may show a depiction of this banded armour corselet, which had the strips attached to a leather or fabric backing that extended below the waist as a skirt. The bands also continued down past the hips to protect that area of the body as well. It is also interesting to note that the row of buckles down the middle of the cuirass are somewhat similar to the same used on the top part of the so-called *lorica segmentata*, the famous segmented plate armour of the Roman imperial legionaries. Sarmatian horsemen also utilized other types of armour, including mail armour by the first century BC. At first, scale cuirasses were still worn over mail armour that protected the limbs and extended as a skirt over the thighs. However, over time mail became so popular among the heavy horsemen that in the second century AD it began to completely replace the previous scale armours. Though just as in earlier periods most Sarmatian warriors could not afford such expensive heavy armour, so those cavalrymen had to rely on much cheaper options. Also beginning around the second century AD, the most common replacement for iron armour among the Sarmatians was a scale cuirass constructed with horn or the hooves of horses. Both of the ancient writers Pausanias and Ammianus Marcellinus described Sarmatian troops as wearing such armour.[6]

Like metal body armour, metal helmets were also mostly reserved for the Sarmatian aristocracy. In the early history of the Sarmatians, such helmets were usually obtained from the Greek colonies along the coasts of the Black Sea, just as with the Scythians, and many of the first helmets found on Sarmatian archaeological sites were in the Corinthian style. Another Greek helmet type utilized by the nomadic horsemen was the Pilos. Sarmatian metal helmets that did not originate from the Greeks were often Celtic Montefortino types of both A and B styles, or were in the Etrusco-Italic style; and since many of the remains of these helmets display a less-than-expert craftsmanship, it is believed that most of these latter types were constructed locally. Helmets that were not made in regions of strong Sarmatian influence were probably imported from the Galatians or another Celto-Germanic tribe. By the last quarter of the first century BC, nearly all of these early Sarmatian helmets were replaced by the *spangenhelm* type, which was made with one or two horizontal loops that had three or four bands riveted to them in order to hold curved, iron plates. Depictions of this helmet that quickly became widely popular among the Sarmatians can be found not only on Trajan's Column but also on several Bosporan tomb artworks and funerary reliefs.[7]

Although many experts do not consider Sarmatian horsemen to be classified as cataphracts, there is some evidence to suggest that the wealthiest noble warriors outfitted their mounts with armour; the most prominent proof would be the images of scale barding on Trajan's Column. Furthermore, the Bosporan funerary stele from the first century AD that depicts a lancer atop a horse wearing barding is also very important due to the strong ties between the Sarmatians and the Bosporans. Some discoveries from excavations of Sarmatian sites may be the remains of horse armour, especially the finds uncovered at a gravesite on the Kuban in 1896; however, the theories on the exact nature of all of these finds remain unproven. The last evidence of barding for the mounts of the heavy cavalrymen comes from the written accounts of Valerius Flaccus in the first century AD, as well as the later descriptions of the Sarmatian tribal group known as the Alans by Isidore of Seville and Constantius.[8]

The last piece of armour that may have been in the equipment of the Sarmatian heavy cavalrymen was the shield. In the accounts of Strabo in the first century BC and Cassius Dio in the second century AD, two Sarmatian tribes, the Roxolani and the Iazyges respectively, are described as carrying shields. On the other hand, Tacitus states that the Sarmatian lancers did not carry shields, which could mean that the light cavalrymen only utilized the equipment for the most part, instead of the more heavily armed lancers. This would make sense for the primary weapon of the Sarmatian heavy cavalrymen was the *kontos*, which was almost always used in combat with both hands. Yet the Sarmatian horsemen did not quickly adopt the large weapon for in the accounts of their early history the writers used the Greek term *longche* (spear or javelin) and the Latin word *hasta* (spear) to describe the weaponry of the nomadic warriors, such as Strabo and then Ovid in the beginning of the first century AD. However, as the century progressed, elite aristocratic warriors arose from within the Sarmatian ranks and threw away their light spears for the *kontos,* as they wore the most heavy armour they could afford. Like the *kontos* of the Seleucid and Parthian cataphracts, the heavy lance that the Sarmatians adopted was also about 3.6 metres (12 feet) in length on average, though it is also possible that some of the heavy horsemen wielded lances that were exceptionally long. Based upon artwork found on ancient Bosporan walls of the second century AD, some of the heavy lances of the Sarmatians were as long as 4.5 metres (14 ft. 9 in.).[9] The huge size of some of the Sarmatian lances was most likely the reason why the Roman writers distinguished their *kontoi* as the 'contus sarmaticus' in Latin.[10] Since many Sarmatian lancers were not wealthy enough for the most complete sets of armour for themselves, and only a very few could supply their mounts with barding (especially constructed of metal), the heavy cavalrymen are more properly referred to as *kontophoros* (Greek) or *contarius* (Latin), which means 'bearer of the *kontos* (*contus*)', rather than as cataphracts. By the second half of the first century AD, these were the terms used to describe the Sarmatian lancers in the written record, such as in the Roman accounts of Tacitus, Arrian and Ammianus Marcellinus.[11]

The first time that armoured Sarmatian horsemen armed with lances entered the ancient written record was when a contingent of them were hired as mercenaries by the ruler of the minor Armenian kingdom of Iberia, King Pharamenes, in AD 35. The Iberian king then used the mercenary lancers against the Parthian empire in battle. When the Sarmatian heavy cavalry faced the Parthian horse-archers, the mounted ranged troops expected the tribal warriors to act like most of the other Central Asian peoples of the time and exchange arrow fire. However, the Parthians were surprised to find the Sarmatian horsemen charging straight at them with their long lances. Once the two cavalry forces were engaged in brutal combat, King Pharamenes then made the decisive order to have his infantry enter the combat. The Parthians could not withstand the combined assaults and the battle was won.[12]

   The Romans faced the new Sarmatian lancers on the battlefield for the first time in the beginning of the spring of AD 69 when 9,000 of the nomadic warriors, from the Sarmatian tribe known as the Roxolani, invaded the Roman province of Moesia. After they finished raiding the surrounding territory, the Sarmatians attempted to travel back over the Danube River to their own lands, but were intercepted by the Roman legionaries. Warmer weather had caused the riverbank to thaw, making the ground thick with mud. The Roman historian Tacitus has provided an account of the battle in his book, *The History*:

> *But as on this occasion the day was damp and the ice thawed, what with the continual slipping of their horses, and the weight of their coats of mail, they could make no use of their* conti *[lances] or their swords, which being of an excessive length they wield with both hands. These coats are worn as defensive armour by the princes and most distinguished persons of the tribe. They are formed of plates of iron or very tough hides, and though they are absolutely impenetrable to blows, yet they make it difficult for such as have been overthrown by the charge of the enemy to regain their feet. Besides, the Sarmatians were perpetually sinking in the deep and soft snow. The Roman soldier, moving easily in his cuirass, continued to harass them with javelins and lances, and whenever the occasion required, closed with them with his short sword, and stabbed the defenceless enemy; for it is not their custom to defend themselves with a shield.*[13]

   The Sarmatians may not typically have been as heavily armoured as the cataphracts of the period, yet the heavy weight of their armour still ended up as a major weakness for them. Unable to combat the lighter legionaries on the slick terrain, the Sarmatians sustained heavy losses and were defeated.[14]
   Nearly a hundred years after the battle with the Roxolani, another Sarmatian tribe, called the Iazyges, penetrated the Roman borders by crossing the Danube River again; this time in the winter of 173/174 when the waterway was frozen over. Like the Roxolani, the Iazyges raided Roman territory and were then pursued by imperial forces as they headed back to the Danube. However, once they reached the frozen river, the Sarmatian warriors turned to face the Roman army on the ice, confident in the ability of their mounts to fight on the slippery surface. As the Romans approached, the Sarmatian horsemen charged into the infantrymen in the centre and on the flanks. The legionaries responded quickly, however, most likely forming into a square that

successfully repelled the lancers' assaults. Surprisingly, the Roman soldiers in the front of the infantry formation were even helped by their comrades behind them who provided their shields for the men of the front lines to stand on for more stability upon the slick ice. After the Romans withstood the charge, more and more of the horses of the Iazyges increasingly began to slip on the frozen surface, which the Romans exploited to the fullest. When the legionaries counterattacked, they frequently ripped the Sarmatian riders off their mounts and once the invaders were dragged to the ground, many were killed. Some of the Iazyges managed to retreat but a great many were slain.[15]

After the Roman victory, it took two more years before the two sides were willing to negotiate peace terms, as stated by Cassius Dio in his *Roman History*:

> *Indeed, the emperor had wished to exterminate [the Iazyges] utterly. For that they were still strong at this time and had done the Romans great harm was evident from the fact that they returned a hundred thousand captives that were still in their hands even after the many who had been sold, had died, or had escaped, and that they promptly furnished as their contribution to the alliance eight thousand cavalry, fifty-five hundred of whom he sent to Britain.*[16]

The most fascinating aspect of these terms is the transfer of 5,500 armoured Sarmatian lancers to the Roman province of Britain in 175. Some scholars believe that these warriors formed the basis of the Arthurian legends with their mounted knights. Not only is there evidence that the Sarmatians served in the imperial forces of Britain all the way up until the fifth century but later Roman cataphracts were also stationed on the island, which may have then augmented the mythic stories in the following centuries. More information about ancient Sarmatian culture gives further credence to the theory, for there were two major aspects that have a striking similarity to the tales of King Arthur. First and foremost, the ancient Sarmatians worshipped a sword thrust into the ground, much like the 'sword in the Stone'. Another interesting fact is that the Sarmatians commonly used standards with the image of a dragon, or *draco*, a mythical creature that was a common theme of the Arthurian tales.[17] Whether the Sarmatians truly inspired the Arthurian legends or not, it is almost certain that the descendants of the 5,500 mounted warriors who continued to serve in the Roman armies greatly influenced the heavy cavalrymen and the later cataphracts stationed there.

The Armenians

The kingdom of Armenia remained an important state in the east throughout the Ancient era and Late Antiquity. Armenia was often caught in the power struggle between the Romans in the west, and in the east, first the Parthians and then the Sassanians, though the Armenians remained a dangerous enemy with their deadly cataphracts. The Armenian cataphracts of the third century AD gradually began to adopt Sassanian-style equipment, such as the Assyrian-looking helmet that was often utilized throughout the early phases of the re-emergence of the Persian Empire. The Armenian heavy cavalrymen also wore a long cuirass of lamellar armour that covered the thighs all the way down to the knees. Underneath the lamellar was a coat of mail with long sleeves that extended to the wrists. To protect the legs, the cataphracts also wore mail leggings that covered the feet as well. Although much later, an eleventh century representation of the Armenian heavy cavalryman, the bas-relief of Goliath at Gagic, Lake Van, may provide an example of what these earlier cataphracts looked like in the Late Antique period. The mount of the cataphract was armoured with a facemask over the head and a neck guard, along with armour that protected the entire chest; all of which were very similar to the armour that was used by the Sassanian cataphracts.[18]

The Kingdom of Palmyra

Like Armenia, Palmyra was a minor eastern state that adopted its own version of the most renowned warriors in the region, the cataphracts of the Parthians and Sassanians. Palmyra was a powerful and prosperous city located in Syria, which due to its small size when compared to the superpowers of the region, was often under the hegemony of a larger empire. For a few centuries at the end of the first millennium BC, the city was under the rule of the Seleucid empire, until it gained its independence when Syria became a province of the Roman Empire in 64 BC. However, in the first century AD the kingdom of Palmyra was incorporated into the Roman Empire and primarily became a client state of its new ruler. As a vassal kingdom of the Romans, Palmyra supplied the empire with mounted troops to fight in their wars for as long as it remained under Roman hegemony. Yet it was not until the third century AD that native Palmyran cataphracts, who fought for their own kingdom, appear in the historical record.[19]

The Palmyran cataphracts most likely rode armoured steeds that wore barding similar to the remains uncovered at Dura Europos. Also, based upon the cuirasses with *pteruges* worn by the Palmyran gods on the third century AD votive reliefs, now located in the Louvre, there is a possibility that some of the elite heavy cavalrymen of the kingdom may have worn the Hellenistic style of corselet, like their former over-lords, the Seleucids. However, it is more likely that the Sassanians were a greater influence on the Palmyran cataphracts of the third century AD, especially regarding the kind of sword carried.[20] In fact, not only the swords, but also nearly all of the other arms and armour of the elite Palmyran heavy cavalrymen probably had a strong Persian influence. Like those of their Sassanian counterparts, and other contemporaneous cataphracts, the swords of the elite Palmyran heavy cavalrymen were secondary arms, while the lance was their primary weapon.[21]

Shortly after his great victory over the Romans at the Battle of Carrhae-Edessa circa 260, Sassanian Emperor Shapur I was attacked by a Palmyran army, which forced the ruler to shift his focus away from the defeated Romans to the small kingdom instead. In 260/261, the king of Palmyra, Odenathus (r. 260–67), gathered his forces, including many cataphracts, and then struck the baggage train of the Sassanian army in Syria. Shapur counterattacked with his army, though the emperor was unsuccessful and, ultimately, was forced to return back to his own lands further east. For almost five long years, the kingdom of Palmyra fought the substantially larger Sassanian empire until the conflict ended in a stalemate in 265.[22]

Due to the weakness of the Roman Empire at the time, especially after enduring several serious defeats against the Sassanians, King Odenathus of Palmyra was appointed the *Corrector Totius Orientis*, meaning the 'Supervisor of the Whole East', by the Roman emperor. The title gave the Palmyran king independent authority over a huge tract of land that extended from the edge of Egypt in the south, all the way up to the region of the Black Sea in the north. Yet even though he was granted an immense amount of power by the emperor, Odenathus still remained a vassal to the Romans. The subordinate position of the kingdom of Palmyra ended in 267, however, when, after the king's death, Queen Zenobia (r. 267–72) tried her best to free the kingdom from the Roman yoke. First, the Palmyran queen took the offensive and conquered the rest of Egypt that was not previously under her control. The Romans were not able to respond to the Palmyran rebellion for a few years until after Emperor Aurelian (r. 270–75) defeated both the Vandals and the Alemanni and then led his forces to the east in 272.[23]

Aurelian sent one of his generals to reclaim Egypt, while the Roman emperor led a greater force through Asia Minor to reach the kingdom of Palmyra. As the Roman army advanced into Palmyran territory, nearly all of the towns and cities in their path quickly switched to the side of the great western empire without putting up any resistance. However, when Aurelian and his men approached the important city of Antioch, the Romans found the Palmyran army in their way while they traversed through the Orontes River valley. Not only were all of the troops led by Zenobia mounted upon steeds, but also many of the cavalrymen were heavily armoured cataphracts. Yet even though specific information is unknown about the number of soldiers who fought for each side, it is likely that Aurelian brought many horsemen with him as well to combat the numerous mounted warriors of the eastern kingdom. It can be stated with certainty though that the Roman cavalry did not include any cataphracts.[24]

Before the Battle of Immae began, the Roman emperor intently watched the enemy forces, especially the many Palmyran cataphracts, which opposed his troops, in order to finish devising his battle plan. As stated in the account of Zosimus in his *New History*, Aurelian then arranged his troops in the way that he felt was best to overcome the opposing cataphracts and then the combat commenced:

> But observing that the Palmyrene cavalry placed great confidence in their armour, which was very strong and secure, and that they were much better horsemen than his soldiers, he planted his infantry by themselves on the other side of the Orontes. He charged his cavalry not to engage immediately with the vigorous cavalry of the Palmyrenians, but to wait for their attack, and then, pretending to fly, to continue so doing until they had wearied both the men and their horses through excess of heat and the weight of their armour; so that they could pursue them no longer. This project succeeded, and as soon as the cavalry of the emperor saw their enemy tired, and that their horses were scarcely able to stand under them, or themselves to move, they drew up the reins of their horses, and, wheeling round, charged them, and trod them under foot as they fell from their horses. By which means the slaughter was promiscuous, some falling by the sword, and others by their own and the enemies' horses.[25]

Aurelian brilliantly managed to turn the Palmyran cataphracts' best attribute into their greatest weakness with much success. Worn out by the heavy weight of their armour, the cataphracts were then quickly defeated, which, according to the later Roman writer Festus, accounted for a large part of the Palmyran forces:

> Aurelian defeated [Zenobia], relying on many thousands of [cataphracts] and archers, at Immae, not far from Antioch.[26]

With so many of their troops defeated, the rest of the Palmyran army was forced to flee; thus, the Romans won the major encounter at Immae.

After the defeat, Zenobia left the people of Antioch to their own devices while the Palmyran queen desperately tried to regroup her forces. It is possible that the queen managed to augment her army so that it increased to number as many as 70,000 men, but even if this number is not a major exaggeration, the Romans were also able to gather reinforcements; therefore, Aurelian's army may have been out-numbered, but it was still a large host as well. Some of the new units incorporated in the Roman army may have even been Sarmatian lanc-ers that Aurelian hoped would have great success against the Palmyran armoured horsemen. Even so, the Palmyrans still had a considerable number of cataphracts, so their heavy cavalry was almost certainly more numerous than the Romans'. The two augmented armies then met again at the Battle of Emessa in that same year of 272. At the second major confrontation between the Romans and the warriors of Zenobia, Aurelian ordered his troops to employ the same tactics that were so successful in the previous battle. However, when the Roman cavalry feigned retreat again in order to exhaust the cataphracts, this time the Palmyran armoured horsemen managed to reach the Roman mounted troops and made contact with a powerful charge. After slamming into the Roman cavalrymen, causing panic and disorder to spread through-out their ranks, the Palmyran cataphracts proceeded to hack their way through the enemy in the vicious mêlée.[27]

Many Roman cavalrymen were slain by the formidable Palmyran cataphracts before the imperial infantry was able to intervene in the fighting to aid their mounted comrades. Since the Palmyran armoured horsemen were fully engaged in close combat with the enemy cavalry-men, the cataphracts were no longer in their tight, cohesive formation, so the Roman foot soldiers exploited the situation as much as possible. First, the Roman infantrymen assaulted the cataphracts from the rear. Then, the majority of the foot troops used the tactic of targeting areas of both the riders and mounts that were the least armoured, which was increasingly becoming one of the most common ways that were used to overcome the cataphracts. However, it was the Palestinian contingent

leucid arms and armour captured by the Romans after their victory at Magnesia in 190 BC, depicted in a relief from the stoa of the temple of Athena Polias Nikephorus, first half of the d century BC. Illustration by Mark Birge-Anderson.

rracotta plaque of a Parthian cataphract hunting a lion, from Babylonia, 2nd century AD. itish Museum, London.

Depiction of a fully armoured cataphract. Redrawn version of a crude graffito found at Dura Europos, 2nd – 3rd century AD. Illustration by Mark Birge-Anderson

A fragment of ancient Roman scale armour (lorica squamata Museum of Somerset, Taunton, U

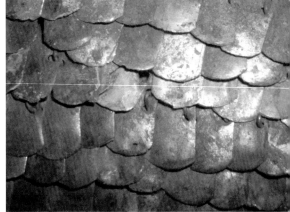

Sarmatian cataphracts flee from Roman cavalry during the Dacian wars (AD 101-106) from the reliefs on Trajan's Column, Rome, constructed in AD 113.
Photo by Conrad Cichorius, 1896.

XXXVII

Sassanian cavalryman with a *kontos* attacking a fully armoured Parthian rider. Silver plate with gold coating. Azerbaijan Museum, Tabriz, Iran. Photo by Alborz Fallah.

Relief from Firzubad, Iran, depicting the victory in AD 224 of the Sassanian emperor, Ardashir I (r. 224-242), and his son, Prince Shapur, over the cavalry forces of the Parthian emperor, Artabanus V (r. 208-224). Illustration by Eugene Flandin, 1840.

elief from Naqsh-i Rustam, Iran, depicting the Sassanian emperor, Bahram II (r. 274-293), combat with a foe carrying a broken *kontos*.

Relief from Naqsh-i Rustam, Iran, showing a Sassanian emperor, Hormuzd II (r. 303-309
unhorsing an unknown opponent.

A relief of a Sassanian ruler armoured as a *clibanarius* from Taq-i Bustan, Iran. It depicts eith
Khosrow II (r. 590-628) or Peroz I (r. 459-484). Photograph by Javad Yousefi.

Drawing of a relief, which depicts laminated limb armour and a helmet with a metal facemask, from the Column of Arcadius, constructed in 5th century Constantinople. Even though it was destroyed by earthquakes, it was preserved in a series of drawings.

Mosaic depicting a Late Roman armoured cavalryman mounted on an armoured horse. Photograph courtesy of Simon MacDowall.

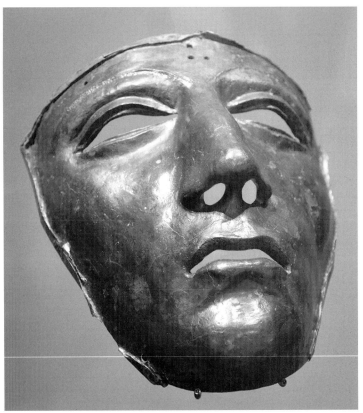

Facemask for Roman cavalry, early 1st century AD, from Kalkriese. It was originally made of iron with silver overlay but the silver was later removed. Museum und Park Kalkriese, Germany. Photograph by Carole Raddato.

Roman cavalry facemask helmet found at Noviomagus, 1st century AD. Museum Het Valkhof, Nijmegen, Netherlands. Photograph by Carole Raddato.

Insignia of the *Magistri Officiorum* showing the arms and armour of the Roman state factories (*fabricae*) from the *Notitia Dignitatum*, late 4th/ early 5th century AD. MS. Canon. Misc. 378, Roll 159 B, Frame 34. Bodleian Library, Oxford.

Weapons and armour of Late Roman soldiers, including laminated limb defences worn by the cataphracts, from the *Notitia Dignitatum*. MS. Canon. Misc. 378, Roll 316.2, Frame 2. Bodleian Library, Oxford.

A 14th century illustration that shows a fully armoured Byzantine warrior mounted on a unarmoured horse. *Alexander Romance* manuscript. San Giorgi de Greci, Venice.

The cavalry of Alexander the Great anachronistically depicted as cataphracts in a 14th centur illustration from the Byzantine *Alexander Romance* manuscript. San Giorgio de Greci, Venic

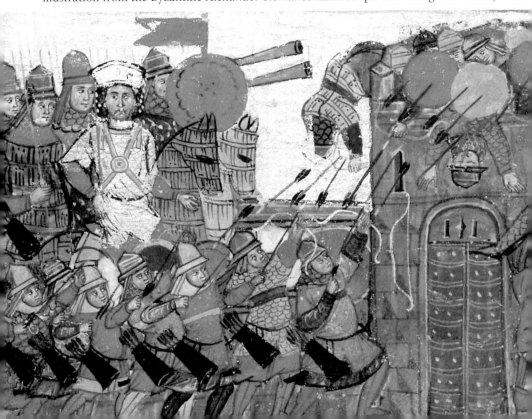

among the Roman forces that did the most damage to the Palmyran cataphracts by using staves and clubs. The blunt weaponry may not have been able to penetrate the heavy armour of the cavalrymen but the powerful blows still did a considerable amount of damage to both the riders and mounts underneath the layers of protection. When enough of their comrades had been slain by the Roman infantrymen, the rest of the surviving Palmyran horsemen fled in terror.[28]

After suffering two major defeats, Zenobia tried to escape from the Romans pursuing her, but the queen was quickly found and then forced to participate in the triumph of Emperor Aurelian. On the other hand, the Palmyran queen was not treated like the typical captured enemy leader and was allowed to live. Not only that, but Zenobia even married a Roman senator and spent the rest of her life in the imperial capital. Having dealt with the eastern threat of Palmyra, Aurelian and his forces were then able to shift their focus to the major rebellion in Gaul.[29] The kingdom of Palmyra may have ultimately lost its conflict with the Roman Empire but its cataphracts definitely managed to kill many imperial troops in the process. From then on, the minor eastern state was never again a major threat to the great western power. However, a new and formidable adversary had already arisen in the East, with its own lethal cataphracts and clibanarii, the Sassanians.

CHAPTER FIVE

THE SASSANIAN PERSIAN CATAPHRACTS AND *CLIBANARII*

The Sassanian Empire

The first ruler of the Sassanian Persian Empire, Ardashir I (r. 224–42), initially rose to power after successfully rebelling against his father, and the true heir of his people, his older brother. After their deaths, Ardashir became the king of Persis in 211/212 and then began his fight with the Parthians shortly afterwards, gradually increasing the territory under his control. When the Parthian Emperor Artabanus confronted King Ardashir at the Battle of Hormozgān in 224, and was subsequently killed, Ardashir became the emperor of the new Sassanian Empire at Ctesiphon. Not long after the creation of the revived Persian state, Emperor Ardashir continued to focus on expanding his territory by invading Armenia. At first, the Parthian royal family members that ruled over Armenia managed to put up fierce resistance against the invaders and even gained support from the Romans, Scythians and Kushans. However, after the three allied states suffered heavy losses against the Sassanian army, all of them gradually withdrew their forces from the conflict. Armenia resisted for ten long years but was eventually overtaken. Ardashir also turned his attention towards the border with the Roman Empire, where he had great success. By 235, Mesopotamia and much of the territory along the boundaries was seized by Sassanian forces, including the important cities of Nisibis, Carrhae, Dura Europos, and Hatra.[1]

Origins of the *Clibanarii*

After the death of Emperor Ardashir in 241, his son and co-ruler, Shapur I (r. 240–270), ascended the throne of a fledgling, yet huge, empire with a large, powerful army under his command. Although the empire that Shapur ruled over was still new, his father had created a strong, stable state built upon several, long-standing foundations established by the previous Parthian government. Many aspects of the Parthian military were carried over into the Sassanian armies as well, including the elite, heavily armoured aristocratic cavalrymen, the cataphracts. The early Sassanian version of the cataphract had many similarities to its Parthian predecessor; however, as the empire grew older and evolved, so too did these elite horsemen who fought in the imperial armies throughout the following centuries.

As the arms and armour of the Sassanian heavy horsemen changed, a new word began to emerge in the Greco-Roman accounts regarding the East, which was used to describe the armoured mounted troops who fought in the region; the new Latin term for the Sassanian cataphract-type of warrior was *clibanarius* (pl. *clibanarii*). There are several different theories regarding the origin of the word, as well as for the exact differences between the older *cataphracti* and the new *clibanarii*. Initially, it was thought that the term was a derivation of either an older Persian or Latin word. The first was the Old Persian word for 'warrior', which is *grivpan*. The second possibility for the origin of the term *clibanarius* was the Latin term to describe a 'field oven', known as a *clibanus*; the thinking behind this being that the word was used because it must have felt like standing in an oven to be so heavily armoured under the hot sun in the Middle East.[2] On the other hand, even if *clibanarius* did come from the Latin masculine noun *clibanus* or *cliuanus*, the latter term most likely meant 'more complete armour', as opposed to the Latin word *lorica*, which was used to describe only a 'cuirass' or 'corselet'.[3]

Even though the first Sassanian elite heavy cavalrymen were referred to as *catafracti*, the Romans may have begun to use the term *clibanarii* to describe the eastern armoured horsemen as early as the third century AD, for it is possible that the Roman Emperor Diocletian (r. 284–305) incorporated the first unit of *clibanarii* into the Roman military.[4] Interestingly, in a description of the *clibanarii* (in the Roman army, not Sassanian) by the Roman historian Ammianus Marcellinus, he stated:

> *And scattered among them were the cataphracts, whom they call* clibanarii, *all masked, furnished with protecting breastplates and girt with iron belts, so that you might have supposed them statues polished by the hand of Praxiteles, not men. Thin circles of iron plates, fitted to the curves of their bodies, completely covered their limbs; so that whichever way they had to move their members, their garment fitted, so skillfully were the joinings made.*[5]

The exact difference(s) between the earlier *cataphracti* and the newer *clibanarii*, used by either the Sassanians or the Romans, has been a topic of much debate between modern scholars. The fact that Ammianus used the phrase 'the cataphracts, whom they call *clibanarii*', along with other evidence, has led several scholars to the conclusion that there was very little differentiation between the two types of heavy cavalry-men, if there were any differences at all. On the other hand, many other experts believe that the *clibanarii* were either as heavily armoured, or even more heavily armoured than the earlier cataphracts; these schol-ars often also state that the *clibanarius* rode an armoured mount. Other theories attribute the differences between the two types of heavy cav-alrymen to the equipment carried, specifically whether or not either a bow, shield and/or a lance was used in combat, or in the tactics employed on the battlefield. If the *clibanarii* and the earlier cataphracts were in fact the same kind of mounted warrior with very few differ-ences, especially in terms of arms and armour, the two different terms could simply be attributed to regional preference; the word *cataphracti* remained in use throughout the western regions of the Roman Empire, while heavily armoured cavalrymen were increasingly referred to as *clibanarii* in the east. However, eventually the term *clibanarii* grew in popularity to such an extent that at least by the sixth century AD, the word had replaced the earlier term *cataphracti* throughout the Greco-Roman world.[6]

The Sassanian *clibanarii* typically wore *spangenhelm*-type metal hel-mets that originated from the interactions with the Sarmatians and other Iranian warriors. The earliest depiction of the Sassanian *spangenhelm* can be found on the terracotta of a soldier from Tepe Yahya of the fourth century AD. The helmet was usually 20cm (8in) wide and 22–24cm (8–9in) tall. The style of *spangenhelm* most used by the heavy cavalry-men was the Bashlyk type, characterized by a higher cone shape. Like the Sarmatian heavy cavalrymen, the Sassanian *clibanarii* preferred to utilize the *spangenhelm* for it provided much protection and was more easily mass-produced than the other options available to the heavy horsemen. To construct the helmet, the Sassanians took at least four, or as many as six, pieces of metal and riveted them together by using a frame. Because the *spangenhelm* was made of several separate pieces it was not as difficult to create as the one-piece and two-piece helmets also in use. The wealthiest of the *clibanarii* decorated their *spangenhelm* with jewels, precious metals and important symbols or images. The most common ornaments were feather motifs from Iranian mythical creatures, such as the simurgh and the griffin – like varanga. Extremely thin plates, only 0.1 to 0.2mm thick and made of gold or silver, were also occasionally overlaid upon the iron pieces of the helmet. Some helmets, such as those worn by Emperor Bahram II (r. 274–293) and his bodyguards, contained stylized wings on each side. The royal *spangen-helm* depicted on the Taq-i Bustan relief is one of the best examples of highly decorated Sassanian helmets. Not only was the helmet embellished with a globe on top that had ribbons attached to it, but there was also a jewel directly on the middle of the forehead, along with two rows of pearls beside it.[7]

Even though one-piece helmets were harder to construct, they must have been common amongst the early Sassanian *clibanarii* for that appears to be the main type of helmet worn by the horsemen on the Bishapur, Firuzabad and Naqsh-i Rustam reliefs. Another type of protective headgear worn by the earliest heavy cavalrymen of this period is known as a ridge helmet, which was constructed with two pieces. To make the Sassanian ridge helmet of the third century, two riveted bands of iron connected two solid pieces that were each formed to cover half of the skull. A mail aventail was also attached; this protected the neck but left the face exposed aside from the solid nose guard that extended down from the top of the helmet. The ridge helmet on average was about 26cm (10in) in height and 16cm (6in) in width. An example of the helmet was found on the cavalryman at Dura Europos, which may have either been a Parthian, Sassanian or Roman cataphract/*clibanarius*.[8]

The helmets of the *clibanarii* may have also contained a mask to fully protect the face of the rider, yet this was certainly not always the case. The faces of both of the Sassanian emperors in the Firuzabad relief of the third century AD and the Naqsh-i Rustam relief are fully visible without any facemasks attached to their helmets. On the other hand, in the third-century *Aethiopica* of Heliodorus and the fourth-century accounts of Ammianus Marcellinus, the Sassanian *clibanarii* are described as having a metal facemask attached to their helmets that covered every part of the head except for the eyes. These facemasks were probably a prominent feature of the most heavily armoured Sassanian cavalrymen of these two centuries, especially during the reign of Emperor Shapur II (r. 309–379). Furthermore, the heavy horseman depicted in relief at Taq-i Bustan near Kermanshah, which is likely to be Emperor Khosrow II (r. 590–628) but could also instead be an image of Emperor Peroz I (r. 459–484), is shown wearing mail that also protected his entire face, leaving only two holes for the eyes. The aventail provided much protection for it was often two or even three layers thick. The late Sassanian *spangenhelm* type of helmet shown on the relief also has a unique feature in that the metal eye slits are a part of the helmet, with the layers of mail attached underneath them. Another change made to the latest version was that it was more hemispherical, as opposed to the earlier conical style.[9]

Most of the rest of the body of a Sassanian *clibanarius* was armoured with segmented iron plates over a full coat of mail that covered the arms past the elbows, sometimes all the way to the knuckles, and extended below the knees as well. During the reign of the first Sassanian emperor, Ardashir I (r. 224–242), mail production was established and the armour quickly became one of the most popular types among the heavy cavalrymen. However, along with the iron plates commonly used to protect the torso, mail was often augmented with other solid metal protection, such as vambraces on the arms. The Sassanian heavy horsemen may have also worn a gauntlet known as the *bazpan*, similar to those utilized by the Parthians; this armour consisted of mail augmented by metal strips that protected the hands of the rider. Based on the depiction of the *clibanarii* in the Firuzabad relief, it is possible that the most heavily armoured of the cavalrymen wore a full plate cuirass; however, it is more likely that the image merely shows a textile garment worn over the mail coat, especially since such Hellenistic breastplates were so uncommon in western Asia. Yet even if the *clibanarii* wore cloth over their armour, this too may have been augmented with padding, or even had plates sewn into the fabric to increase the protection it provided.[10]

Lamellar and scale armours were also used by the Sassanian *clibanarii*; however, these armours were certainly used considerably less than they were by the earlier Parthian cataphracts. When the heavy cavalrymen did wear a lamellar cuirass, it was often only short-sleeved, as depicted on reliefs of the fourth century AD, and may have even had a mail coat underneath it at times. The lamellar of the Sassanians was highly influenced by the armour worn by the warriors of Central Asia. It was commonly constructed with small plates of iron, bronze or leather that were laced together both horizontally and vertically; but it could also be made by longer plates that were either tied or sewn together and attached to a backing often made of leather. The armour used least by the Sassanian *clibanarii* was made of scales. The armour was constructed with smaller and larger scales laced horizontally upon a backing. The last armour that may have been occasionally worn by the heavy cavalrymen at the end of this period was the laminated armour that consisted of several circular, metal hoops that covered the limbs. There is an image of a Sassanian warrior painted on a wooden shield from the eighth century AD, after the Arab conquest, found in the ruins of Mug Castle, now in modern day Uzbekistan. It depicts the heavy horseman in a coat of laminated armour with sleeves that reached the wrists and a striking similarity to the banded armour cuirass of the Sarmatian heavy cavalrymen. The arms of the late *clibanarii* were further reinforced with one of the first representations of the tubular armour known as *basuband*.[11]

Whereas most of the arms and armour of the *clibanarii* were similar to the earlier cataphracts, one major new addition was the inclusion of a shield, as depicted on the Taq-i Bustan relief. While the earliest heavy cavalrymen did not carry a shield, the late Sassanian *clibanarii* carried a small, round shield that was shaped like a buckler and most likely worn on the left forearm to deflect enemy arrows. Another difference from the cataphracts was that the mounts of the Sassanian heavy cavalrymen might have worn much lighter armour than those of the earlier cataphracts, with most of the protection constructed from leather, or the armour could even have merely been a fabric barding; on the Firuzabad relief, the horses are armoured with felt.[12] Yet this was definitely not always the case, especially during the later periods of the Sassanian empire. Over time, lamellar barding, known as *bargostvan* and made of overlapping rows of curved bands attached to a strong fabric, became a prominent feature of the mounts of many Sassanian *clibanarii*. In the fourth century, facemasks were commonly used to protect the heads of the horses as well. By the fifth century, both half-trappers and full trappers were utilized by the *clibanarii*. As shown on the Taq-i Bustan relief, partial lamellar armour that only covered the entire front of the horse, from the legs to the chest, neck and the head, became highly popular for it greatly increased the speed of the horse since it did not have the added weight of the armour on the rest of its body. If lamellar was not utilized, the horse armours were often made of iron or bronze scales sewn onto a tough, linen-like backing that was bound at the edges with rawhide that was sometimes red in colour.[13]

One final change made by the Sassanians, which became a key component to the weaponry of especially the late *clibanarii*, was the inclusion of the bow and arrows. Like the Parthian horse-archers, the Sassanians used bows constructed with wood, horn and sinew in Central Asian styles; however, armoured mounted troops began to use the bows instead of just light cavalrymen. The Sassanian bow was held in a bowcase, known as a *kamandan*. Along with the bow and case, the heavy horsemen also carried a quiver called a *tirdan* that usually held thirty arrows. Although early Sassanian *clibanarii* carried both the *tirdan* and *kamandan*, it was not until later in the empire that the mounted riders began to suspend the archery equipment from their belts in the same manner as that commonly practised by the horse-archers of Central Asia. With the quiver and bowcase attached in that way, both of them hung to the right side of the rider. The arrows utilized by the heavy cavalrymen were made of wood, fletched with three vanes and were typically 80–85cm (31–33in) long, similar to the ones fired by the Achaemenid Persian archers centuries before. Depending on the situation, the Sassanians used a number of different types of arrowheads, including bladed points described as iron-bladed, gold-notched, lead-poisoned, falcon-winged, horn-handled or vulture-feathered. To nock the arrow on the bowstring, it was Sassanian practice to use a cut on a reed joint. Though ambidexterity with the bow was acknowledged as an incredibly valuable skill, it was rare among the *clibanarii*; most were trained to hold the bow in the left hand and fire the missiles with the fingers of the right hand on the bowstring. If the hands of the heavy cavalryman were lightly armoured, or completely unarmoured, leaving the vital fingers used to draw the bow exposed, the archer covered the tips of the important digits with protective guards. A small chain was also worn around the wrist that was attached to the fingertip guards so they did not fall off while the *clibanarius* was in combat.[14]

To draw the bow, the Sassanians used the middle and ring fingers on the string while the index finger pointed straight along the side of the arrow shaft. It is uncertain exactly how the thumb was used but it probably helped the index finger keep the arrow firmly nocked. To ensure the most rapid rate of fire possible, it was also Sassanian practice to hold three extra arrows in the same hand as the bow.[15] The heavy cavalrymen were proficient with the bow as early as the third century AD; bows and quivers are depicted on the earlier Firuzabad relief and the weaponry is also seen on the late Taq-i Bustan relief a few centuries later. Furthermore, the horseman on that eighth century shield from Mug Castle has two unstrung bowstaves in a case on his left hip. Along with archery equipment, the weaponry of the heavy cavalryman also included a slightly curved scimitar in the late Sassanian style and possibly a mace as well. However, in between the era of the Firuzabad relief and the late *clibanarii* shown at Taq-i Bustan, there may have been a period when the heaviest armoured cavalrymen did not carry bows at all and only fought with close combat weapons like maces, swords and *kontoi* (heavy lances), especially in the fifth century AD.[16]

Among the various secondary arms carried by the Sassanian heavy cavalrymen, the most important was the sword. The first swords used by the *clibanarii* were similar to the ones carried by the Parthians before them, with straight, long blades and broad guards. On the other hand, the early Sassanian swords quickly began to adopt many characteristics similar to Sarmatian blades, such as globe-shaped pommels and wider guards. The Sassanians probably gained these influences from the Kushans, instead of direct interaction with the Sarmatians, because the first iron longswords that the Sassanians possessed with these features most likely came from encounters with the former group. Sarmatian styles were not always adopted, however, for some early Sassanian blades contained much smaller guards, similar to the Eastern types utilized by the Han Chinese. However, the Sassanians, for the most part, continued to make changes influenced by Sarmatian styles, especially when they modified the older Parthian blade to make the sword even longer and slimmer at 1–1.11 m (39–43in) in length and 5–8.5cm (2–3in) wide. Furthermore, early heavy cavalrymen suspended their swords from the belt in the same manner as the Sarmatians, often slung vertically to the left since the *tirdan* and *kamandan* archery equipment occupied the right side of the rider. To hang their swords in this way, a metal slide was mounted onto their scabbard, which was also then attached to their belt, yet allowed the scabbard to move along it. The image of Emperor Shapur I (r. 242–270) at Naqsh-i Rustam provides a visual representation of a sword suspended from the belt in this manner. The practice most likely continued among the Sassanians at least until the reign of Shapur II in the fourth century AD, or it possibly persisted even after his successor, Ardashir II (r. 379–383), came to power.[17]

By the fifth century, the Sassanians were introduced to a new suspension method for their swords, known as the double-locket or two-point system. The innovation may have first been encountered through interactions with Turkish or Avar tribal groups of Central Asia; however, it is likely that they were introduced to the new method during their conflicts with the Hephthalites. With the two-point system, the *clibanarii* attached their scabbards to their belts using two straps that they could adjust, which allowed them to change the angle of tilt of the sword in its scabbard. Thus, the improved equipment may have increased the speed at which the heavy cavalrymen were able to draw their swords. Even if it did not improve the performance of the horsemen by much, the innovative Turko-Avar method quickly replaced the old suspension system on the battlefield regardless. On the other hand, the old vertical suspension method continued to be used in ceremonies by the Sassanians; evidence of this can be found on the image of the investiture of Khosrow II at Taq-i Bustan. In images at Taq-i Bustan that are not religious ceremonies, the two-point method is also seen in use.[18]

In the later part of the era, the Sassanian *clibanarii* adopted a different type of sword that was typically 1.05m (41in) long and no longer contained a guard for the hilt. The wooden grip of these late Sassanian iron swords also contained a unique feature in that two distinct indentations were made: a larger one for the majority of the fingers to comfortably fit in and a smaller one just for the index finger as the hand gripped the hilt. The chopping power of these new blades was increased as well for the hilts curved slightly downward towards the end, creating an angle with the blade that put more of its weight into the blow. Thus, with these swords, the force behind the attacks of the heavy cavalrymen increased, making them more deadly as they cut down the enemy from atop their mounts. However, many of the late Sassanian swords may have been rather straight, which would have also made them effective thrusting weapons. Since the swords of the *clibanarii* were not only weapons, but also important symbols of wealth and status, the scabbards of the blades were sometimes highly ornate; the most common decoration was a v-shaped chape. Like the *spangenhelm* helmets worn by the late heavy horsemen of the period, the scabbards were also often decorated with the varanga or simurgh-feather designs, which often were located on the front of the scabbard. On the other hand, common decorations for the back of the scabbard were spiral designs similar to the artistry of the Celts. The wealthiest *clibanarii* plated their scabbards with thin sheets of solid gold or silver that were wrapped around and trimmed with a flat strip to cover the gap where the edges of the plates met.[19]

In addition to the sword, the late Sassanian *clibanarii* often carried smaller bladed weapons or daggers as well. These secondary blades were commonly carried using the two-point suspension system also utilized for swords, as seen at the site of Balalyk Tepe near Termez, Panjikent and at Varakhshah. Other auxiliary weapons included maces, axes or whips. Maces were the most commonly used of these. They were made of iron and often 40–55cm (16–21in) long. It is also possible that the Sassanians carried a whip or lasso like the Sarmatians and other mounted warriors of the Central Asian Steppes. In his *De Re Militari*, Vegetius mentioned how effective lassos were against cataphracts which were used to grab hold of riders' necks and pull them off their steeds. The only evidence of the Persians utilizing whips comes from the late tenth or early eleventh century epic poem, the *Shahnameh*, written by Firdawsi. However, whips are mentioned frequently in the poem which covers earlier Persian history, so the *clibanarii* may have been armed with the weapon as well. The last and most unique of the auxiliary arms possibly carried by the late *clibanarii* was the missile-launching device known as the *panjagan*, meaning 'five device'. The exact specifications of the invention are unknown since there are no surviving remains but the written accounts state that the contraption could fire five missiles at once. Therefore, heavy cavalrymen armed with the missile weapon instead of the bow could not only fire many more shots at a much higher rate, but they could also spread their fire over a wider area as well.[20]

Regardless of the addition of a bow and the various secondary arms, the long lance (*kontos*), adopted from the Parthians, was the chief weapon of the Sassanian *clibanarii* for most of their existence. As depicted on the Naqsh-i Rustam relief, the heavy cavalrymen often held the lance in both hands to the side of their steed's head when charging against mounted opponents. The *kontos* continued to be used by the Sassanian horsemen even after they adopted the shield, most likely due to the change of the type of saddle utilized. As depicted on the Firuzabad relief, the front horns of the saddle firmly held onto the legs of the rider. As time progressed, further advances in saddle technology gave the rider more balance to make it easier to wield the *kontos* in one hand and a shield in the other. The relief at Taq-i Bustan shows the weapon used in this way, the lance is aimed forward to the side of the horse's head, but held in only the right hand of the rider. It may also be that the introduction of stirrups made it possible for the late Sassanian *clibanarii* to wield the *kontos* in a one-handed grip; however, there is no conclusive evidence that proves that the horsemen ever used stirrups. For example, the legs and feet of the *clibanarius* at Taq-i Bustan are too damaged to prove one way or the other. Even if the late Sassanian heavy cavalrymen did utilize stirrups, they were most likely not in use until near the end of the era.[21]

The ability of the *clibanarii* to wield *kontoi*, bows and swords, along with shields, is primarily due to the successful development of the saddle by the Sassanians. They often placed a cloth over their steed before putting the saddle on top the mount, which was secured into place by both a girth strap around the stomach and a breast strap across the chest. By the third century, the saddle utilized by the Sassanians had four horns, of which the front pair curved over the thigh to grip the legs more firmly. Even without stirrups, a warrior who rode on this saddle could still charge with the lance while leaning forward without losing his balance. However, in the late Sassanian period a new saddle was adopted with a raised bow that replaced the front horns of the older version. The raised-bow saddle gave the *clibanarii* even more balance when charging with their *kontoi*, however, there was on major drawback; with the new saddle, the Sassanians removed the horns located in the back but did not replace them with a raised bow or anything else. Some scholars, such as Michalak and Herrmann, see this development as an important clue, in the absence of other evidence, that stirrups had by now been adopted. They theorize that the rear horns were no longer needed since the stirrup provided the required stability instead.[22] Of course stirrups would not *necessarily* render the rear saddle bow obsolete. Western knights used the stirrup and raised cantle together, pushing forward against the stirrups, forcing themselves back against the cantle to brace themselves against the impact of their charge.

Like the Parthian cataphracts, the Romans faced the Sassanian type of the heavily armoured cavalrymen on multiple occasions, for the great western and eastern empires waged several wars against each other over the centuries. Also, just as with the Parthian heavy cavalrymen, the Romans had great respect for the extensive armour of the Sassanian *clibanarii*. The Romans encountered the *clibanarii* of the Sassanian armies in the earliest years of the eastern empire and the ancient Roman account known as the *Scriptores Historiae Augustae* mentioned the importance of the heavy cavalrymen's armour to the westerners in the aftermath of one of these early conflicts:

> *10,000 of their* cataphractarii, *whom they call* clibanarii, *we have slain in battle, and with their armour we have armed our men.*[23]

Even though the Roman account boasted of the great victory the imperial army won against the *clibanarii*, the Sassanians achieved much more overall success against the Romans in the first decades of their rule, such as with the victories of Ardashir I.

After the territorial gains made by his father in Mesopotamia, Shapur I went on the offensive in the beginning of his reign; first, he captured the vital Kushan city of Peshawar, and then seized the Indus valley and Bactria.[24] Yet these early successes were combined with the losses the Sassanian empire sustained against the Romans. After the achievements made by Roman Emperor Gordian III (r. 238–244) in his eastern campaign against the Sassanians in 243, the Roman army he led managed to reach Misiche, located to the north of Ctesiphon, in the next year and were confronted there by Shapur and his soldiers. Gordian was well aware of the superior cavalry strength of the Sassanian army, so the emperor may have recruited an elite contingent of Gothic auxiliary armoured horsemen to combat the Persian heavy cavalry, especially the *clibanarii*. Due to their experience fighting Sarmatian armoured cavalry, in what is now modern day Ukraine, the Roman emperor believed that Gothic mounted troops had the ability to withstand the elite *clibanarii* of the Sassanians. When the Sassanian and Gothic heavy cavalry met at Misiche, the Germanic troops proved to be no match for their Persian counterparts, who not only had more extensive armour but were also more skilled in shock combat tactics with the lance. Furthermore, archers in the Roman army may have discovered, like the Parthians had in 224, that the combined lamellar, laminated and mail armour utilized by the Sassanian *clibanarii* provided such extensive protection that the arrows of the Romans rarely penetrated through the thick layers to strike the warrior underneath. In the end, the Gothic cavalry, along with the archers, legionaries and the rest of the Roman forces, were overwhelmed and defeated at Misiche.[25]

Roman Emperor Gordian may have lost his life while in combat, or was murdered by his own men after the battle. Gordian's successor, Philip the Arab (r. 244–249), chose to pay tribute to the Sassanians rather than continue the fight. However, the conflict was renewed when Shapur invaded the Roman-controlled part of Mesopotamia almost a decade later in response to Roman moves against Armenia. A huge Roman army consisting of 60,000–70,000 soldiers intercepted the Sassanian invasion force at the Battle of Barbalissos in c.253, but in the end was completely crushed by the Neo-Persians. The Sassanian army followed up the victory with the capture of Antioch and Dura Europos by 256 AD. With the Romans defeated and thoroughly embarrassed by the fledgling successor state to the Parthians on more than one occasion, the new Roman Emperor Valerian (r. 253–260 AD) desperately needed a victory to salvage the empire's martial reputation. Therefore, Valerian raised another enormous army of 70,000 men and began his eastern campaign by ousting the Sassanians from Antioch shortly after it was taken. The Sassanians countered the Roman assault by putting Carrhae and Edessa under siege, forcing Valerian and his men to meet them there. At the battle of Carrhae-Edessa in 260 or 261, the Sassanian army inflicted another of the most disastrous defeats ever experienced by the Romans, like Crassus' loss centuries before. In the latest catastrophe, not only was the Roman emperor captured, but so too were senators, generals and many other important Roman officials that travelled with the army. Unfortunately for Shapur, immediately after this epic victory over the Roman Empire, he was embroiled in the frustrating conflict with the kingdom of Palmyra from 260/261 to 265 AD.[26]

It was not until nearly 100 years later in the fourth century that another major war broke out between the Sassanian Empire and the Romans, in which the *clibanarii* frequently played a prominent role in the fighting, according to the ancient accounts. In 359, the Sassanian Emperor Shapur II (r. 309–379) invaded Mesopotamia and besieged the city of Amida. The Roman soldier and historian, Ammianus Marcellinus, personally witnessed the invasion and siege, specifically mentioning Sassanian *clibanarii*, or cataphracts, as part of the enemy forces in his account of the events from the *Rerum Gestarum*:

> *While all this took place in the course of half an hour, our soldiers in the rear, who occupied the higher part of the hill, cry out that another force, of cataphracts, was to be seen behind the others, and that they were approaching with all possible speed.*[27]

After the Sassanians surrounded Amida, Ammianus and the rest of the defenders fiercely resisted the attackers from behind the city walls. To speed up the process, the Sassanians stormed the walls with towers and other siege engines, supported by the *clibanarii* and infantrymen, but the besiegers were hard-pressed by the heavy missile fire of the defenders:

> *But when their approach brought them within bowshot, though hold-ing their shields before them the Persian infantry found it hard to avoid the arrows shot from the walls by the artillery, and took open order, and almost no kind of dart failed to find its mark; even the cataphracts were checked and gave ground, and thus increased the courage of our men.*[28]

In the end though, the valiant defence of Amida was made in vain, for after seventy-three days the army of Shapur II eventually took the city. Although Amida was one of the greatest prizes gained in the western campaign of Shapur II, the city was not the only place attacked by the Sassanian emperor. Along with seizing Singara and the Roman fortress of Vitra, Shapur II also assaulted the fortified town of Bezabde with his *clibanarii*, as recorded by Ammianus: [29]

> *On his first attack the king himself, with a troop of cataphracts gleaming in full armour and himself towering above the rest, rode about the circuit of the camp, and with over-boldness advanced to the very edge of the trenches. But becoming the target of repeated missiles from the ballistae and of arrows, he was protected by a close array of shields placed side by side as in a tortoise-mantlet, and got away unhurt.[30]*

The Sassanian forces eventually overcame the defences of Bezabde as well and then went on to storm the town.

Shortly after he became the Roman emperor, Julian the Apostate (r. 361–3) responded to the invasion of Shapur II and the capture of Amida by gathering a huge force of 65,000 soldiers from both mobile forces and troops stationed in forts on the borders. By 362, Julian invaded the Sassanian Empire with the large Roman host. The emperor then split his army in two and first led one 35,000-strong force to the Euphrates River, following it south to reach the city of Ctesiphon. Furthermore, 1,000 ships cruised down the river alongside and in support of the ground forces. Once he reached Ctesiphon, Emperor Julian managed to defeat the Sassanian forces outside the fortifications, but after the survivors retreated back within the city walls, the Romans struggled greatly in their attempts to take the capital. Meanwhile, the second half of the army, consisting of 30,000 troops and commanded by Procopius, headed towards northern Mesopotamia to first join with the Armenians before it reunited with the rest of the Roman forces.[31]

As the Romans surrounded Ctesiphon, Shapur II kept his distance with his swift cavalry forces, which included most of his *clibanarii*. Instead of facing the full Roman army on the battlefield, the Sassanian emperor ordered his heavily armoured horsemen to utilize their deadly shock combat tactics by slamming into the enemy troops and causing as much damage as possible before quickly retreating to safety. The rapid strikes of the *clibanarii* were a dreadful nuisance to the Roman soldiers, yet the attacks did not cause any considerable damage to the army. However, since the defences of Ctesiphon were too strong and Procopius had thus far failed to return with the other half of the army, Julian and his generals decided to lead the army away from the city in the hope of meeting the Sassanians on the field to win a decisive battle against their mighty eastern rival. Therefore, Julian made an order for the Roman ships on the Euphrates to be destroyed so that the Sassanians could not seize them. Then, the Roman army advanced deeper into Sassanian territory only to find the surrounding countryside scorched to the ground everywhere they went before they had arrived. This terrible revelation was compounded with the fact that the Romans were still being pursued by the Sassanians, whose cavalrymen, headed by the *clibanarii* armed with their heavy lances, struck the most vulnerable points of the Roman army as it was on the move. When the Sassanian horsemen attacked in this manner, they most likely formed up with the heaviest armoured *clibanarii* in the centre, while the less armoured cavalrymen were placed on the wings, probably armed with bows instead of lances. The rapid assaults of the Sassanian cavalry caused even more damage than usual because large war elephants also supported the horsemen by crashing into the Roman lines as well.[32]

Yet, even though the Sassanian forces had their successes against the Romans as they made their rapid strikes, the Roman invaders remained extremely dangerous as well. The legionaries were particularly deadly in close combat fighting, so the Sassanian cavalrymen were careful to avoid engaging too many of them at one time. After centuries of dealing with Seleucid, Armenian, Parthian and Sassanian cataphracts, the Roman heavy infantrymen had discovered ways of overcoming the heavy armour of their mounted opponents. Like the Gaulish auxiliaries led by Publius Crassus at the Battle of Carrhae in 53 BC, the legionaries learned to dive underneath the armoured horses of the heavy cavalrymen and stab upwards into their exposed bellies. Additionally, the heavy infantrymen had also learned that the visibility of the riders was extremely limited due to the small size of the eye slits on their helmets, which the legionaries exploited as much as possible at close-quarters. On the other hand, the fact that the *clibanarii* were able to charge into the Roman marching columns is further evidence that the heavy armour they wore may have been so strong that most archers in the Roman army could not penetrate it with their arrows, and were, therefore, unable to repel the charges of the *clibanarii* before they made contact with their lances. And although there were several occasions in which the heavily armoured horsemen felt it was more prudent to simply make a tactical retreat in the face of a Roman cavalry attack, more often than not, the cavalrymen who fought for the Romans were no match for the Sassanian *clibanarii* and were unable to prevent the devastating charges into the legionary ranks.[33]

The scorched-earth strategy of the Sassanians worked in forcing the Romans to retreat from their lands without facing the lethal legionaries in a pitched battle, mostly because the Romans were quickly running out of food. Yet, as Julian withdrew with his forces, Shapur II continued to follow the Roman troops, which finally led to another major battle on the Tigris River in 363. The Sassanians were located on the opposite bank across from the Romans. As most of their troops moved into formation, Sassanian archers were placed alongside the river in order to shield the movements of their comrades behind them. The front line of the main Sassanian army, stationed much further from the riverbank than the archers, was comprised of the formidable *clibanarii*.[34] Ammianus describes the scene:

> The Persians opposed to us serried bands of cataphracts in such close order that the gleam of moving bodies covered with closely fitting plates of iron dazzled the eyes of those who looked upon them, while the whole throng of horses was protected by coverings of leather.[35]

The heavily armoured Sassanian cavalrymen were supported by a horde of militiamen armed with spears standing among them, along with a line of elephants placed behind the cavalry/infantry formation. Moving as stealthily as possible, the Roman army crossed the river at midnight and managed to break up the line of bowmen standing on the other side. By the middle of morning on the next day, the entire Roman army had made it across, then managed to regroup and advanced towards the main body of the Sassanian forces. A contingent of javelineers successfully hid the approach of the Roman army to such an extent that the Sassanians were caught off-guard and were not able to fire nearly as many arrows into the advancing enemy as they normally would have. Without having to endure numerous volleys of missiles, the Roman legionaries more easily broke through the Sassanian front lines, leading to the total collapse of the eastern army. Panic rapidly spread amongst the fleeing troops until their collective escape devolved into a stampede, increasing the number of Sassanian warriors killed in the combat. Once the carnage was over, as many as 2,500 Sassanians lay slain on the battlefield, while the Romans reportedly lost a mere 75 men.[36]

After their victory on the Tigris River, the Romans continued their long retreat until the Sassanian army confronted them again at Maranga on 22 June. Nearly the entire front of the Sassanian army was comprised of *clibanarii*; the heavy cavalry in the centre were armed with lances, while those on the flanks fought as armoured horse-archers. Again,

Ammianus described the terrifying warriors who more resembled statues than men:

> *Moreover, all the companies were clad in iron, and all parts of their bodies were covered with thick plates, so fitted that the stiff joints conformed with those of their limbs; and the forms of human faces were so skillfully fitted to their heads, that, since their entire bodies were plated with metal, arrows that fell upon them could lodge only where they could see a little through tiny openings fitted to the circle of the eye, or where through the tips of their noses they were able to get a little breath. Of these some, who were armed with* conti *[heavy lances], stood so motionless that you would think them held fast by clamps of bronze.*[37]

Yet infantry archers also supported the mass of horsemen, and elephants were placed behind all of them as a rearguard. The Romans were outnumbered so the infantry formed into a crescent shape in the hope of preventing the Sassanian forces from encircling them. As at the previous battle on the Tigris River, the Roman soldiers, by charging at the Sassanian front lines as quickly as possible, were able to surprise the enemy troops and engage them before their deadly archers were able to release many arrows. Since the *clibanarii* were also unable to utilize shock tactics with their lances while locked in close combat with the legionaries, they too were unable to reach their full potential in the encounter. Therefore, while casualties remained low, Shapur II and his men made a tactical retreat, using the horse-archers to cover their escape.[38]

Even though the Romans had won another small victory at the Battle of Maranga, the *clibanarii* and the other Sassanian forces continued to make lightning-strike raids on all sides of the retreating marching columns of the Romans. To Shapur II, the conflict was a war of attrition that would be won by gradually wearing the Roman army down, which made a huge negative impact on the morale of the soldiers. On the other hand, the rapid assaults failed to cause any major damage to the overall forces, and the Roman army had not suffered any serious losses in the battles of the campaign thus far. And even though they were very low on food supplies, Julian also still desired one last final showdown to break the Sassanian army and effectively conquer their empire, so it was only a matter of time until the Roman commander was able to draw his rival into another battle.[39]

As the Roman army marched on, it came under a fierce assault by the Sassanians four days later near Samarra on 26 June. The Sassanian *clibanarii* viciously charged the Roman marching columns on all sides with their long, deadly lances, while war elephants assaulted the enemy lines as well. The Roman legionaries stalwartly repelled the attacks all around them until one of the flanks began to break under the onslaught. Therefore, Julian rushed towards his overwhelmed men to do whatever he could to turn back the tide.[40] As recorded by Ammianus, the lance charges of the Sassanian heavy cavalrymen were relentless while the Roman emperor desperately tried to rally his men:

> *While [Julian] was hastening to restore order there without regard to his own peril, a Parthian band of cataphracts on another side attacked the centre companies, and quickly overflowed the left wing, which gave way, since our men could hardly endure the smell and trumpeting of the elephants, they were trying to end the battle with* conti *(heavy lances) and volleys of arrows.*[41]

Yet the moment that ultimately led to the Roman defeat was caused because, in his haste, Julian recklessly charged into the thick of the combat without putting his armour on. When the *clibanarii* slammed into the Roman lines, one lance managed to pierce through the extremely vulnerable Roman emperor; Julian died from the mortal wound later that day.[42]

The death of the emperor was a catastrophe, but the Roman army was not broken. The soldiers quickly proclaimed that the commander of the imperial guard, Jovian (r. 363–364), was to be the new emperor and the army continued its retreat out of the Sassanian territory. The raids and assaults of the *clibanarii* and other Sassanian forces did not cease either. Here Ammianus describes an attack launched as the Roman army resumed its march:

> *But when we accordingly were just beginning to leave, the Persians attacked us, with the elephants in front. By the unapproachable and frightful stench of these brutes, horses and men were at first thrown into confusion, but the Joviani and Herculiani, after killing a few of the beasts, bravely resisted the cataphracts.*[43]

By the end of the encounter, the Romans had successfully driven the Sassanians away, though their losses were great. The Romans then moved on and the Sassanians continued to harass them. However, the need for food became so great for the Roman soldiers that Emperor Jovian was forced to make an embarrassing peace agreement with

Shapur II. In order to stop the incessant Sassanian assaults, the Roman emperor was required to hand over important territory, including Nisibis and Singara. The Romans were then finally able to escape without any more violent interference from the Sassanians.[44] Yet Shapur II had not yet finished terrorizing the Romans, for he still desired retribution for the invasion carried out by Julian. Ammianus again mentioned the elite heavy cavalrymen as a vital part of the invasion forces led by the Sassanian emperor:

> *At the end of the winter [Shapur II], king of the Persian nations, made immoderately arrogant by the confidence inspired by his former battles, having filled up the number of his army and greatly strengthened it, had sent his cataphracts, archers, and mercenary soldiers to invade our territories.*[45]

Throughout the summer and the rest of 371 both sides fought fiercely to a stalemate until they agreed to an armistice before the coming of winter.

After the war with Rome, the focus of the Sassanian Empire was forced to shift towards the east where there were invasions, first by the Kushans and then the Hephthalite Huns, for the rest of the fourth century. The first major invasion of Persian territory by the Huns occurred near the end of the century and the invaders managed to reach Mesopotamia before Sassanian forces defeated them in 395. The empire was also embroiled in several internal conflicts throughout this period, which continued to occur in the fifth century as well. The Sassanian Emperor Wahrām V (r. 420–438 AD) successfully managed to consolidate his power and end the internal strife within his empire, along with putting an end to the expansion of the new Hephthalite empire. However, when a new series of conflicts with the Huns erupted during the reign of Emperor Peroz I in the later half of the fifth century AD, the Sassanians suffered several major defeats. Accounts of these battles, as well as specific information about the wars with the Huns, is scarce, yet a possible reason for the sudden superiority of the Hunnic warriors over the Sassanians may have been due to a drastic increase in the effectiveness of their horse-archers because of the adoption of stirrups. With the revolutionary equestrian equipment, mounted archers gained a considerable amount of stability, which greatly improved the accuracy of their shots. Since their heavy armour already made them much less mobile than the Hunnic horse-archers, the protection became more of a hindrance for the elite *clibanarii* because the extensive armour was also unable to protect them nearly as much as it was against the archers of the Roman army. Furthermore, the ability of the horse-archers to outrun the Sassanian heavy horsemen almost completely removed the threat of their cavalry charges. Ultimately, the Sassanians were so overmatched against the superior Hunnic horsemanship and equestrian tactics that, in 484, Emperor Peroz died in combat against them. A major result of these disastrous wars, as well as other increasingly frequent conflicts with the Turko-Hunnic peoples of Central Asia, was that the Sassanian *clibanarii* gradually evolved into a much more composite type of cavalry with different arms and armour more influenced by Central Asian styles. At the same time, the overall preference for the lance began to decrease among the Sassanian heavy cavalrymen, as the bow became more important, even though the horsemen remained heavily armoured.[46]

In the fifth century AD, the western half of the Roman Empire collapsed and, as a result, the centre of Roman power completely transferred to the eastern capital of Constantinople. In 531, the Sassanian Empire again came into conflict with the eastern Romans (also known as the Byzantine Empire), after their army, led by Azarethes, invaded the Commagene region, located in modern day northeastern Turkey, and threatened to invade Syria. In response, the great Byzantine general Flavius Belisarius gathered an army of 20,000 imperial and auxiliary soldiers, both infantry and cavalry, which intercepted the Sassanian forces near Callinicum. The Sassanian army was comprised entirely of 15,000 cavalrymen, 5,000 of which were Arab Lakhmid allied forces led by Al-Mundhir, while the rest were Persian aristocratic warriors under Azarethes, many of which were armoured *clibanarii*. While Al-Mundhir and his Lakhmid warriors were placed on the left wing, the Sassanian general and the most heavily armoured *clibanarii* were stationed in the centre of the army formation, defended by a trench that was dug in front of their position, and the rest of the Sassanian heavy horsemen occupied the right wing. Byzantine heavy infantrymen faced the Sassanian *clibanarii* on that flank next to the Euphrates River. The centre and right wing of the Byzantine army was first comprised of their best mounted warriors, led by Belisarius, in order to combat the elite *clibanarii*, then there were the allied Hunnic warriors, the Lycaonian infantrymen and, finally, 5,000 Arab Ghassanid horsemen on the extreme right, facing their Arab rivals, the Lakhmids.[47]

The two armies confronted each other on a battlefield with the ground sloping upward to the west, while the Euphrates River was located to the east. The Battle of Callinicum began with an intense duel between the bowmen of both armies, with the Sassanian horse-archers gaining the upper hand, for they not only had greater skill in archery than the Byzantine troops, but the wind also happened to be in their favour. While the continuous volleys of arrows fired managed to distract Belisarius, Azarethes stealthily moved his best *clibanarii* to the left flank, alongside the Lakhmids, in order to engage the Ghassanids. He managed this without the Byzantine general noticing. With the Lakhmid mounted troops equipped similarly to the Sassanian heavy horsemen, the armoured cavalry was able to quickly overcome and rout their Arab rivals. The defeat of the Ghassanids then opened the way for the Sassanian *clibanarii* to occupy the higher ground to the west. From their superior position, the heavy horsemen assaulted the right flank of the Byzantine forces, routing the Lycaonian infantrymen in the process.[48]

The defeat of their right wing meant that the Byzantine army had decreased in size, but it was not yet completely broken; both allied Hun and eastern Roman infantrymen held their ground against the charge of the Sassanian *clibanarii*. To withstand the cavalry charge, the Byzantine soldiers formed into a tight infantry formation with their shields locked together and their backs towards the Euphrates River. The foot archers of the eastern Roman army also fired straight at the charging heavy cavalrymen to disrupt their formation as they rushed forward. The first charge of the Sassanian *clibanarii* not only failed to break through the shield wall, but they also suffered heavy losses as well. The *clibanarii* persisted in their assaults, making several more failed attempts to crush the remaining Byzantine infantrymen and losing even more men in the process. Eventually, Belisarius managed to organize a retreat and lead his battered men across the Euphrates to escape from the battle. Under the command of Azarethes, the Sassanian army had achieved another victory against the Romans, but the cost was great.[49]

Around 558, the Sassanian Emperor Khosrow I (r. 531–579) attempted to stabilize the eastern territories of his empire by establishing an alliance with the western Turkish khanate against the Hephthalite Huns. After the combined forces overcame the Huns, the Sassanians and the Turks divided the conquered territory between them. However, the partnership was short-lived, for in the 580s the Turks began to threaten the northeast borders of the Sassanian Empire. Then, in 588, the Huns, who lived in the territory previously conquered by the Turks and had subsequently become their vassals, invaded the Sassanian lands. The formidable general Bahram Chobin was chosen to command 12,000 elite Sassanain cavalrymen and these quickly advanced to confront the invading forces. As at the Battle of Callinicum, many of the Sassanian horsemen, possibly as many as several thousand, were *clibanarii*. When the Sassanian army met the Huns and their western Turk overlords on the field of battle in April, Bahram defeated them decisively. The Sassanians took the city of Balkh shortly after and then, in 589, the Persian forces won another victory near Herat. Bahram followed up his victories by crossing the Oxus River to invade and conquer the eastern Turks; the deadly general may have even personally killed their *khagan* with an arrow while in combat.[50]

In the *Strategikon*, a Byzantine military treatise written at the end of the sixth century, there is an interesting section that may confirm that the evolution of the Sassanian *clibanarii*, from lancers highly skilled in shock tactics, to armoured horse-archers, was complete:

> *[The Sassanians] wear body armour and mail, and are armed with bows and swords. They are more practised in rapid, although not powerful archery, than all other warlike nations.*[51]

The treatise continued to describe the transformation of the mounted warriors to troops based entirely on archery, for it claimed that the late Sassanian *clibanarii* had completely replaced the lance in exchange for the bow:

> *[The Sassanians] themselves do not make use of lances and shields. Charging against them is effective because they are prompted to rapid flight and do not know how to wheel about suddenly against their attackers, as do the Scythian nations.*[52]

If the relief of the *clibanarius* from Taq-i Bustan is, in fact, from the reign of Emperor Khosrow II (590–628), this description contradicts the visual representation, for the lance is clearly depicted on the relief. Therefore, it may be possible that while some of the last imperial *clibanarii* still carried lances, the bow had predominately become the favoured weapon among most of the late Sassanian heavy cavalrymen, for it was the main weapon used to combat the mounted horse-archers of Central Asia. Yet even if their tactics had shifted to focus primarily on rapid-fire archery, the armoured horsemen were still a major threat in battle. Furthermore, the late Sassanian *clibanarii* focused on ways to overcome enemy lancers without having to face their charges head on:

> *In fighting against lancers [the Sassanians] hasten to form their battle line in the roughest terrain, and to use their bows, so that the*

charges of the lancers against them will be dissipated and broken up by the rough ground.[53]

When war erupted between the Sassanian Empire and the Byzantines for the final time in the beginning of the seventh century AD, it was most likely the armoured horse-archer version of the *clibanarii* who fought against the Eastern Romans.

In 590, shortly after his successes against the Huns and Turks, the victorious general Bahram Chobin seized the throne from the new rightful ruler of the Sassanian Empire, the newly crowned Khosrow II. In desperation, the deposed emperor turned to the ruler of the Byzantine Empire, Maurice (r. 582–602). The emperor of the Eastern Romans agreed to help Khosrow by providing soldiers in exchange for a substantial amount of territory. With the Byzantine support, the Sassanian emperor quickly defeated the usurper and reclaimed his throne. Then, a little over a decade after Khosrow returned to power, it was the Byzantine Empire that was struck with instability after the assassination of Maurice. In 603, the Sassanian ruler exploited the situation and invaded Byzantine territory. Since the Byzantines were embroiled in civil war, the Sassanians had much early success and already by 611 their forces had completely expelled the Eastern Romans from Mesopotamia, tightened their hold over Armenia and seized Caesarea at Cappadocia.[54]

By 613, Byzantine Emperor Heraclius (r. 610–641) was able to finally respond by first combining his forces with those of his brother, Theodore, along with the soldiers of the Byzantine general, Nicetas. With numerous cataphracts of the horse-archer type, and the rest of the Sassanian army under his command, general Farrokhan 'Shahrbaraz' (meaning 'the Boar of the Realm') continued to defeat the Byzantines on several more occasions. The Sassanians' success was almost halted in 619 though, when an allied Turkish-Hephthalite army struck while the imperial forces were distracted by their war with the Byzantines. However, Armenian general Smbat Bagratuni led the Sassanian army, including 2,000 Armenian heavy cavalrymen, and defeated the Turk and Hun attackers near Tus. Shortly afterward, the victorious Armenian general crushed another Turkish-Hunnish army and then slaughtered many as they attempted to retreat. In the end, Bagratuni was so successful that, for the rest of its existence, the Sassanian Empire no longer had to deal with any threats on their northeastern borders and could shift back to focus solely on the conflict with the Byzantines.[55]

However, the Byzantines began to seize the momentum in July 622, after Heraclius defeated the Sassanians for the first time in the war. The battle was followed up by a decisive Byzantine victory, even after the three Sassanian generals, Shahrbaraz, Shahin and Shahraplakan, had united their forces to face Heraclius. The success of the Byzantines was all the greater for Shahraplakan being slain in the combat. Shahrbaraz survived though and managed to turn the tide back in the Sassanian's favour, even reaching as far as Constantinople in 626. However, his relationship with Khosrow II deteriorated, causing the Sassanian general to make his own peace terms with the Byzantines shortly after. With Shahrbaraz and Shahraplakan out of the picture, only Shahin was left to fight Heraclius and his army, until Theodore and his men defeated the last, great Sassanian commander. The Byzantine army then carried out a major invasion of the Sassanian Empire and overcame any remaining resistance. At this point, the situation became so dire at the palace that the Sassanian people deposed Khosrow. By 629, the Sassanians were ultimately forced to make peace with Heraclius.[56]

After their initial victories against the Byzantines, the armies of the Sassanian Empire never managed to take full advantage of their success and, in the end, lost the long war with their ancient western rival. Even in victory, though, the empire of the Eastern Romans was also greatly weakened after the costly, lengthy conflict. With the two greatest superpowers of the region so vulnerable, Arab armies did manage to take advantage of the weakened states of both empires in order to invade vast stretches of territory in the name of Islam. While many Byzantine lands were also conquered in the invasions, the Eastern Roman Empire would survive for centuries yet. By contrast, the Sassanian Empire did not last. After the Sassanians suffered several defeats to the formidable Arab forces, the final emperor, Yazdegird III (r. 632–651), escaped to the east until he was killed by the hands of his own countrymen at Merv in 651. Although the death marked the end of the Sassanian Empire, warriors armed and armoured as cataphracts remained in the region, as evidenced by the eighth century AD wooden shield painting found in the ruins of Mug Castle. Furthermore, the victorious Arab soldiers seized most of the former Sassanian *clibanarii* equipment to utilize for themselves. However, the true medieval successors to the heavily armoured cavalrymen, who, most importantly, were still called cataphracts, were the armoured horsemen of the Byzantine Empire.[57]

CHAPTER SIX

IMPERIAL ROMAN
CATAPHRACTI,
CATAPHRACTARII AND
CLIBANARII

The Roman Empire

By the end of the reign of Emperor Trajan in 117, the territory of the
Roman Empire had increased to its greatest extent. But as we have
seen (see Chapter 3), land was not the only major addition made to
the empire at that time. After numerous violent encounters with the
deadly Parthian cataphracts, as well as the Sarmatian armoured lancers, the Romans finally decided to create their own unit of cataphracts,
known as *ala I Gallorum et Pannoniorum catafractata.*[1] This first known
Roman cataphract unit was most likely introduced during the reign of
Emperor Hadrian in the second quarter of the second century AD and
was stationed in Moesia Inferior. Early evidence of this unit is from the
funeral stela of the prefect M. Maenius Agrippa, although it is possible that cataphracts may have been a part of the Roman army before
the creation of *ala I Gallorum et Pannoniorum catafractata,* perhaps in the
reign of Hadrian's predecessor, Trajan, or even earlier than that.[2] When
the ancient historian Flavius Josephus witnessed the Roman siege of
Jotapata in 68, his account contained a particularly interesting moment:

> [Vespasian] *made the most courageous of the horsemen get off their
> horses, and placed them in three ranks over against those ruins of the
> wall, but covered with armour on every side, and with* kontoi *[heavy
> lances] in their hands.*[3]

Completely armoured like cataphracts, the dismounted heavy cavalrymen of the Roman army charged at the breached walls, while the
defenders poured extremely hot olive oil down on them from above.
Some of the hot oil managed to get under the armour of the unlucki-
est attackers, burning through their skin as if it was on fire itself, but

the improvised infantrymen were sufficiently well protected to storm the fortifications. However, it is possible that these heavily armoured warriors were not Roman soldiers at all, but rather mounted troops provided by allied rulers who simply fought in the Roman army.[4]

Another heavy cavalry unit created around the same time as the first Roman cataphracts, specifically during the reign of Emperor Trajan in the early second century, were also armed with the *contus* (*kontos* in Greek) like the cataphracts and Vespasian's armoured dismounted horsemen. The new unit was known as *ala Ulpia contariorum milliara civia Romanorum*, with the word '*contariorum*' meaning the cavalrymen fought with the *contus* (heavy lance). In general, mounted warriors in the Roman army who wielded the *contus* were known as a *contarius* (pl. *contarii*), or 'contus-bearer'. The main difference between the Roman *contarii* and cataphracts was that the latter heavy cavalrymen were much more armoured than the former. While the *contarii* did wear armour, they were much more like the majority of the Sarmatian mounted lancers who were too poor to provide their steeds with expensive barding, while the cataphracts were armoured like the wealthiest aristocratic warriors, with both riders and horses covered with extensive protection. With heavier armour, the cataphracts could be even more deadly at shock combat than the *contarii*, though there were also far fewer of the super-heavy cavalrymen for they were far more expensive to equip for combat.[5]

Because such heavily armoured cavalrymen as the cataphracts were added into the Roman army, the Greek military writer Aelian distinguished the two different kinds of cavalry in his second century work, *Tactics*:

> *The forces of cavalry as being ordered by troops, are either cataphracts, or not cataphracts. They are cataphracts, that cover their own and their horses' bodies all over with armour.*[6]

In *Ars Tactica*, Arrian also provided a short description of the Roman cataphracts during this period:

> *The cataphracts provide both armoured horses and riders, the latter with breast plates of metal scales, linen or horn and thigh protectors; the horses with side-protectors and forehead-protectors.*[7]

The vast majority of the Roman cavalry were of the second kind described by Aelian without heavy armour for both the riders and mounts. Many of these were light cavalry units who were more skilled and equipped for ranged combat or skirmishing than for shock combat.

Therefore, the cataphracts played a vital role that had been missing in the Roman army before their arrival, for the heavily armoured horsemen were more specialized for shock tactics than any previous unit.[8]

Yet, even though the cataphracts were the most armoured Roman cavalrymen up to the time of their creation, the early Roman version still tended to be less armoured than the Parthian and later Sassanian types, with more similarities to the Sarmatian heavy horsemen. The imperial cataphracts of the west wore metal *spangenhelm*-type helmets and full coats of armour, commonly made of scales and used predominately to protect the torso but also portions of the limbs as well, along with greaves and thigh guards. Just as with the Sarmatian horsemen, other parts of the earliest Roman cataphracts were left exposed. Yet, especially by the fourth century, though possibly even earlier, the cavalrymen increasingly began to wear laminated arm protection that extended to the wrist.[9] Furthermore, although metal facemasks attached to helmets is a feature much more commonly attributed to later Roman cataphracts and *clibanarii*, it is possible that some of the earlier heavy cavalrymen might have adopted the intimidating protection as well due to the growing number of archaeological remains of the impressive headgear that have been uncovered, some of which are dated to as early as the second century.[10]

The mounts of the early cataphracts were occasionally armoured too; however, barding was utilized much less frequently than with the foreign eastern versions. Ancient depictions of Roman cataphracts and their mounts upon funeral *stelae* of the units *equites catafractarii Ambianenses* and *equites catafractarii Pictavenses* show the steeds unarmoured while the riders are armoured. On the other hand, the number of metal facemasks discovered at archaeological sites suggests that the steeds usually wore these at least. Arguably one of the most characteristic features the earliest imperial cataphracts shared with both the Sarmatians and the eastern heavy cavalrymen of the Parthians and Sassanians was that the primary weapon of the Roman variants was also the long heavy lance (*contus*), which was most likely approximately 3.6 m (12 ft) in length like the weapons of their eastern adversaries. The Roman heavy horsemen commonly carried the *spatha* style sword along with the lance as well. Similar to the early Sassanian *clibanarii*, the first Roman cataphracts utilized a saddle with two frontal horns and two horns in the back that gripped the thighs of the rider, making it easier to fight with the *contus*. The horns were also very useful for they allowed the rider to attach further equipment to the saddle.[11]

Even though the Romans had finally adopted cataphracts in the second century AD, the military still utilized very few units of them until the middle of the following century. Several inscriptions prove the existence of another Roman cataphract unit known as *ala nova firma miliaria catafractaria Philippiana*, which was created in the mid-third century. The cataphract unit originated in the east, yet from 234 to 238 the contingent was ordered to fight the Alemanni and other tribes in Germania. After Germania, the unit of cavalrymen moved first to Pannonia and then later it was stationed in Arabia. At some point during the reign of Emperor Philip the Arab (r. 244–9), further evidence of the cataphract unit was left, for its prefect made an inscription in Bostra.[12] Cataphracts also fought in the army of Emperor Maximinus Thrax (r. 235–8) when he returned to Italy, as recorded by the ancient historian Herodian:

> On each flank marched the squadrons of cataphracts, the Moroccan javelin men, and the archers from the East.[13]

However, it was not until later in the third century that all cavalry units in the Roman military drastically rose in both importance and number throughout the empire as the new emperor, Gallienus (r. 253–68), attempted to transform the Roman armies to make them much more mobile. Before this time, the Roman army relied predominately upon the heavy infantrymen of the legions, but cavalrymen were a much higher priority in the new model army of Gallienus. His reforms were intended to improve the quality and performance of all horsemen in the Roman armies and, as a result of this, the cataphracts achieved a more prominent position within the military overall.[14]

The Roman *Cataphractarii*

In the second half of the third century, the Romans began to use a term that was an even more Latinized version of the original Greek word *kataphraktoi* than *cataphracti*. The new term was *cataphractarii*, which was used for one of the first Roman cataphract units, the previously mentioned *ala nova firma miliaria catafractaria Philippiana*. The word has not only been found on several funerary stelae and on papyri discovered in Egypt, but *cataphractarii* were also mentioned in the ancient written accounts on several occasions.[15] In the *Scriptores Historiae Augustae*, 100 *cataphractarii* were stationed in Dalmatia for Emperor Claudius II Gothicus (r. 268–270 AD):[16]

> *You will assign him from the district of Dardania 200 foot-soldiers,*
> *100* cataphractarii, *60 horsemen, 60 Cretan archers, and 1,000 new*
> *recruits, all well armed.*[17]

The ancient Roman account also provided a number for the Roman *cataphractarii* during the reign of Emperor Aurelian (r. 270–75): 'You will have the Third Legion, the Fortunate, and 800 *cataphractarii*'.[18]

The number of cataphracts may have greatly increased under Aurelian because after he defeated Queen Zenobia of Palmyra, many of her soldiers were made to serve in the Roman army, including many heavy cavalrymen.[19] In 273, the *cataphractarii* were then included in the emperor's triumphal procession through the capital:

> *Then came the Roman people itself, the flags of the guilds and the*
> *camps, the* cataphractarii, *the wealth of the kings, the entire army,*
> *and, lastly, the senate (albeit somewhat sadly, since they saw sena-*
> *tors, too, being led in triumph) – all adding much to the splendour*
> *of the procession.*[20]

Cataphractarii were mentioned in the fourth-century accounts of Ammianus Marcellinus as well, along with Roman *cataphracti* and *clibanarii*. Yet *cataphractarii* was a term used almost exclusively to describe Roman mounted troops, not the heavy cavalrymen from other foreign armies like the other two terms, which were frequently used to describe the cataphracts of the East.[21]

Many scholars have theorized that what distinguished the *cataphractarii* from the Roman *cataphracti* and *clibanarii* was that they wore less protection; especially for their mounts, which were typically unarmoured. *Cataphractarii* was also a term used predominately to describe Roman heavy cavalrymen in the West, who in turn were equipped with more Roman-style arms and armour than their eastern counterparts in the army. Since they were more properly equipped to fight in the West, the *cataphractarii* were not armed with the bow, which was almost exclusively utilized by Roman heavy cavalrymen in the East at that time.[22] (To clarify, the mounted Roman soldiers called *cataphractarii* certainly did not carry bows in the first centuries of their existence – though as discussed later in the next chapter, Eastern Roman warriors armoured like *cataphractarii* were armed with bows in the early Byzantine period.) Like the cataphracts, and most of the *clibanarii*, the primary weapon of the *cataphractarii* was the *contus*. The *cataphractarii* typically served in the mobile field armies, known as *comitatenses*, or the forces stationed in frontier forts, known as *limitanei*.[23]

In the latter half of the third century and into the fourth century, there were several *cataphractarii* units created with names that may indicate a Gallic origin, such as the *equites catafractarii Ambianenses*, *equites catafractarii Pictavenses*, *equites catafractarii Albigenses*, and *equites catafractarii Biturigenses*. It is interesting to note that these *cataphractarii* may have come from Gaul, for that was also the region that many of the Sarmatians settled in exchange for service in the Roman army. With their experience fighting as armoured lancers, the Sarmatians were ideal *cataphractarii*, especially since the Sarmatian heavy cavalrymen were often less armoured than typical cataphracts, and rarely rode armoured mounts.[24] More solid evidence supporting the theory that the *cataphractarii* did not ride armoured horses comes from the stelae of three of the horsemen from these units. Even though the images of the soldiers on these stelae depict their full uniform and equipment, their mounts are unarmoured.[25] In addition to the funeral stelae, depictions of *cataphractarii* are also located on both the Arch of Constantine and the Column of Marcus Aurelius at Rome, the Arch of Galerius at Salonika and the Tropaeum Traiani at Adamklissi. The heavy cavalrymen in the images typically wore a mail or scale cuirass and metal helmets, rode unarmoured horses, and were armed with lances or spears, along with shields. The *cataphractarii* remained an important part of the Roman military for a few centuries until eventually the term fell completely out of use in the ancient accounts by the end of the fifth century AD.[26] The word that would then take the place of not only '*cataphractarii*', but also of the earlier term '*kataphraktoi*', in the Greco-Roman written record, was '*clibanarii*'.

The Roman *Clibanarii*

It is possible that Emperor Constantine the Great (r. 306–37) adopted the first Roman *clibanarii* early in the fourth century but, if not, then it was certainly his predecessor, Diocletian, who created them even earlier at the end of the third century. One major reason why Emperor Diocletian is attributed with the creation of the Roman *clibanarii* is that he was also responsible for the construction of arms and armour factories (*fabricae*) in the East, such as the workshops that were located in Nicomedia and Daphne (Antioch). Furthermore, in the ancient document known as the *Notitia Dignitatum*, which was created over a century later but still contained information on earlier Roman army units, those two cities are mentioned as still having factories dedicated to the manufacture of heavy armour for the *clibanarii* (*fabricae clibanariae*) that may have been the same workshops established by Diocletian.[27]

As the fourth century progressed, the term *clibanarii* gradually increased in popularity until it became the preferred term to describe the most heavily armoured Roman cavalrymen. Then, especially after the word *kataphraktoi* completely disappeared from the ancient accounts in the fifth century, *clibanarii* became the only term to describe armoured riders who rode armoured mounts in the Roman army. Aside from their extensive armour, there were other ways that the *clibanarii* differed from the *cataphractarii*; while there were *clibanarii* known as *scutarii clibanarii* (armed with shields) and *sagittarii clibanarii* (armed with bows), the *cataphractarii* rarely carried such equipment or weaponry in the earliest centuries of the Roman cataphracts. Furthermore, *clibanarii* tended to fight in more prestigious units in the Roman army. Unlike the *cataphractarii*, who were predominately limited to the *comitatenses* and *limitanei*, some units of *clibanarii* served as *palatini* (cavalrymen in the main Roman field army) and there was even an elite unit of the heavily armoured horsemen in the *scola* (imperial guard). Also, there were four *fabricae clibanariae* dedicated to the manufacture of armour for the *clibanarii* (including the workshops possibly established by Emperor Diocletian in Nicomedia and Daphne), which may be an indication that they wore special armour, or that the protection of the super-heavy cavalrymen was so extensive that it took incredibly skilled artisans to create.[28]

Since the early Roman version of the *clibanarii* were much more heavily armoured, their arms and armour differed from the earlier cataphracts and *cataphractarii*, which were based on the more lightly equipped Sarmatian lancers. For example, the heavy cavalrymen who fought in the *Scola Scutariorum Clibanariorum*, one of the imperial guard units that was made as a replacement to the disbanded Praetorian Guard, may have worn ridge-style, plumed helmets with all sorts of additional protection attached; this would have included a metal facemask, cheek protectors, and a solid plate aventail, or a full mail aventail that would either have left some of the face exposed or covered everything except for the eyes, as with late Sassanian heavy cavalrymen. Scholars often link the highly stylized Roman facemask finds with their use solely in parades since it is predominately in the accounts of those celebrations that the descriptions of the facial protection appear. However, due to the large amount of remains uncovered, it is unlikely that the metal masks were merely parade equipment, especially because it is highly likely that Seleucid and

Parthian cataphracts, whom the Romans had encountered on several occasions since the early second century BC, wore metal facemasks in battle. The torsos of the *clibanarii* were armoured with cuirasses, most likely of lamellar construction that was further augmented with mail. As was common with many of the different types of ancient cataphracts and *clibanarii*, mail was used to protect especially vulnerable areas of the body, but this was unnecessary for much of the limbs of the Roman *clibanarius*, because most of his arms and legs were covered with laminated armour that extended down to protect much of his hands as well, and the armour even covered the feet. The horses were probably fully armoured with a whole-body trapper and facemask, both made of either iron or bronze scales, which practically covered the entire animal, except for the belly and legs, such as that shown on the mount in the Dura Europos graffito of the third century. Heavy lances (*conti*) continued to be the favoured weapons for most of the heavier-armoured Roman *clibanarii*.[29]

Even if the first official units of Roman *clibanarii* were introduced later during his reign, Constantine the Great had to face the elite heavy cavalrymen in the army of his major imperial rival in the west, Maxentius (r. 306–312 AD), who ruled from the city of Rome. The civil war between the two adversaries escalated until their armies confronted each other at the Battle of Turin, which was fought near the city in 312.[30] The later *Panegyric of Constantine*, attributed to Nazarius and written after Constantine won the civil war, celebrated the emperor's victory over Maxentius and his formidable *clibanarii*:

> *So many soldiers filled the open plain that he who saw them arrayed would not fault their confidence. What a spectacle that is said to have been, how dreadful to behold, how terrible, horses and men alike enclosed in a covering of iron! In the army they are called* clibanarii: *the men are covered with mail in the upper part, a corselet which extends down to the horses' chests and hangs to their forelegs protects them from injury of a wound without impeding their gait. Nevertheless, neither the fact that their armour doubled the terror inspired by so large a number nor that numbers added force to their arms frightened you, Emperor. For it is certain that valour shows a spirit proportionate to the type of engagement because it regulates its capacities in accordance with the course of events: in small matters it is lax almost to negligence, in affairs of moderate importance moderately attentive; when great things come it is aroused according to the magnitude of the task to be endured. That display of armour,*

that army covered with iron, which would have been a painful sight to unwarlike men, stimulated the spirits of invincible ones, because the soldiers infected by the Emperor's example took fire with all their courage when they encountered an enemy whom it was fitting to defeat. You yourself take over the cataphracts, where the greatest strength of the opposing battle line lay. Their training for combat is to preserve the course of their assault after they have crashed into the opposing line, and since they were invulnerable they resolutely break through whatever is set against them. But you, most prudent Emperor, who knew all the ways of fighting, got assistance from your ingenuity: that it is safest to elude those whom it is most difficult to withstand. By drawing your lines apart you induce an enemy attack which cannot be reversed; next by leading your lines back together you hem in the men whom you admit to your game. It did them no good to press forward, since your men purposely gave way; iron's rigidity did not allow a change in direction for pursuit. Thus our men assailed those who were delivered to them with clubs equipped with heavy iron knobs which wore out an invulnerable enemy with their beating, and when they were inflicted especially on their heads they forced those whom the blows had confused to tumble down. Then they began to fall headlong, to slide down backward, to totter half-dead or dying to be held fast by their saddles, to lie entangled in the confused slaughter of horses, which in unbridled pain, when their vulnerable points had been discovered, cast their riders everywhere. When all had been killed to a man and your soldiers were untouched, people transferred the horror inspired by their armour to wonder at the victory because those who where considered invulnerable had died without wounding anyone on your side.[31]

In this account, the few vulnerable areas of the horses were once again specifically targeted, as had been done several times in the past to defeat the cataphracts. Additionally, the utilization of clubs or rudimentary maces was certainly a more unusual solution to overcome the heavy armour of Maxentius' *clibanarii*, but the Roman infantry had also used such weaponry before, against the Palmyran cataphracts. Constantine knew that his soldiers would have great difficulty in trying to penetrate the thick armour of the heavy cavalrymen with the blades of their weapons. The iron-tipped clubs would also fail to break through the layers of protection, but like the Palestinian contingent discovered at the Battle of Emessa in 272, the hard blows from the blunt weapons were able to incapacitate the armoured riders, or even knock them off their mounts. Yet out of the different methods used, the most brilliant aspect of Constantine's tactics to overcome the *clibanarii* was to allow them to think they had broken through his lines with their charge, only to then surround and assault them from all sides at close range. Yet, even though Maxentius was defeated at Turin, he and his army remained relatively intact. Therefore, Constantine and his outnumbered forces confronted Maxentius' army again at the Battle of Milvian Bridge and completely crushed them at that encounter, which occurred later that same year of 312.

The great emperor may have made it seem almost easy to defeat the *clibanarii*, but Constantine certainly understood the worth of the formidable armoured cavalrymen and played a pivotal role in the process of them becoming an important part of the Roman military, such as the creation of the *Scola Scutariorum Clibanariorum*. By the reign of Constantine's son, Emperor Constantius II (r. 337–61), the *clibanarii* were an integral part of the Roman army. When the Roman Empire was once again embroiled in a civil war after the usurper Magnentius seized the western half of the empire in 350, Constantius had a substantial amount of the super-heavy horsemen in his army to deal with the rebel forces of the rival claimant to the imperial throne. In his second panegyric of Constantius, called *The Heroic Deeds of the Emperor Constantius, or on Kingship, Oration II*, the later Roman Emperor Julian, also known as Julian the Apostate, gave another short description of these horsemen:

> *Of these troops some carry lances and are protected by cuirasses and helmets of wrought iron-mail. They wear greaves that fit the legs closely, and knee-caps, and on their thighs the same sort of iron covering. They ride their horses exactly like statues, and need no shield.*[32]

Not only does Julian go into much more detail in his description of the heavily armoured cavalrymen cited earlier in the first chapter, but the idea that the emperor employed particularly heavy horsemen is reinforced in the writing of Libanius, for he stated:

> *[Constantius] clad the bodies of his cavalry in steel with greater care than the Persians themselves, who protected from wounds the very horses by means of armour.*[33]

With such formidably armoured mounted troops, Constantius confidently advanced to deal with the usurper.

The emperor, with his *clibanarii*, confronted Magnentius at the Battle of Mursa in Pannonia on 28 September 351.[34] As written by Julian the Apostate, in his *Panegyric in Honour of the Emperor Constantius*, it was the *clibanarii* fighting for Constantius that won the battle:

> *Neither side gained the advantage, till the* [clibanarii] *by their archery, aided by the remaining force of cavalry, who spurred on their horses to the charge, had begun to inflict great loss on the enemy, and by main force to drive the whole army before them.*[35]

It was not just the typical heavily armoured cavalrymen that were a vital part of the victory, but rather it was the unique *sagittarii clibanarii* of the emperor, who were used in conjunction with assaults from the Roman heavy cavalry armed with lances, which led to Constantius' success at the encounter. After the Battle of Mursa, it took one more major confrontation before the ultimate victor was the last ruler left standing. In defeat, Magnentius had fled to Gaul; therefore, in 353, the last battle was fought at Mons Seleuci located in the French Alps. Once again, Constantius was victorious, so the usurper committed suicide and the war was over.[36] In 357, the emperor held his triumph and the *clibanarii* were among the troops who marched in the parade.[37] It was in his account of this procession that the Roman writer Ammianus Marcellinus gave his full description of the Roman cataphracts cited previously (see Chapter 5), which contained the fascinating line, 'the cataphracts, whom they call *clibanarii*'.

Even after the Romans fully embraced the heavily armoured *clibanarii*, the empire still utilized the lighter versions of cataphracts as well. For example, the Roman cataphracts of the Scythae regiment in the first half of the fourth century were of the more lightly armoured version. These horsemen wore a helmet and cuirass but probably little other armour, leaving most of the face, neck and limbs exposed. Furthermore, the mount was completely unarmoured. The segmented iron helmet had a nose-guard attached, along with cheek-protectors that extended down from the brim of the helmet to cover the temples as well. However, no further protection was attached to the helmet in order to guard the rest of the exposed areas of the neck and lower skull, as a mail aventail would have done. Bronze scale armour was utilized for the torso, made with the scales riveted to one another. To compensate for the lighter armour, these later Roman type cataphracts carried a large, round shield. The heavy cavalrymen were armed with both the traditional short *gladius* sword and the longsword called the *spatha*, which was typically used by Roman mounted troops. Like the *clibanarii* of the Sassanian Persian Empire, the Roman cataphracts replaced their older four-horned saddle with a new, partially wood-framed one that provided much less balance than the previous model. Therefore, some scholars have theorized that the Romans also possibly adopted the stirrup at this time in order to gain the desired stability for mounted combat. However, as with the contemporaneous Sassanian heavy cavalrymen, there is no solid evidence to prove this theory because Roman artwork of the period does not depict the revolutionary equestrian equipment.[38]

Before Julian became the sole emperor of Rome in 361, he was appointed into the slightly less prestigious position of caesar by Constantius in 355, and thus, given command over Gaul. As Libanius stated in his *Funeral Oration upon the Emperor Julian*, the new commander led a powerful army, for among the troops were included many *clibanarii*:

> He possessed a military force as great as had previously kept these empires in order, and numerous foot soldiers, numerous cavalry, whose invulnerability, by reason of their armour, is, I think, most formidable.[39]

However, it was not just the super-heavy cavalrymen that fought for Julian. Ammianus Marcellinus also mentions the *cataphractarii* as having been included in the caesar's forces on several occasions. The first time that the heavy horsemen appear in the accounts of the Roman historian was after a report that the Alemanni had besieged the city of Autun in 356, when Julian quickly gathered his forces to break the siege:

> And to avoid any delay, he took only the cataphractarii *and the crossbowmen, who were far from suitable to defend a general, and traversing the same road, he came to Auxerre. There with but a short rest (as his custom was) he refreshed himself and his soldiers and kept on towards Troyes; and when troops of savages kept making attacks on him, he sometimes, fearing that they might be in greater force, strengthened his flanks and reconnoitred; sometimes he took advantage of suitable ground, easily ran them down and trampled them underfoot, capturing some who in terror gave themselves up, while the remainder exerted all their powers of speed in an effort to escape. These he allowed to get away unscathed, since he was unable to follow them up, encumbered as he was with heavy-armed soldiers.*[40]

It is interesting to note that since Julian needed to act quickly, he decided to take only his *cataphractarii*, and not the *clibanarii* who were also in his army. This section of Ammianus' account reinforces the theory that one way to distinguish the two different kinds of heavy cavalrymen was that the *cataphractarii* were more lightly armoured than their primarily Eastern counterparts, even though the historian still described them as 'heavy-armed soldiers'.[41] Once the Romans reached the main Germanic army, the two forces collided and the Romans stood victorious, thus relieving the city of Autun.

Two years after his appointment as caesar, in 357, Julian led his troops across the Jura Mountains to reach an enormous Alemanni army, which greatly outnumbered his 13,000 soldiers. Ammianus recorded the march of the Roman army and specifically mentioned the important placement of the *cataphractarii* on the flanks of the columns as they advanced towards the enemy:

> *Already the beams of the sun were reddening the sky, and the blare of the trumpets was sounding in unison, when the infantry forces were led out at a moderate pace, and to their flank were joined the squadrons of cavalry, among whom were the* cataphractarii *and the archers, a formidable branch of the service.*[42]

The tribal warriors in the Germanic army under the command of their king, Chnodomar, numbered at least 35,000 men; however, it is possible that the Alemanni forces may have even amounted to as many as 60,000 warriors. After crossing the Rhine River, the Germanic army had ravaged the surrounding countryside, forcing Julian to respond. The Roman army marched 21 miles to reach the Alemanni; therefore, the general wanted his men to rest for a night before fighting the battle. Yet most of the army, from the officers to the lower ranks, wanted to catch the Alemanni before they were able to flee back over the Rhine. The Roman soldiers got their wish, for Julian then led them out to engage the Germanic warriors at the Battle of Strasburg (or Argentoratum).[43]

The Alemanni had dug trenches in front of the soldiers on their right wing, not only to provide protection for the men on that flank but also attempting to hide warriors who waited to make a surprise attack on the advancing Roman soldiers as they approached. All of the horsemen of the Germanic army were on the left side, along with light infantrymen spread throughout the cavalry for support, as described by Ammianus:

> *And among them here and there they intermingled skirmishers and light-armed infantry, as safe policy certainly demanded. For they realized that one of their warriors on horseback, no matter how skillful, in meeting one of our* clibanarii, *must hold bridle and shield in one hand and brandish his spear with the other, and would thus be able to do no harm to a soldier hidden in iron armour; whereas the infantry soldier in the very hottest of the fight, when nothing is apt to be guarded against except what is straight before one, can creep about low and unseen, and by piercing a horse's side throw its unsuspecting rider headlong, whereupon he can be slain with little trouble.*[44]

Although they were formidable warriors with a terrifying presence that was unique to ancient battlefields, knowledge of the weaknesses of the cataphracts was spreading across the known world of the time. Just as the Gauls attacked the exposed bellies of the horses ridden by the Parthian cataphracts at Carrhae in 53 BC, these were also the tactics that the Roman legionaries adopted to use first also against the Parthians, and then later to combat the cataphracts of the Sassanian Empire. Ammianus' statement shows that the Alemanni, and possibly other Germanic warriors, had also learned to exploit the vulnerable areas of the cataphracts' mounts with soldiers on foot. Combining skirmishers and other foot soldiers with cavalry was a tactic that had been used by Germanic armies for centuries, so it was very convenient for them that it worked so well against the cataphracts. Yet, as with all Roman armies, as well as most of the armies that fielded cataphracts, the heavily armoured horsemen were not the only cavalrymen, for there were also more lightly equipped mounted troops under Julian's command at the battle.[45]

Every Roman cavalry unit was placed on their right wing to oppose the Germanic horsemen. It is unknown if Julian did this because he wanted to combat the enemy cavalrymen with his own mounted troops, or whether he may have possibly chosen the formation because a captured German spy had informed him of the Alemanni plans to dig the trenches in front of their own right wing. Even though the Romans had marched out to meet them, it was the Germanic warriors who struck first. The horsemen of the Alemanni army charged the Roman cavalry so quickly that the Germanic warriors may have even caught the imperial mounted troops while they were completely immobile, causing chaos and confusion to rapidly spread throughout the Roman ranks. As the brutal combat intensified between horsemen of both armies, the Alemanni attacked with such intense ferocity that it intimidated the Roman soldiers considerably. Those Roman horsemen who were not lucky enough to wear the heavy armour of the *clibanarii* or *cataphractarii* desperately clung to their shields, holding them close to their bodies in the hope that the equipment would provide enough protection for their heads under the vicious assaults.[46]

The Roman infantrymen along the left flank of the cavalry tried to help their mounted comrades, but it was to no avail, as recorded by Ammianus:

> *Now that had happened for the reason that while the order of their lines was being re-established, the cataphracts, seeing their leader slightly wounded and one of their companions slipping over the neck of his horse, which had collapsed under the weight of his armour, scattered in whatever direction they could.*[47]

Up to this point, the cataphracts and the rest of the Roman mounted troops had withstood the brutal assault of the Germanic warriors, but the drawn-out combat had taken its toll on the heavy cavalrymen. Therefore, not only did witnessing their commander getting wounded cause a drastic drop in morale among the armoured horsemen, but also the Roman cataphracts and their mounts were most likely extremely exhausted from fighting for so long while wearing their heavy armour, which is also a possible explanation for why the horse of one of the cataphracts collapsed in the account of Ammianus. Although the cataphract contingent broke and was nearly routed, once the armoured horsemen reached the Roman infantrymen held in reserve behind them, the heavy cavalrymen quickly regrouped and managed to rejoin their comrades who were still in the thick of the fighting at exactly the right moment. When the cataphracts re-entered the fray, the momentum of the combat then began to shift in the Romans' favour due to the fierce counterattack of the combined infantry and cavalry forces of the Roman army. The Alemanni tried their best to withstand the renewed vigour of the Roman army, but their efforts were futile. In the end, Julian won a spectacular victory over his Germanic foes.[48] In the end of his account of the battle, Ammianus included the number of Roman casualties, along with the list of slain officers, which included the commander of the *cataphractarii*:

> *Now there fell in this battle on the Roman side 243 soldiers and four high officers: Bainobaudes, tribune of the Cornuti, and also Laipso;*

and Innocentius, commander of the cataphractarii, *and one unattached tribune, whose name is not available to me.*[49]

The *cataphractarii* and *clibanarii* under Julian were truly tested at Strasburg and, although they nearly failed, the fact that the armoured horsemen did eventually rally in order to a play an important role in the spectacular Roman victory should not be forgotten.

After the Battle of Strasburg, the next time that the Roman cataphracts were mentioned by Ammianus was in 370, when the Saxons invaded northern Gaul. The Romans confronted the invaders and shortly thereafter a truce was agreed upon by the two sides; in exchange for young warriors to serve in the Roman military, the Saxons were granted safe passage to return to their homeland. Yet the peace established was only a Roman ploy to lull the Germanic warriors into a false sense of security, for as the Saxons made the return journey home, Roman soldiers hid in a secluded valley and waited for the Germanic tribesmen to approach. However, the plan to ambush the marching Saxons nearly failed when some of the legionaries prematurely rushed out to engage the German army before it had reached the designated place where the Romans were supposed to surround them. Ammianus recorded that it was at this moment, when the foolish infantrymen were cut off from the rest of the Roman army and left completely exposed to endure a vicious assault by the Saxon warriors, that the Roman cataphracts came to the rescue:

> But after suffering great losses they were routed and would have perished to a man, had not a troop of cataphracts, which had been similarly stationed on another side, near a byway, to cause danger to the savages as they passed by, been aroused by their cries of terror, and quickly come to their aid. Then the contest became hotter and the Romans with fortified courage pressed upon the Saxons from all sides, surrounded them, and slew them with their drawn swords; not one of them could again return to his native home, not a single one was allowed to survive the slaughter of his comrades.[50]

In contrast to what occurred at Strasburg, in this encounter it was the infantry who were routed while the cataphracts remained a cohesive, deadly force who were primarily responsible for the success of the ambush.

The Cataphracts of the *Notitia Dignitatum*

Some time between 396 and 425, an administrative document was compiled that contained vital information about the organization of the Roman government for both the western and eastern parts of the empire.[51] Known as the *Notitia Dignitatum,* the rare ancient document provides extremely valuable information on Roman army units of the period, including the *clibanarii* and *cataphractarii.* Therefore, the *Notitia Dignitatum* is the primary source of information regarding the organization of the units of heavy cavalrymen beginning with the end of the third century to throughout the entire fourth century AD. Listed below are the *cataphractarii* and *clibanarii* units in the *Notitia Dignitatum:*[52]

Cataphractarii
East
- *equites catafractarii Biturigenses* (comitatenses) – *magister militum praesentalis I*
- *equites catafractarii* (comitatenses) – *magister militum praesentalis II*
- *equites catafractarii Ambianenses* (comitatenses) – *magister militum praesentalis II*
- *comitates catafractarii Bucellarii iuniores* – *magister militum per Orientem*
- *equites catafractarii Albigenses* (comitatenses) – *magister militum per Thracias*
- *ala I Iovia catafractariorum, Pampane* – *Dux Thebaidos*
- *equites catafractarii, Arubio* – *Dux Scythiae*

West
- *equites catafractarii iuniores* – *vexilatio* in *Britannia*
- *equites catafractarii, Morbio* – *Dux Britanniarum*

Clibanarii
East
- *comites clibanarii* – *magister militum praesentalis I*
- *equites primi clibanarii Parthi* (comitatenses) – *magister militum praesentalis I*
- *equites Persae clibanarii* (palatini) – *magister militum praesentalis II*
- *equites secundi clibanarii Parthi* (comitatenses) – *magister militum praesentalis II*
- *equites promoti clibanarii* (comitatenses) – *magister militum per Orientem*

- *equites quarti clibanarii Parthi* (comitatenses) – *magister militum per Orientem*
- *cunea equitum secundorum clibanariorum Palmirenorum* (comitatenses) – *magister militum per Orientum*
- *scola scutariorum clibanariorum* – *magister officiorum*

West

- *equites sagittari clibanarii* – *magister equitum praesentalis Africa*
- *equites Africae clibanarii*

According to the information on the cataphract units of the *Notitia Dignitatum*, it is possible that the Roman heavy horsemen were led by regional commanders, hence the titles *Dux Thebaidos, Dux Scythiae, Dux Britanniarum*, etc., with *'Dux'* meaning the rank of the military leader of each of the specified regions. It is unknown exactly how many of the heavy cavalrymen served in the units; however, it is possible that each one numbered around 300 men. It is also interesting to note that the Roman soldiers who fought as cataphracts during this period were not only recruited from the eastern provinces, but also from the western territories as well, which suggests that cataphract warfare was no longer primarily exclusive to the eastern sections of the Roman military as it had been early on. On the other hand, just as the *cataphractarii* were more western oriented with units using Gallic-sounding names, the *clibanarii* were the opposite, with units that obviously had strong connections to the Parthians (*Parthi*), Persians (*Persae*) and Palmyrans (*Palmirenorum*). And ultimately, the Roman cataphracts in general were also predominately stationed in the east, most likely to combat the more numerous heavily armoured cavalrymen who fought for the eastern armies located throughout the region.[53]

The fact that many of the Roman cataphract units in the *Notitia Dignitatum* are referred to as *equites* may indicate that they were created in the fourth century. Furthermore, it is possible that one of these units, called the *equites catafractarii, Arubio*, and led by the *Dux Scythiae*, was the same as the unit mentioned in an inscription at Chârsovo in Bulgaria from the fourth century AD, which was referred to as the *numerus catafractariorum*. Although, like the inscription in Bulgaria, there is another inscription that is located at Histria, which mentions a unit called the *vexillatio XII catafractariorum*. However, since this fourth century cataphract unit stationed in Moesia is never mentioned in the *Notitia Dignitatum*, it is possible that the detachment no longer existed by the time of the creation of the document. On the other hand, some of the units of the *Notitia Dignitatum* were also created at the end of the third century AD and were still a part of the Roman army when the document was compiled. For instance, the unit known as *ala I Iovia catafractariorum*, stationed at Thebaid in Egypt, probably originated before the creation of the other cataphract units called *equites*. Not only was *ala* an earlier term than *equites*, which was used predominately in the third century instead, but the title *Iovia* may also indicate an origin as early as the reign of Emperor Diocletian. Units known as *ala* also usually consisted of 500 troops; however, the *ala I Iovia catafractariorum* was probably the same size as the other contemporaneous units listed in the *Notitia Dignitatum*, despite its older name.[54]

An ancient papyrus has been also been discovered, which has given incredible insight on the career of an individual Roman cavalryman, whose ascension through the ranks of the army eventually led him to the prestigious position as cataphract. Interestingly, the horseman lived around the same time that the *Notitia Dignitatum* was compiled, from the end of the fourth century to the beginning of the fifth century. After ten years of service in a different type of Roman cavalry unit, the experienced horseman, named Serapion, was allowed to join the cataphracts. To serve first as a different type of cavalryman for such a long period of time before becoming a cataphract was most likely very typical in the careers of these elite mounted troops. For even with the gradual improvements in saddle technology, the heavily armoured horsemen had to be extremely skilled equestrians to not only wield the *contus*, but also to ride mounts with such extensive barding; especially if the stirrup had not yet been adopted by the Romans. Serapion was a particularly talented cavalryman, for after only two years as a cataphract, he was promoted to become a cavalry officer with the rank of *decurio*.[55]

Although he does not use the term *clibanarii* to describe them, the descriptions by the court poet Claudius Claudianus provide evidence that the most heavily armoured horsemen in the Roman army still wore extremely extensive protection at the end of the fourth century AD. Claudian first wrote about the cataphracts in his work called *In Rufinum*:

> *Over against them the cavalry seek to restrain their eager steeds by holding tight the reins. Here nod the savage waving plumes whose wearers rejoice to shake the flashing colours of their shoulder-armour; for steel clothes them and gives them their shape; the limbs within give life to the armour's pliant scales so artfully conjoined, and strike*

terror into the beholder. It is as though iron statues moved and men lived cast from the same metal. The horses are armed in the same way; their heads are encased in threatening iron, their forequarters move beneath steel plates protecting them from wounds; each stands alone, a pleasure yet a dread to behold, beautiful, yet terrible, and as the wind drops the parti-coloured dragons sink with relaxing coils into repose.[56]

Furthermore, in another work known as the *Panegyricus de Sexto Consulatu Honorii Augusti,* the court poet gives another short, colourful description of the Roman cataphracts:

When [an innocent maid] sees the mail-clad knights and brazen-armoured horses she would fain know whence that iron race of men is sprung and what land it is gives birth to steeds of bronze. 'Has the god of Lemnos', she would ask, 'bestowed on metal the power to neigh, and forged living statues for the fight?' Joy and fear fill her mind; she points with her finger how Juno's bird decks the gay crests upon their helmets, or how, beneath the golden armour on their horses' backs, the red silk waves and ripples over the strong shoulders.[57]

From Claudian's words, it is clear that the riders of the super-heavy Roman cataphracts still wore extensive protection and rode heavily armoured mounts around the time that the *Notitia Dignitatum* was compiled in the early fifth century.

On the other hand, a Roman cataphract fighting in the *Sagitarii Juniores Orientalis* at the beginning of the fifth century was much less well armoured. The mounted warrior might have had a facemask attached to his helmet that probably had a similar look to the Anglo-Saxon helmet found at Sutton Hoo. The heavy cavalrymen were most likely armoured with a mail hauberk as well, but this torso protection probably did not have a cuirass over it. Though less heavily armoured, the cataphracts may have still utilized laminated limb armour for both the arms and the legs. Like the earlier cataphracts of the Scythae regiment from the prior century, the steeds of these horsemen were also unarmoured. The heavy cavalrymen of the *Sagitarii Juniores Orientalis* probably carried large round shields and were armed with Germanic style swords, bows and smaller secondary arms, such as axes.[58]

Vegetius, as one of the last military writers of the late Roman Empire, is one of the few primary sources on contemporary Roman cavalry during the fifth century. When he wrote about the Roman cavalry of his age in general, in his treatise titled *De Re Militari*, Vegetius made an interesting statement:

> *On cavalry there are many precepts, but since this branch of the military has progressed in its training practices, type of armour and breed of horses, I do not think there is anything to be gained from books, for the present state of knowledge is sufficient.*[59]

Throughout most of the history of ancient Rome, the numerous, deadly legionaries of the legions, or the infantry in general, was the dominant arm of the Roman military. However, according to Vegetius, the Roman army had clearly changed by the fifth century AD. Not only does the military writer believe that cavalry had improved to a level unprecedented before his lifetime, but Vegetius also lamented how far the once-great Roman legionaries had fallen by the time he wrote his treatise. The situation with the Roman infantrymen during this period was so bad that the ancient writer described them as being almost useless; he stated that discipline was so lax that most of the foot soldiers did not even wear their helmets and cuirasses in battle because the armour was too heavy. The cavalry, including the cataphracts, had finally become the most important branch of the Roman armies.

Vegetius also briefly mentioned cataphracts in the *De Re Militari* as well. One of the occasions is the description of a rare and extremely innovative way in which cataphract-type warriors were utilized by the Roman army:

> *Pairs of cataphract horses were harnessed each to a chariot; mounted on [the horses] were cataphract cavalrymen who aimed* sarissae, *that is very long pikes, at the elephants. Being covered in iron they were not harmed by the archers riding the beasts, and avoided their charges thanks to the speed of their horses.*[60]

As stated by the Roman writer, the cataphract/chariot combination was one of the ways in which the Romans may have attempted to combat the huge war elephants utilized by their eastern enemies, particularly in the armies of the Sassanian Empire. Depictions of these unique cataphract warriors and their scythed vehicles are located in the *Notitia Dignitatum*, which may suggest that the heavily armoured pair of lancers were more than just an idea and may have actually even been used by the Romans in combat. In his other short statement on cataphracts in the *De Re Militari*, Vegetius wrote about the traditional heavy cavalrymen. Yet, while the late Roman writer acknowledged their strengths, he was also critical of their weaknesses:

> *Cataphracts are safe from being wounded on account of the armour they wear, but because they are hampered by the weight of their arms are easily taken prisoner and often vulnerable to lassos. They are better in battle against loose-order infantry than against cavalry, but posted in front of legionaries or mixed with legionaries they often break the enemy line when it comes to* comminus, *that is, hand-to-hand fighting.*[61]

After both fighting the cataphracts and using their own versions of the heavily armoured cavalrymen, Roman military experts like Vegetius were well aware of how invulnerable they could be with such extensive armour. The Romans had also witnessed how devastating the full cavalry charge of the cataphracts could be when, centuries earlier, the Seleucid emperor Antiochus and his heavy horsemen broke through and routed the legionaries of the Roman left wing at the Battle of Magnesia in 190 BC.

Direct experience utilizing the cataphracts may have also reinforced the idea to many Romans that the mounted troops were too expensive to field for what was gained in return on the battlefield. The legionaries had proved on several occasions that no matter how heavily equipped cataphracts were, the armoured cavalrymen still had considerable difficulty trying to break through the lines of highly trained heavy infantry armed with shields in a tight formation, even when the horsemen used the heavy lance. Furthermore, the infantry of the Gauls, Germans and Romans had also shown that they could bypass the extensive protection of the cataphracts by targeting the vulnerable areas of the mounts, or by using strong, blunt, metal weapons that may not have been able to penetrate the thick cataphract armour but could incapacitate a rider with fierce blows that had the potential to even knock him off his horse. When knocked to the ground, the cataphract commonly became prone and completely lost his advantage. Yet even if the rider managed to stay on top of his mount when he was struck with maces, eventually his greatest attribute became his main weakness, for the extreme weight of the armour quickly caused fatigue, followed by severe exhaustion in prolonged combat; even more so in the extreme heat of the Middle East and other hot climates around the Mediterranean Sea. But the Romans knew that the cataphracts were far from useless in certain situations, and as stated by Vegetius, the heavy cavalrymen were especially valuable against any infantry in a loose formation, especially if they were not as well trained as the legionaries. It also makes perfect sense that the military writer would make a point of stating that when the cataphracts, the elite heavy cavalrymen of the Roman army, fought with the best Roman heavy infantry, the legionaries, the two forces were a supremely lethal combination on the battlefield.

It might be due to the several weaknesses of the armoured cavalrymen that the cataphracts were not often utilized by the Romans at the end of the fourth and throughout the fifth century, for the heavy horsemen were rarely mentioned in the written records of the period. For instance, even if they were a part of the Roman army at the major Battle of Adrianople in 378, the cataphracts do not specifically appear in the account of the encounter, and thus, certainly did not make a significant impact in the combat that led to one of the greatest defeats in Roman history.[62] On the other hand, another very likely reason for the absence of the expensive armoured cavalrymen was the declining state of the Roman Empire throughout most of the following century after the disastrous defeat. The situation worsened considerably for the Romans on 24 August 410 when the ancient capital was seized by the Goths and then sacked by the Germanic warriors for three days afterwards. Then, in 455 AD, the city of Rome was sacked and plundered again, this time by the Vandals who wreaked even more havoc than the previous Germanic tribe by carrying out their destructive acts for fourteen days. When civil war erupted in 472 between two claimants for the throne in Rome, the western half of the empire was on the brink of a collapse from which it would never recover. In 476, the last ruler of the western empire was deposed, which meant the end of Roman rule over all of the territories in the west.[63] However, the Roman Empire would live on in the east, ruled from the new magnificent capital city of Constantinople. Later known as the Byzantine Empire, the successor state of the Eastern Romans continued many of the practices of their predecessors, which included the use of the metal-encased horsemen called cataphracts. The Byzantines' continued reliance on the fully armoured cavalrymen for several centuries proves that when the Eastern Romans could afford them, the imperial armies still believed the cataphracts were worth the heavy price, despite their weaknesses.

CHAPTER SEVEN

THE BYZANTINE *KATAPHRAKTOI* AND *CLIBANARII*

The Byzantine Empire

On 11 May 330, Roman Emperor Constantine the Great transformed and vastly expanded upon the ancient Greek city of Byzantium, founding the new enormous, political centre of the east, which he named Constantinople.[1] Over time, Constantinople not only became the eastern capital of the empire, but eventually the most important imperial city overall, even surpassing the old centre of Rome. When the traditional capital fell, along with the rest of the western half of the empire, the great city founded by Constantine remained as the new, sole capital of the surviving Eastern Roman Empire, now commonly referred to as the Byzantine Empire. Although now centred in Greece, the Byzantines considered themselves the only true successors to the ancient Romans, thus, nearly all aspects of imperial Roman culture and society continued to evolve in the remaining territories of the east. One of the military practices that transferred from the late Roman period to the early Byzantine was the use of the armoured *clibanarii*.

Early Byzantine *Clibanarii*

By the 6th century AD, in the beginning of the Byzantine era, the armies of the Eastern Roman Empire finished the gradual transition, which initiated in the 3rd century, from infantry-centred forces to a military dominated by cavalrymen.[2] During this period, the Byzantine Empire also experienced a massive resurgence in power during the reign of Emperor Justinian the Great (r. 527–65). Under his rule, the empire of the Eastern Romans not only prospered but also managed to reclaim much of the lost territory in the west. A major reason why the new emperor was so successful in his military exploits was due to the reforms of the military made early in his reign. In the reorganized Byzantine armies, the field forces were still required to be highly mobile and were therefore comprised primarily of cavalrymen, including the heavily armoured *clibanarii*. On the other hand, the numbers of the elite heavy cavalrymen were limited for several reasons. The first two were issues that the Romans had experienced with the cataphracts for centuries; both their high cost and the length of time it took to properly train a mounted warrior to fight in such heavy armour. Furthermore, when the empire was in its state of decline, it had lost much of the land that was ideal for the breeding of large warhorses used for the cataphracts. The scarcity of proper mounts was a major problem for Justinian, who made efforts to make the region of Cappadocia the primary source of the heavy cavalry steeds.[3] Yet, even if Justinian struggled to find heavy warhorses at times during his reign, it is still very possible that the Byzantine military managed throughout the rest of the sixth century to arm approximately fifteen per cent of the cavalry units in its mobile field armies as cataphracts troops.[4]

The arms and armour of the Byzantine *clibanarii* were similar to the late Roman version, but with alterations as well. For example, a heavy cavalryman who fought in the *Leones Clibanarii* unit during the reign of Emperor Justinian I would have commonly worn lamellar armour, especially in Central Asian styles. The lamellar cuirass often protected the arms to the elbows and extended past the waist to the mid-thighs of the rider. The *spangenhelm*, in Italo-Germanic styles, was a popular type of helmet utilized by the heavy cavalrymen, but it often did not contain a facemask during that period. Protection for the mounts, in terms of barding, was similar to the late Sassanian *clibanarii* in that the armour covered the front part of the horse, specifically the head, neck and chest; this too was most likely lamellar in construction. The Byzantine horsemen fought with lances, but continued the practice of having more diverse martial skills for they were also armed with bows and arrows that were highly influenced by Turkic and other Central Asian warriors, as well as long swords of a type that was used by the Iranian peoples and tribal groups of the steppes.[5] Some units of the heavily armoured *clibanarii* were most likely a part of the Byzantine forces in the battle of the Casilinus (Volturnus) River in 554 AD, and the battle of Solachon in 586 AD, though they did not distinguish themselves in the combat from the other Byzantine mounted troops in the written accounts of Late Antiquity.[6]

Near the end of the sixth century, Emperor Maurice (r. 582–602) ascended the Byzantine throne. One of the greatest acts attributed to the new ruler of the empire was the creation of one of the best military treatises made in antiquity, called the *Strategikon*. Although the term *clibanarii* is not used to describe them, a significant portion of the treatise was dedicated to the units of heavily armoured cavalry, including a description of the horsemen's armour, as well as some information on when, and from whom, their equipment was to be acquired:

> With individual training progressing satisfactorily, the soldiers must be armed by their commanding officers. The proper equipment needed on campaign may be gotten ready in the leisure of winter quarters. Each soldier should have the equipment corresponding to his rank and his pay and perquisites. This is especially true of the commanders of a meros, a moira, or a tagma, and of hekatont-archs, dekarchs, pentarchs, and tetrarchs, and of the bucellary [personal bodyguard units recruited directly by officials and generals] and federate troops. They should have hooded coats of mail reaching to their ankles, which can be caught up by thongs and rings, along with carrying cases; helmets with small plumes on top… It is not a bad idea for the bucellary troops to make use of iron gauntlets and small tassels hanging from the back straps and the breast straps of the horses, as well as small pennons hanging from their own shoulders over the coats of mail. For the more handsome the soldier is in his armament, the more confidence he gains in himself and the more fear he inspires in the enemy.[7]

Although not all mounts of the Byzantine heavy cavalry wore extensive barding, there were still a significant amount of horses armoured like the steeds of the earlier *clibanarii*:

> The horses, especially those of the officers and the other special troops, in particular those in the front ranks of the battle line, should have protective pieces of iron armour about their heads and breast plates of iron or felt, or else breast and neck coverings such as the Avars use.[8]

The Byzantine armoured horsemen and their mounts in the *Strategikon* may have typically worn slightly less protection than earlier Roman versions, like the contemporaneous Sassanian *clibanarii*, though they certainly wore heavy armour. The weight of the extensive protection was so high on some occasions that pack animals 'may be needed to carry the coats of mail and the tents'.[9] Furthermore, even though the lance was still utilized by the Byzantine mounted troops, the bow continued to rise in importance for the heavy cavalrymen of both empires as well:

> *Bows suited to the strength of each man, and not above it, more in fact on the weaker side, cases broad enough so that when necessary they can fit the strung bows in them, with spare bow strings in their saddle bags; quivers with covers holding about thirty to forty arrows; in their baldrics small files and awls; cavalry lances of the Avar type with leather thongs in the middle of the shaft and with pennons; swords; round neck pieces of the Avar type made with linen fringes outside and wool inside. Young foreigners unskilled with the bow should have lances and shields... Apart from the foreigners, all the younger Romans up to the age of forty must definitely be required to possess bow and quiver, whether they be expert archers or just average. They should possess two lances so as to have a spare at hand in case the first one misses. Unskilled men should use lighter bows. Given enough time, even those who do not know how to shoot will learn, for it is essential that they do so.*[10]

Because they wore less armour than the *clibanarii* and frequently utilized the bow, a better term used to describe the heavy cavalrymen of the *Strategikon* may be *cataphractarii sagittarii*.[11] It is also very clear that the Avars highly influenced the weaponry and equipment of the armoured horse-archers and cataphract lancers of the Byzantines. Conflicts with the Avars, Huns and other mounted warriors from the steppes of Central Asia forced the Byzantines to adopt the tactics and weaponry of their mounted, nomadic foes and, thus, was also the main factor behind the creation of the archer/lancer hybrid cataphract units.[12]

Aside from arms and armour, the description of the heavy horsemen also recommended clothing and other important equipment:

> *The men's clothing, especially their tunics, whether made of linen, goat's hair, or rough wool, should be broad and full cut according to the Avar pattern, so they can be fastened to cover the knees while riding and give a neat appearance. They should also be provided with an extra-large cloak or hooded mantle of felt with broad sleeves to wear, large enough to wear over their armament, including the coat of mail and the bow. Then, in case it should rain or be damp from the dew, by wearing this garment over the coat of mail and the bow they may protect their armament and still not find it awkward to use the bow*

or the lance. Such cloaks are necessary in another way on patrol, for when the mail is covered by them, its brightness will not be seen at a distance by the enemy, and they also provide some protection against arrows… Besides the leather cases for the coats of mail, they should have light wicker ones. During battle or on raids they may be carried behind the saddle arch by the horse's loins. Then if, as in the case of a reversal, the men with the spare horses are missing for a day, the coats of mail will not be left unprotected and ruined and the soldiers will not be worn out by the constant weight of the armour.[13]

The *Strategikon* continued with the saddles, as well as the other related equestrian equipment, for the *cataphractarii sagittarii*, including the revolutionary stirrup:

The saddles should have large and thick cloths; the bridles should be of good quality; attached to the saddles should be two iron stirrups, a lasso with thong, hobble, a saddle bag large enough to hold three or four days' rations for the soldier when needed. There should be four tassels on the back strap, one on top of the head, and one under the chin.[14]

Ever since the battle of Panion in 200 BC, the cataphracts and *clibanarii* of the Seleucids, Parthians, Sassanians, the earlier Romans, and several other kingdoms, had proven over the centuries that heavily armoured warriors could fight on armoured mounts without stirrups, even with the enormous *kontos* (*contus*). Yet, even though the cataphracts certainly existed before the Romans adopted stirrups in the sixth century AD, there is no doubt that the introduction of this significant piece of equipment greatly improved the performance of the armoured horsemen. First of all, the most obvious benefit was that it was considerably easier for such a heavily equipped warrior to mount his horse by using the stirrup as a stable platform to step up on to. Furthermore, while in combat, stirrups made it easier for the cataphracts to use all of their various weaponry. With the increased stability provided by the stirrup, lancers no longer had to wield their primary weapon in both hands, but instead could be armed with both a shield and the lance. In addition, the heavy cavalrymen could put more of their weight into the strikes of their swords, maces and other sidearms, making heavier blows with the potential to cause greater injury to enemy soldiers. However, what was most important for the *cataphractarii sagittarii* was that stirrups gave mounted archers much more manoeuvrability in their saddle to fire in all directions and even allowed the most skilled riders to stand up, which gave them more stability in order to improve their aim considerably.[15]

When the Sassanians invaded the Byzantine Empire in 603, initiating the decades-long war between the two great superpowers of Late Antiquity, it was the composite lancer/archer version of the Byzantine cataphract that fought against their eastern adversary. However, for the first two decades of the war, the Byzantine forces did not fare well against the armies of the Sassanian Empire. Even after the ruler of the Eastern Romans, Emperor Heraclius, personally got involved in the situation in 613, the Sassanians continued to win the war. It was not until the end of the decade that the Byzantine emperor realized he must put his soldiers through an intensive period of re-training if they were to have any hope of defeating the Sassanians. Therefore, Heraclius left on 4 April 620 and gathered his forces at a location near Caesarea in Cappadocia to begin the process of improving the martial capabilities of his troops. As a vital part of his armies, the cataphracts also underwent further training that especially improved two major aspects of their combat: both their proficiency with the lance, in conjunction with stirrups, for enhanced shock tactics, as well as extensive training with the bow.[16]

Although it is possible that the Sassanian heavy cavalrymen had also adopted stirrups by this point, there is no solid evidence to prove this. Thus, if it's true that the Sassanian horsemen did not utilize the revolutionary equestrian equipment, the use of stirrups would have given the Byzantine cataphracts a considerable advantage over their mounted opponents.[17] On the other hand, even if both armies had access to the equipment, the new cavalry tactics employed by the Byzantine armoured horsemen alone may have been sufficient enough to overcome the late Sassanian *clibanarii*. If it was, in fact, solely the use of enhanced shock tactics that gave the Byzantines the advantage, it may have been due to the Eastern Roman lancers' greater ability to charge into the especially vulnerable rear or flanks of the Sassanian armoured cavalrymen.[18]

Another advantage that the Byzantine cataphract may possibly have had over the Sassanian version might actually be their archery technique. Even if the Sassanian horse-archers were the masters of rapid-fire archery, as according to the *Strategikon*, their method of shooting the bow differed in that they drew their bowstrings with the three lower fingers on their hand. By contrast, the Byzantine armoured horse-archers adopted the same draw technique that was utilized by the Huns, later known as the 'Mongolian draw'. Using this method, the archers of the Eastern Romans pulled the bowstrings with their thumbs instead of their fingers, which may not have been the fastest technique, but it was the way to cause the most potential damage on a shot from a compound bow. Also, once again, if the Byzantine archers had stirrups and the Sassanians did not, that would have made Eastern Roman archery even more superior to that of the Neo-Persian Empire.[19]

The intensive training and drills were carried out for about six or seven months before Heraclius led the army out of Cappadocia to begin campaigning again around the beginning of winter at the end of 620. In 622, Heraclius and his men encountered the Sassanian forces under the command of the general Shahrbaraz, who after making a failed attack on the Byzantines, fled into the protection of the nearby mountains. While the Byzantine army remained on the level plain, the Sassanian warriors frequently left the safety of their mountainous refuge to make assaults on the army in the field. Yet in each attempt, the Byzantines overcame their attackers and successfully drove them off back into their favoured rough terrain, which negated the effectiveness of the Eastern Roman lancers, as described in the *Strategikon*. However, it was not just with the lance that the Byzantine cataphracts repelled the attacks of the Sassanians, for the use of the Hunnic draw employed by the Eastern Romans may have also allowed them to shoot farther than the enemy archers. On the other hand, the Byzantine army was either unable or unwilling to rout the Sassanians from out of their mountainous refuge. The first major battle that the newly trained army participated in took place near Ophalimos when general Shahrbaraz led his forces down out of the mountains to attack the Byzantines on the plains. On this occasion, however, the Byzantines managed to make a surprise attack that caught the Sassanians completely off-guard and halted the momentum of their cavalrymen. It was when the Sassanian horsemen were in this vulnerable state that the Byzantine heavy cavalry made at least one successful charge that broke the Sassanian army, leading to victory for Heraclius and his men.[20] These violent encounters with the Sassanians also demonstrated how effectively armoured the Byzantine cataphract remained even in its new lancer/archer hybrid incarnation. According to the *Chronicle* of Theophanes, while the Byzantine emperor was in the thick of the combat, his horse was struck several times but was never wounded:

> *[Heraclius' horse] took a lance thrust in the flank and received many sword blows to the face, but because he was wearing armour of layered felt, he was unharmed, nor did the swords have any effect.*[21]

In 625, when both of the generals, Shahrbaraz and Shahin, pursued Heraclius, the Byzantine emperor retreated to the safety of a wooded hill near Tigranocerta. From this superior position, the Byzantine archers dug in and began to launch volleys of arrows down upon their pursuers. Since the Eastern Roman archers had a greater range than their enemies, the Sassanians could not get close enough to damage the Byzantine forces. Without any cover for protection, the Sassanian warriors were slain on the open plain below until they were eventually routed.[22]

After Heraclius led his army deep into Sassanian territory, the decisive battle of the war was fought near Nineveh in 627. After successfully distracting the Sassanian forces by raining arrows down upon them, while either using fog or kicking up dust to conceal their actions, the Byzantines managed to get into position and outflank them. When the Byzantines appeared to flee, the Sassanian army pursued them into an open plain but then the Byzantines suddenly turned and confronted the Sassanians, showing that the retreat was actually a feint. Before the Sassanians realized what was happening, they found themselves surrounded and began to sustain heavy casualties. The Sassanians fought fiercely for a time until they could no longer take the onslaught and were forced to retreat.[23] The conflict between the Byzantines and Sassanians did not end immediately afterwards, but the Byzantine victory at the Battle of Nineveh marked the effective end of true Sassanian resistance.

The Byzantines may have finally overcome their ancient nemesis, yet the prolonged conflict left the empire of the Eastern Romans severely weakened as well. Thus the jubilation they felt because of this accomplishment was extremely short-lived, for as early as 634 not only was Syria invaded, but the militant Arab followers of the Prophet Muhammad also conquered Damascus. The Islamic conquests continued for many years in several directions from out of the Arabian Peninsula; very few states of Late Antiquity managed to resist, let alone survive. Unlike the Sassanian Empire, the Byzantines ultimately endured the Arab invasions, though it was at a great cost; nearly all of the eastern imperial territories were seized by the conquerors. For the rest of the seventh century, the empire suffered through a period known as the Byzantine 'Dark Ages' and yet, since the Arabs failed to take the capital, Constantinople, the Eastern Romans survived and slowly began to recover.[24]

Long before the disastrous Arab conquests that devastated the Byzantine Empire, the term *clibanarii* completely fell out of use in the written records by the end of the sixth century.[25] Even though they were not called *clibanarii*, the Byzantines fielded many of the lancer/ archer hybrid cataphracts throughout the Sassanian-Byzantine War, yet the amount of heavily armoured cavalry in the overall army decreased greatly after they were severely defeated by the Arab armies. Heavy horsemen still remained a vital component of Byzantine armies over the following centuries; however, none wore such extensive protection to be deemed as either *cataphracti* or *clibanarii* by the early medieval writers of the period that was known as the Byzantine Dark Ages. It was not until the ninth century that the elite heavy cavalrymen of the Imperial Tagmata (full-time professional army) were again armoured much more like cataphracts, along with their mounts. Regarding the armour, segmented metal helmets were worn, as well as mail hauberks that extended to the middle of the thigh and had sleeves that only reached the elbows. Below the helmet, a full mail aventail commonly protected the face and head, leaving only two openings for the eyes. The top layer of armour over the torso comprised of a small, sleeve-less lamellar cuirass. Underneath the cuirass, the heavy horsemen also wore a quilted *epilorikon* with long sleeves that could be laced up if needed. The elite mounted troops fought with swords and lances, but also carried a shield. The facemask that covered the head of the steed was often made of bronze, while the barding that protected the rest of the horse's body was commonly made with layers of felt that were both stitched and glued together.[26]

The condition of the Byzantine Empire continued to improve in the ninth century, thus, by the beginning of the tenth century, the economy was also in a much better state. With the improved economic conditions, a greater number of wealthy landowners emerged than those that existed in the previous two centuries, and these could afford to field a much larger number of cataphracts than those that had served in the army since the seventh century AD. The number of cataphracts available to the Byzantine military was augmented even further as a result of legislation passed in the early ninth century, which encouraged poorer soldiers to pool their resources together in order to arm and armour some of their number to fight as cav-alrymen, sometimes even as cataphracts later in the tenth century.[27] The previous term used to describe the Roman heavily armoured cavalrymen, *clibanarii*, was not revived in the medieval Byzantine accounts of the tenth century for these new Byzantine cataphracts. Since the empire of the Eastern Romans was moved to the Greek lands of the east, surrounding the new capital of Constantinople, Greek was the official language of the medieval Byzantine Empire.

Therefore, an even more ancient Greek term was resurrected to describe the late Byzantine cataphract. Coming back full circle, the last heavily armoured horsemen in the Greco-Roman accounts were predominately known as *kataphraktoi*, beginning in the tenth century. However, even though the medieval Byzantines did not again use the Latin word *clibanarii* for their cataphracts, a Greek variation of the term was used to describe the essential lamellar armour cuirass worn by all of the late Byzantine cataphracts, the *klibanion*.[28]

Late Byzantine *Kataphraktoi*

Most likely during the reign of Emperor Leo VI Sophos (r. 886–912), the cataphracts had officially returned to the armies of the Eastern Romans. The late Byzantine cataphracts primarily wore mail armour (*lôrikion alusidôton*) that not only covered the torso and arms to the wrist, but the protection also extended all the way down the ankles. Further armour was also commonly worn over the mail, such as a lamellar cuirass (*klibanion*) and lamellar protection for the limbs as well. An even greater amount of protection was added on top of the *klibanion* of the heavy horsemen, for first, splinted armour was attached to the upper sleeves and then later scales, or inverted lamellar pieces, were often attached to the upper arms, as well as to the skirt. Though there were also a good number of the cataphracts who wore scale armour (*lôrikion folidôton*) instead of mail, which sometimes only protected the torso as a cuirass and thus provided less protection than those armoured with a coat of mail; yet even with this limited armour, the scale armour was also augmented with lamellar limb armour as much as possible. Armour for the lower legs of the rider (*podopsella*) and the forearms (*kheiropsella*) were often used, along with the armour for the upper sleeves of the *klibanion*.[29]

The helmets utilized by the Byzantine cataphracts often had mail attached to them that protected the entire head and face of the rider, except for openings for the eyes; the most heavily armoured cataphracts had double-layered mail protection, as recommended by Nikephoros Phokas in his military treatise, the *Praecepta Militaria*:

> They must have iron helmets heavily reinforced so as to cover their faces with chain mail two or three layers thick so that only their eyes appear.[30]

Not only have remains of this kind of helmet been found, such as the those uncovered at Yasenovo in Bulgaria, along with several other discoveries of Caucasian helmets, but also depictions of cataphracts wearing these helmets can be viewed in the Madrid Skylitzes manuscript. The most superbly armoured cavalrymen were also equipped with greater leg protection, with full lower leg armour known as *khalkotouva*.[31] Just as with nearly all of the other Byzantine horsemen, the cataphracts also carried a cloak that was often waterproof. Although not often worn in combat, the garment was a valuable piece of equipment for the long marches carried out by every soldier. Before battle commenced, the cataphracts commonly rolled their cloaks up and stored them behind the saddles of their mounts with straps. Standard military issue cloaks, sandy-brown in colour, were provided for the warriors who needed them, however, many of the heavy cavalrymen wore their own garments, which were usually in bright colours and decorated with hems and panels. The most important of the decorations was the *tablion*, the central panel that showcased the rider's main emblem.[32]

During the reign of Emperor Leo VI, the Byzantine cataphracts, in general, were typically much more heavily armoured than they tended to be later in the tenth century. Nearly all of the heavy cavalry of Leo's reign wore both a full padded garment and an entire mail shirt underneath their lamellar *klibanion* and upper sleeve armour. On the other hand, after the reforms enacted by Emperor Nikephoros II Phokas (r. 963–9) the weight carried by the cataphracts decreased due to the changes he made to the armour they wore. The newer cataphract replaced the mail shirt and the full padded garment with a smaller, short-sleeved arming jacket or *zoupa* instead; over which he still wore a *klibanion*, but this armour for the Nikephorian cataphract was supplemented with padded lower sleeves and skirts that were faced with mail, along with splinted upper sleeve armour.[33] According to Nikephoros Phokas, the *klibanion* was an essential piece of equipment for the cataphracts:

> *Each warrior must wear a* klibanion. *The* klibanion *should have sleeves down to the elbows. Down from the elbows they should wear arm-guards which – both these and the skirts hanging from the* klibania *– have chain mail and are made of coarse silk or cotton as thick as can be stitched together. Over their* klibania *they should wear* epilorika *of coarse silk or cotton. Their hands should go out through the shoulder slits. Their sleeves should be hung behind on their shoulders.*[34]

Especially due to the removal of the mail shirt, the weight of the armour decreased significantly; however, less protection left several areas of the body vulnerable, such as the armpits and elbows. It is possible, though, that the Byzantines did the same thing as the Western European knights by attaching mail facings to these vulnerable areas.[35]

Although less armoured than the version seen in Leo's reign, the cataphracts during the reign of Phokas were a near perfect balance between encumbrance and protection; therefore, they still wore a very comprehensive set of armour. Though complex, the arming process of the late Byzantine cataphracts was developed in a way to allow the heavy cavalrymen to arm themselves individually as much as possible, without needing the assistance of another to put on their armour. The system began with the short-sleeved, padded jacket (*zoupa*) for the torso. Also known as the *peristhêthidion*, this was either a solid garment pulled over the rider's head, or the jacket was buttoned up instead. It was important for the heavy horseman to make sure that the jacket was as close to the same size as his lamellar *klibanion* as possible in order for the armour to fit properly. Next came splinted greaves (*podopsella*) worn on the lower legs, though later in this era some of the cataphracts may have upgraded their armour to solid metal greaves. After the *podopsella*, the rider then put on a padded skirt (*kremasmata*); at first this was augmented with mail but near the end of the era many late Byzantine cataphracts substituted the mail with either a scale or lamellar covering as an alternative. The padded skirt was most likely attached to the bottom of the *zoupa* on the torso in order to keep it in place around the waist and over the thighs. One of the most vital components of the armour was put on next, the *klibanion*. Due to a series of technological innovations that began in the eighth century, the Eastern Romans created a type of lamellar armour used for the cuirass that was far superior to any other lamellar they had ever developed. The new lamellae plates were fixed to a leather backing in rows that were both riveted in place at top and bottom and also attached with the common laces used primarily in the past before the rows were suspended, which made the armour somewhat resemble brigandine armour that had been turned inside out. It is unknown exactly how the *klibanion* was put on; however, since it is likely that the lamellar cuirass needed to be fastened with a series of buckles and straps along the sides, this armour was one piece that the cataphract may have required some assistance to put on properly. Luckily, cataphracts were nearly always accompanied by a groom whose function was to help with such matters, or their 'spear companions' who fought alongside them could help as well if need be.[36]

After the *klibanion*, the next items worn by the cataphract were known as *manikellia*, which protected the upper arms. They were initially attached directly to the lamellar cuirass, but over time an armoured shoulder piece was adopted that the upper sleeve protection was attached to instead. Typically, the *manikellia* were splinted armour, however, the late Byzantine cataphracts often wore upper sleeve guards constructed of inverted lamellae plates or scales near the end of the period. The entire torso of the rider, including the arms and the legs down to the knees, was then covered with further protection in the form of a large padded coat known as an *epilôrikion*. Then the last major piece of armour was put on, the helmet, which kept the entire head and face very protected, especially due to the thick mail skirt attached to it that left only the eyes vulnerable. To keep the rings of the mail skirt holding onto the helmet, they were often supported by a wire that ran through a channel that was slotted throughout the brim of the helm. Armour for the forearms (*kheiropsella*) made of padding covered with mail was often put on last and probably attached to the sleeves of the *zoupa*, which was also probably done with some help from one of the cataphract's comrades; Byzantine cataphracts may have also worn mailed gloves (*kheiromanikia*), which, if so, might have been put on after the forearm armour. From the tenth to the twelfth century, most of the heavy cavalrymen were armoured in some variation of this manner.[37]

Since the quality and quantity of the arms and armour of the cataphracts almost always depended largely upon the personal wealth of the rider, some of the richest warriors were able to afford the full mail coat and chose to wear it underneath their *klibanion*, even with the added weight that came with it. The most heavily armoured cataphracts of their time were therefore protected more like the earlier heavy horsemen who fought under Emperor Leo, and thus gained the benefit of having much more protection for particularly vulnerable areas like the armpits and elbows.[38] Furthermore, the mail skirts attached to the helmets of the heavily armoured cavalrymen may have even been three layers thick for some of the warriors. The super armed and armoured cataphracts during this era, especially after the reforms of Nikephoros Phokas, may have been referred to as *klibanophoroi* (the Greek version of the Latin term *clibanarii*) to distinguish them from the other cataphract cavalrymen. The *klibanophoroi* were rare in the Byzantine ranks and most likely only fought in the Tagmata regiments.[39] In fact, the most heavily armoured cataphracts were so rare and expensive to field that they only constituted five per cent or less of the overall forces in the Byzantine army, probably within only three Tagmata units at most, each numbering between 384 and 504 men.[40]

The mounts of the Byzantine cataphracts were protected as well, though the Eastern Romans continued the popular trend from Late Antiquity and the early medieval period of heavy cavalrymen only protecting the chest, neck and head of the horses, while armour for the rest of the body was very rare and was mostly reserved only for the more heavily armoured *klibanophoroi*. The head armour covered most of the head and was commonly constructed of iron; however, it is also possible that some of the cataphracts continued to use the leather facemasks of earlier Byzantine heavy cavalry horses. Both the chest and neck were often protected with lamellar armour constructed with ox-hide. Sometimes horses wore different armour, such as iron lamellar or mail, though two to three layers of laminated felt glued together was the most common substitute for the ox-hide lamellar.[41] Nikephoros Phokas provided a good description of basic barding that the mounts of the Byzantine cataphracts were expected to have during the period:

> They must have sturdy horses covered in armour, either of pieces of felt and boiled leather fastened together down to the knees so that nothing of the horse's body appears except its eyes and nostrils – likewise their legs below the knees and their undersides should remain uncovered and unconcealed – or they can have klibania [lamellar armor] made of bison hides over the chest of the horse which should be split at its legs and underneath to permit the unhindered movement of their legs.[42]

Just as the full body barding was reserved for the mounts of the wealthiest cataphracts, these were the horses that were given armour made with iron. Therefore, nearly the entire bodies of the horses of the *klibanophoroi* were encased in metal, except for the belly, lower legs, eyes, and nostrils of the animals. The most unique armour added to all of the cataphract mounts, which was almost exclusively used by the Byzantines, were more complete horseshoes that covered the entire underside of the hoof. The full horseshoes were primarily used to protect the horses from caltrops.[43]

The Byzantine cataphracts commonly carried a shield, as stated by Nikephoros Phokas: 'The men should also have shields to turn away arrows'.[44] The shield carried by the elite heavy cavalrymen was at first round in shape and known as the *skoutaria*. These circular shields were usually conical or domed and at least 75–80cm (29–32in) in diameter, though larger shields were also carried that could be as large as 90cm (35in) across. Normally, the shield was strapped to the shoulder of the cataphract, especially while he rode on horseback, and was held in place due to one of his arms placed through one of the arm straps; rings attached to the inside of the shield held rope or leather handles for the cavalryman to hold on to. Worn in this manner, the shield still provided extra protection but allowed the cataphract to freely use both hands. If the cataphract ever dismounted or was thrown from his horse while in combat and forced to fight on foot, the shield was then held in one hand like a buckler, gripped in the fist. However, by the twelfth century, Western European practices influenced the Eastern Romans enough for them to adopt the kite-style shields that then replaced the old *skoutaria*.[45] In as early as 975, some shields were described as having three corners, referring to early versions of the kite shield, such as in the *Sylloge Tacticorum*. The popularity of the Western shields then increased considerably throughout the eleventh century until they became the main type used by the cataphracts. The kite shields of the Byzantine heavy cavalrymen could be as much as 60 cm (2 ft) across, but were often much less broad near the end of the era. These shields were also smaller than the kite types adopted by the Byzantine infantry, and thus were 91–101cm (36–40in) deep.[46]

Like the ancient cataphracts, the late Byzantine *kataphraktoi* carried the traditional *kontos*, which became known as the *kontarion*, that was mostly 3.6m (12ft) long in the beginning of the period and throughout the tenth century.[47] However, some of the later heavy horsemen fought with a *kontarion* that was often smaller, and some had a length of only 2.5m (8ft 2in). This was chiefly due to the fact that the lance had become a less important weapon to the cataphract at that time when compared to other arms in their arsenals. For close combat, the main weaponry of the heavy cavalrymen included two types of swords: the single-edged, slightly curved *paramêrion* and the straight, double-edged *spathion*. The latter blade was a successor to swords utilized several centuries earlier in the early Roman imperial era; however, the *paramêrion* was a much more recent addition to the cataphract armament, for it was adopted by the Byzantines in the late ninth century. On average, both blades were 91cm (36in) long. Nikephoros Phokas recommended that every cataphract should carry both swords in order to be prepared for different situations while in battle, which was possible due to the different ways that the rider could carry each weapon. The attachments on the scabbard of the *paramêrion* were on the same side, therefore, the sword hung nearly horizontal whether it was attached to either a belt or a baldric (shoulder strap). On the other hand, when the scabbard of the *spathion* was attached to a baldric instead of to a belt, the attachments were on each side of the scabbard so that the *spathion* hung vertically as opposed to horizontal. In this way, both swords could be carried by the Byzantine cataphracts for neither one of the weapons hindered the drawing of the other. However, if a cataphract decided to carry only one of the edged weapons instead, the *spathion* could also be suspended from the belt like the *paramêrion* so that it too would be held horizontally. The most heavily armoured cavalrymen were the ones to sometimes choose to bear only one sword, which was commonly the *spathion* attached to their baldric, for the extra protection made it difficult to wear a belt.[48]

Some of the late Byzantine cataphracts carried bows and arrows like the Sassanian and Roman *clibanarii* and *cataphractarii sagittarii*; however, carrying the weaponry was much less common for the heavy cavalrymen of the period. Beginning in the eighth century, overall archery within the Byzantine military was declining, thus, by the reign of Leo VI in the tenth century, the arms of the cataphracts were reformed so that two out of every five of the warriors were equipped with bows only, instead of lances. Armed in this manner, only the best horse-archers among the cataphracts fought with the ranged weaponry, while the rest of the heavy cavalrymen focused exclusively on close combat. This also meant that the lancers were deprived of the powerful ranged weapon, which was exchanged for either two javelins, or a weapon called a *spendobolon*, which was a sling or a staff-sling.[49] Nikephoros Phokas explained how the horse-archers were incorporated into the cataphract formation:

> There must be archers with the kataphraktoi, *in the middle where they can be protected by them. The men in the first, second, third, and fourth lines should not be archers, but from the fifth row on back to the rear. If the total number of* kataphraktoi *in the formation is 504, they must include 150 archers. If it is 384, they must include 80 archers.*[50]

These changes were basically a continuation of the recommendation of Maurice, as recorded in his *Strategikon* of the late sixth century, in which he stated that even though cataphracts should carry both lances and bows, each warrior should use the weapon more suited to their own personal martial skills. The bow utilized by the Byzantines was most likely influenced by the composite bow of the Huns. It was 114–122cm (45–48in) long and given powerful, short limbs that fired 68cm (27in) long arrows. The heavily armoured horse-archers typically carried a quiver full of thirty to forty arrows.[51] The horse-archers among the cataphracts could be equipped similarly to their lancer comrades, though they were typically less armed and armoured. Nikephoros Phokas described the common modifications made to the equipment of the mounted archers:

> *The archers should wear* klibania *(lamellar armour) and helmets only. If possible, their horses should be covered with armour. The archers should wear* kabadia *on their belts to cover a part of their horses and protect themselves from the waist down. If some of them are light horsemen, they must be placed inside the* kataphraktoi. *The men armed with lances or maces and the archers and the light horsemen must also have swords. All should have shields except for the archers.*[52]

The last weapon carried by the Byzantine cataphracts was a smaller sidearm, such as a mace or axe; however the former was much more popular than the latter amongst the heavy cavalrymen. The maces (*vardoukia*) were mostly globular in form, yet flanged types were used by some of the horsemen. The iron heads of many of these maces were attached simply to wooden shafts, but by the tenth century the Byzantine cataphracts were some of the first heavy cavalrymen to use maces that were embellished with hilts and guards similar to those on swords, as well as constructed with iron shafts instead of wood; the Eastern Romans called these unique weapons *spathovaklion* or *sideroravdion*. Yet maces were so prized by the cataphracts, that even if they had wooden shafts, there were some cases in which the mace was given a fine leather handle that was highly ornate with painted decorations, as described by the twelfth-century Arab writer Al-Tartusi. Most of the saddles of the cataphracts had two holsters on either side of the pommel so that they could hold more of these lethal weapons. The far less popular sidearm utilized by the heavy horsemen was the axe. The blades of these axes ranged from either a slightly flared blade to one that resembled the later eastern *tabar*, which was a full, nearly semicircular crescent. Like most battleaxes, the weapons of the Byzantine cataphracts had another fitting that either mirrored the first blade, or gave the axe another dimension, such as a spike, hammerhead or a blade that looked like the point of a spear.[53] Nikephoros Phokas explained how he wanted the cataphracts specialized for close combat to be armed and formed up in battle:

> *The* kataphraktoi *should have the following weapons: iron maces with all-iron heads – the heads must have sharp corners and be three-cornered, four-cornered, or six-cornered – or else other iron maces or sabres. All of them must have swords. They should hold their iron maces and sabres in their hands and have other iron maces either on their belts or saddles. The first line, that is, the front of the formation, the second, third, and fourth lines must have the same complement, but from the fifth line on back the* kataphraktoi *on the flanks should set up like this – one man armed with a lance and one armed with a mace or else one of the men carrying a sabre, and so they should be all the way to the back lines.*[54]

The last sidearm that was possibly used by some of the cataphracts of the period was a war-hammer known as an *akouphion*.[55]

The major reason the Byzantine cataphracts could easily wield both a shield and a lance was due to the stability provided by the continued use of the stirrup. Other equipment that was utilized by the horsemen in order to ride their mounts included saddles, bridles and bits. Saddles were attached to the mounts not only with the common girth straps, but also with straps around the chest and the rump of the horse as well. Wealthier cataphracts decorated the straps with several ornate roundels, while a cheaper option for many of the other heavy horsemen were straps with short pendants. Such ornamentation was critical for the majority of the heavy cavalrymen who required public displays of status to increase their own power and prestige. There were, however, quite a few cataphracts, including the poorest of the warriors, who chose not to use, or more likely could not afford, the adornment and simply utilized plain, leather straps. The saddles of the heavy cavalrymen were highly influenced by Central Asian styles with both a low cantle and pommel, though by the twelfth century the saddle was slightly modified for those cataphracts that only fought with the lance and did not utilize the bow. The lancers did not need to manoeuvre in their saddles nearly as much as horse-archers; therefore, they could utilize saddles similar to the ones used by their counterparts in the West, the knights, which had both higher pommels and cantles. The cavalry seat was constructed in four pieces, including the pommel, the cantle arches, and the side bars. The saddle was curved in order to properly fit around the back of the horse and purposely thickened in the middle to make a better seat for the rider. A slight layer of padding was added to the seats of the saddles for the wealthier warriors, however, most cataphracts simply sat on the wooden frame of the saddle. Like the saddle straps, the bridles used by many of the Byzantine cataphracts were also embellished with metal plaques or roundels, often attached to the junctions of the different pieces, though they could also be in the middle of the bands across the brow of the mount. Aside from the decorations, the only variation between the different bridles was the absence or inclusion of a nose band to go with the standard brow band. The vast majority of the riders used a bit that resembled the snaffle, which lacked any distinctive features, though there were a few cataphracts that used curb bits. As recommended by Leo VI in his military treatise, *Taktika*, saddlebags with at least three days' worth of rations for emergencies were also highly recommended for the cataphracts to carry with them while on campaign.[56]

As the most recent type of cataphract to fight on the battlefields of Europe and the Middle East, more information is known about the lives of individual Byzantine *kataphraktoi* than any of the earlier versions of the heavily armoured horsemen. Some of the best-equipped mounted troops served as full-time soldiers in the imperial capital, or in the garrisons of important provincial cities. Depending on their background, these professional cataphracts could utilize their own arms and armour if they desired, but the Byzantine state also provided full-time troops with whatever equipment they required. In general, these soldiers chose whatever equipment was best, either their own or the military's. On the other hand, most of the late Byzantine cataphracts, like many of the other native cavalrymen who fought for the empire during the period, were part-time soldiers recruited from what was known as the 'theme' system. Themes, or *themata*, were military districts in the imperial provinces with designated farmlands, called *strateia*, that were owned by farmer-soldiers and their families. In exchange for the right to live on and farm the land, the family had to provide an equipped mounted soldier to serve in the Byzantine army. All of the cavalrymen that were recruited, including the cataphracts, not only had to be skilled riders and in top physical shape, but young as well, for men over forty years of age were rarely accepted (although some managed to slip through the cracks and serve longer than they were supposed to). Generally, if a father did not meet these requirements, a son served in his place, usually the eldest. Therefore, the *strateia* often remained in the hereditary possession of one family, passing from fathers to sons. The regional commanders made sure to keep lists, known as the *adnoumia* or muster rolls, of the men who were required to serve, or at least find a substitute.[58]

Like the earlier aristocratic, heavily armoured Parthian and Sassanian mounted warriors, the soldiers who fought as Byzantine cataphracts usually had to be wealthy in order to fulfill that role on the battlefield. Specifically, the *kataphraktoi* not only had to be able to afford their own mount, arms, armour and equipment, but also needed to be rich enough to hire servants, or buy slaves, who could work the land and harvest sufficient agricultural produce to pay for everything. During the reign of Nikephoros Phokas, the most heavily armoured cataphracts required enough land to equal at least 1,152 *nomismata*, or 16 pounds of gold, to properly equip themselves, which is roughly the equivalent of an estate with 30 families working the land. Due to the large size of the *strateia*, and the amount of people that worked there, the wealthy landowners were often required to also supply the imperial armies with resources, money and support staff, including servants, grooms, muleteers and wagon drivers, along with physicians, army medics and even veterinary doctors for the valuable cataphract mounts and the other horses.[59] The Byzantine military also paid the estate owners, or whoever served in their place, for their time in service, so even though there could be many obligations to the state, there was also that monetary benefit as well on top of the valuable land ownership. It is unknown exactly how much the late Byzantine cataphracts earned throughout the period, though the thematic soldiers were typically paid well in general.[60]

As stated above, if the landowner of the *strateia* was too old or sick to serve, any family member could serve in his place. Though the Byzantine state also occasionally forced the replacement of some estate owners who had committed a serious crime. In such cases, ownership still tended to stay within the family, even if it passed to an extended family member. If the master of the estate was not a criminal but was still unable to serve, nor had any family members suitable for service, the owner of the *strateia* had the option of paying a fee instead. When landowners needed to be replaced, most often due to death in battle, and they no longer had any living relatives to take their place, the Byzantine state stepped in and gave the *strateia* to someone else.[61] Landowners were also sometimes replaced when they could no longer afford to provide a cataphract, or any sort of mounted soldier, nor even pay the fine. To prevent this, Nikephoros Phokas tried to institute reforms that made the wealthiest landowners help to provide their poorer comrades with arms and armour, though even with assistance, some were still unable to fulfill their obligation, and thus lost their *strateia* and their farmer-soldier status.[62] Regardless of the numerous qualifications and obligations of the cataphracts from the *themata*, many soldiers still served as the elite heavy cavalrymen in the Byzantine armies of the period. During the reign of Leo VI, some *themata* could supply the Byzantine forces with as many as 4,000 cataphracts, though there was certainly a wide variation in the level of quantity or quality of arms and armour of these mounted soldiers; for example, many of the mounts were probably not completely armoured.[63]

Late Byzantine *kataphraktoi* fought in units of eight men known as *kontoubernia*. The Byzantine armies preferred to place cataphract warriors in units with men from in the same areas; and it was even better if the heavy cavalrymen in the *kontoubernia* were all family members or friends, as Nikephoros Phokas stressed in the *Praecepta Militaria*:

> The kontoubernia *of the* kataphraktoi *must be arranged according to friendship and kinship in battle array, in encampments, and on the march. Each line should have a commander, the bigger lines two apiece, who quarter, live, and march together with them. Not only these officers, but the whole unit, should be under the command of the one head officer and the men should quarter and march together with him.*[64]

These practices were carried out primarily in the hope of optimizing unit cohesion to get the best possible performance from them on the battlefield. However, another major reason the Byzantine military wanted the soldiers to know each other was to prevent enemy spies from infiltrating the ranks. While the *kontoubernia* was on campaign, the eight warriors camped near each other and shared some common equipment to decrease the weight of their overall baggage in the train. There were usually two cataphracts per tent, along with a groom or servant to help with tasks such as preparing food or putting on armour. The three men collectively were known as 'spear companions'.[65]

Thanks to the tenth-century AD military treatises, the *Sylloge Tacticorum*, the *Praecepta Militaria* of Nikephoros Phokas and the *Taktika* of Nikephoros Ouranos, very specific information about the tactics and formations of the late Byzantine *kataphraktoi* is known. These heavily armoured cavalrymen typically attacked with a powerful charge in a triangular wedge formation in the hope to break through the enemy lines, as according to Nikephoros Phokas:

> *It is necessary for the commander of the army to have the triangular formation of* kataphraktoi *at the ready and the other two units*

which accompany it, and, on whichever front the enemy is facing, have them move out through those intervals very calmly in proper formation. Even if the enemy formation is made up of infantry, that is to say heavy infantry, the kataphraktoi *should not be apprehensive but should proceed to the attack very calmly (even if the enemy formation is made up of infantry, as mentioned) and aim the triangular formation of* kataphraktoi *right at the spot where the commander of the enemy army is standing. And then the spears of the enemy infantry in the front lines will be smashed by the* kataphraktoi, *while their arrows will be ineffective, as will the javelins of their javeliners. Then, with the help of God, they will turn to flight.*[66]

The Byzantine Empire was one of the wealthiest states of the Middle Ages; therefore, the imperial troops were almost always equipped with better arms and armour than any of their enemies. Furthermore, infantry was not nearly as well trained as it was in the ancient past and there were no contemporary foot soldiers armed with enormous pikes (the best weapon used against heavy cavalry). Because of this, the combination of their lancers with armoured horse-archers meant the cataphracts were equipped to fight against most kinds of troops (both mounted and on foot), especially in close-quarter combat, yet the late Byzantine *kataphraktoi* were primarily used against infantry. Since most foot soldiers of the age were lightly armoured and armed merely with short spears, or even smaller weapons, the heavily armoured horsemen were almost always able to overcome such forces unless there was a great multitude of them.[67] Nikephoros Ouranos described just how deadly the cataphract wedge, with the numerous lethal weapons they carried, could be when it charged into the enemy forces:

And with God lending us aid through the intercession of His immaculate Mother, the enemy will be routed by this triangular formation of kataphraktoi. *For the enemy's spears and pikes will be shattered by the* kataphraktoi *and their arrows will be ineffective, whereupon, the* kataphraktoi, *gaining in courage and boldness, will smash in the heads and bodies of the enemy and their horses with their iron maces and sabres, they will break into and dismember their formations and from there break through and so completely destroy them.*[68]

One of the most detailed segments of information about the late Byzantine *kataphraktoi* in the *Praecepta Militaria* provides specific information about the battle formation of the heavy cavalrymen. With unique details, such as exactly how many men should be in the formation, more is known about the battle tactics of these armoured horsemen than any other previous cataphract warrior from both Late Antiquity and the Ancient world:

> *Take note that the triangular formation of* kataphraktoi, *if there is a very large body of men, its total must be 504 men, its depth 12 men, which means that the first row of the line is 20 men, the second, 24 men, the third, 28 men, the fourth, 32 men, the fifth, 36 men, the sixth, 40 men, the seventh, 44 men, the eighth, 48 men, the ninth, 52 men, the tenth, 56 men, the eleventh, 60 men, the twelfth, 64 men, so that together the number of men in the whole formation is 504. If such a number of men is not available, this formation must become more modest, so that the first row has ten men, the second, 14 men, the third, 18 men, the fourth…and the entire total of the formation is 384 men. No matter if the contingent is larger or smaller, it is neces-sary to make the first line, that is, the front, conform to the number of the quantity of the host, just as the commander of the host sees fit or prefers. From the second row on down to the back each row must receive an additional two men on the right side and two on the left to make up the triangular formation. The* kataphraktoi *are to be under one commander with assorted officers.*[69]

Formed into their triangular wedge formation, the cataphracts used shock tactics to great effect on the battlefield. Indeed, due to their heavy armour, they were almost entirely restricted to shock attacks and nothing else, for they were much less mobile than the other Byzantine cavalrymen:

> *When [the enemy troops] do turn to flight, it is not the* kataphraktoi *who should undertake the pursuit but their two accompanying units trailing behind them. Likewise, the remaining units should move out through the intervals on both flanks to scatter the Arabitai lest they come up behind the pursuers and strike against them. Do not go chasing after the Arabitai. The commander of the army together with his four units should move out behind the two units escort-ing the* kataphraktoi *and follow them while the* kataphraktoi *take their place with the infantry units and follow the commander of the army. In case the enemy formation moves quickly and joins battle with our heavy infantry with the result that there is not enough room for the body of* kataphraktoi *to go out through the intervals, they*

must head out through the intervals on the flanks in proper forma-
tion with, as noted, the two cavalry units trailing, to annihilate and
destroy the enemy.[70]

After the death of Emperor Leo VI in 912, the Byzantine Empire was
not only wrought with internal turmoil, but also greatly threatened
by the tsar of Bulgaria, Symeon the Great (r. 893–927). Fortunately,
the Bulgarian threat was sufficiently dealt with in the early 920s until
the death of the powerful enemy ruler in 927.[71] The danger of attacks
from Symeon may have been over but the reprieve for the Eastern
Romans was short because another extremely dangerous enemy
had risen to power in the east. This new formidable adversary, Sayf
al-Dawla (meaning 'Sword of the Dynasty'), was a member of the
Hamdanid family that controlled both Aleppo and Mosul. The general already had some military successes against the Byzantines in
the late 930s , though it was not until after Sayf al-Dawla became the
emir of Aleppo (r. 945–67) that the Byzantines considered him their
true nemesis in the east. When the Arab ruler led another particularly
successful raid into Byzantine territory in 953, the new sole emperor
of the Eastern Romans, Constantine VII Porphyrogennetos (r. 945–
959), and the top Byzantine general, Bardas Phokas, had finally had
enough. Therefore, Constantine VII made sure his main military
commander had the resources necessary to raise a large army and
defeat Sayf al-Dawla.[72]

After the Byzantine general Bardas Phokas gathered his numerous
forces, he led them to face the army of Sayf al-Dawla at the Battle of
Hadat in October 954. The Byzantine army consisted of foreign mercenary troops from many different nations, which greatly impressed
their opponents, although the Arabs were arguably even more amazed
by the sight of the many *kataphraktoi* in the Byzantine forces.[73] In a
poem about the battle written for his patron, al-Mutanabbi, the court
poet of the emir, marvelled at the sight of the armoured cavalrymen
who appeared to be clothed in iron upon equally armoured mounts:

> *The enemy came at you, hauling their weapons as if they travelled*
> *on legless horses. When their ranks caught the light, their swords*
> *remained unseen, since their shirts and turbans were also made from*
> *steel.*[74]

What is particularly interesting about the Arabs being impressed by
the cataphracts of the Eastern Romans is that they had their own elite
heavy cavalrymen as well. However, it may be safe to assume that the

armoured horsemen of the Arab army were not as extensively protected as the Byzantine *kataphraktoi*. Regardless of their lighter equipment, it was armoured cavalrymen of the Arab forces who decided the
outcome of the battle, when Sayf al-Dawla led his elite mounted troops
in a powerful charge directed right at the enemy commander, Bardas
Phokas. The heavy cavalry of the Arabs managed to penetrate deep
into the Byzantine ranks and almost reached general Bardas before his
men desperately formed into a solid shield wall to defend their leader.
The loyal troops managed to save their commander's life but the devastating charge had broken the Byzantine forces, so the massive army
was routed.[75]

After his disastrous defeat against the Hamdanid forces at Hadat,
Bardas Phokas was replaced as the supreme general of the army by
his son, Nikephoros Phokas, in 955, and he turned out to be a much
greater military leader than his father. However, the change did not
bring instant success, for Sayf al-Dawla led another successful raid
into the Byzantine Empire in 956. Yet, although the Byzantines were
defeated in another battle near Tall Bitriq that same year, one major
incident in the violent encounter once again demonstrated how truly
effective the heavy cataphract armour of the Byzantines was at that
time. Even after his men had lost the battle, the commander of the
Byzantine army, John Tzimiskes, continued to fight. In the end, the
general was struck several times by his Hamdanid enemies but still
managed to survive the encounter because of his extensive armour.
The poet al-Mutanabbi was so amazed by the incident that he said it
was as if the Byzantine commander was being attacked with feathers
because his armour was so effective.[76]

Even though the Byzantine armies still lost against Sayf al-Dawla
and his men shortly after Nikephoros Phokas had become the head
commander, once he was able to firmly establish his command, and
implement his tactics and reforms to the military, the tide began to
shift in the Byzantines' favour. From 962 to 965, the Byzantine armies
under the leadership of Nikephoros won several victories against the
Hamdanid Arabs and even seized the important fortresses of Adana in
964, and Mopsuestia the following year, both located in Cilicia. It was
also in 963 that the brilliant general succeeded the previous emperor
upon his death to become the new ruler of the Byzantine Empire.
Furthermore, in the spring of that same year, Nikephoros heavily
trained and drilled his soldiers before leading them to battle. It was
most likely as this point that Nikephoros began to implement the
changes to the strategy, tactics and equipment of the overall Byzantine

military in order to conform to the guidelines that he set forth in his *Praecepta Militaria*.[77] These reforms would have included his changes to the arms, armour and tactics of the cataphracts, which would have also lead to the creation of the super-heavily armoured *klibanophoroi*, who wore even more protection than the general *kataphraktoi* troops.[78] After taking the city of Mopsuestia, it would be in the combat outside of the walls of the next major city in the campaign that the revised cataphracts of Emperor Nikephoros Phokas would be able to demonstrate how effective they truly were.

Later in 965, the Byzantine emperor focused his forces on the assault of the city of Tarsos, the capital of Cilicia, even though it was rumoured to be impregnable; the formidable defences of the regional centre were first comprised of a deep trench that surrounded the fortifications, and then there was a two-layered stone wall, filled with murder holes for archers to shoot through when the city was under attack. Furthermore, the citizens of Tarsos were very militaristic people that were fully capable of defending themselves. On the other hand, fortunately for the Byzantine cataphracts, the land surrounding the key stronghold consisted of open, level fields that were ideal for cavalry warfare. Once Nikephoros and his army reached the city, he immediately ordered his men to first construct a fortified camp and then to destroy much of the nearby countryside so that no enemy soldiers could hide behind trees or bushes and easily ambush his troops without warning. The Byzantines did not have to wait long for a response from Tarsos though, for shortly after they finished devastating the land, the Tarsians arrogantly left the protection of their city walls to face the invaders on the battlefield.[79]

The medieval chronicler, Leo the Deacon, has provided an account of the battle at Tarsos in his book, *The History*, including some information on the actions of the cataphracts in the Byzantine army. In the text of the account, Leo is the first Byzantine author to use the new Greek term *pansideroi ippótes* (πανσίδηροι ιππότες) – meaning 'ironclad knights' – to describe the *kataphraktoi*. Even though the word *kataphraktoi* remained in use in the written records of the tenth century, 'ironclad horsemen' was a term used simultaneously that effectively meant the same thing.[80] According to the Byzantine historian, when the Tarsians marched outside their city, Nikephoros and his 'ironclad horsemen' moved out to confront them:

> *The emperor himself led out from the camp the bravest and most robust soldiers, and arranged the divisions on the battlefield,*

deploying the [cataphracts] in the van, and ordering the archers and slingers to shoot at the enemy from behind. He himself took his position on the right wing, bringing with him a vast squadron of cavalrymen, while John who had the sobriquet Tzimiskes, and was honoured with the rank of doux, fought on the left…When the emperor ordered the trumpets to sound the charge, one could see the Roman divisions move into action with incredible precision, as the entire plain sparkled with the gleam of their armour. The Tarsians could not withstand such an onslaught; forced back by the thrusts of spears and by the missiles of the [archers] shooting from behind, they immediately turned to flight, and ingloriously shut themselves up in the town, after losing most of their men in this assault.[81]

The deadly charge of the terrifying ironclad cataphracts, reinforced by the volleys of arrows fired from the archers behind them, quickly overcame the Tarsians, thus, the Byzantines decisively won the battle. Even though some of the surviving citizens managed to escape back into their city, Tarsos was still captured that same year by the Byzantines, along with the seizure of the region of northern Syria. Even before Sayf al-Dawla died in 967, the Byzantines could already advance to Antioch without facing any resistance; therefore, that city also fell in 969. Without its formidable leader, the Emirate of Aleppo became a client state of the Byzantine Empire and was no longer the great threat it once was.[82]

Sayf al-Dawla and the Hamdanid Arabs may have no longer been of any concern, however, a new incredibly dangerous adversary quickly took their place for the Byzantines in 969. Initially, Emperor Nikephoros had requested the ruler of the Kiev Rus', Grand Prince Svyatoslav I (r. 945–972) to be a part of a pincer attack to subdue the Bulgarians, but the prince accepted the offer with far too much enthusiasm and completely conquered Bulgaria on his own. The conquest of the entire Bulgarian kingdom was certainly an unforeseen consequence of Nikephoros' action, which was made worse when the Byzantines soon realized they were the next targets for the highly ambitious Rus' prince and his huge army.[83] According to Leo the Deacon, Nikephoros took immediate actions in preparation for the Rus' attack, including the muster of the cataphracts: 'He began to equip the infantry, to arm the companies, to draw up the cavalry regiment in depth, and to display the [cataphracts]'.[84]

However, the Byzantine emperor was unable to witness the result of his preparations because, before the year was over, he was assassinated. Nikephoros' death left his successor, John I Tzimiskes (r. 969–976), primarily responsible for the defence of the Byzantine Empire when, shortly after, a large Rus' army invaded Thrace in the spring of 970.[85]

Since most of the Byzantine forces were still in the east following the conquest of Cilicia and the fall of Antioch, Emperor John was unable to immediately respond to the Rus' invasion himself. Therefore, the Byzantine ruler ordered two of his best generals, Bardas Skleros and Peter, to gather vital intelligence on the invasion force before his arrival. Not only was the reconnaissance mission successful, but Bardas even managed to win a spectacular victory with only 2,000–3,000 troops against a significantly larger force. The vital win had two major results that were beneficial to the Byzantines; the first was that thousands of the invaders were slain in the encounter, but even better for the empire was that it gave John sufficient time in order to gather an army that could both repel the invasion and then expel the Rus' from Bulgaria as well. By April 971, Emperor John had reached the borders of Bulgaria with possibly as many as 30,000 soldiers in his army.[86]

The Rus' were busy attempting to quell revolts in northern Bulgaria, so the Byzantine army advanced to Preslav, the capital of Bulgaria, before facing any resistance. The Rus' foot soldiers finally confronted the Byzantines outside the walls of the Bulgarian royal city.[87] In the violent encounter that resulted, both the Byzantine and Rus' warriors fought fiercely to a stalemate for some time.[88] Leo the Deacon stated that the decisive moment of the battle did not arrive until Emperor John ordered the *Athanatoi*, an elite cataphract unit from the Tagmata imperial guard, to charge the Rus' left wing:

> *When the battle was evenly balanced on both sides, at this point the emperor ordered the [Athanatoi] to attack the left wing of the [Rus'] with a charge. So they held their spears before them and violently spurred on their horses, and advanced against them. Since the [Rus'] were on foot (for they are not accustomed to fight from horseback, since they are not trained for this), they were not able to withstand the spears of the Romans, but turned to flight and shut themselves up within the walls of the town; the Romans pursued them and killed them mercilessly.*[89]

Just as at the battle outside of Tarsos, the heavily armed and armoured Byzantine *kataphraktoi* smashed through the ranks of the enemy and routed them. The Rus' foot troops were drawn up in a tight formation and even wielded enormous shields that extended down to their feet, yet this was not enough to repel the devastating charge of the cata-phracts. The victory at Preslav demonstrated just how brutally effec-tive the heavily armoured cavalrymen were against infantry who were not nearly as well armed and trained as the legionaries of the ancient Roman Empire of old. After a few more brutal fights, the Byzantines eventually expelled the Rus' from Preslav and captured the city. The surviving Rus' warriors then escaped to rejoin Grand Prince Svyatoslav and the rest of their army to the north at the stronghold of Dorostolon, located near the southern bank of the Danube River.[90]

After taking Preslav, Emperor John led his troops north towards Dorostolon and faced little to no resistance. Although a small group of Byzantine scouts ahead of the main army were successfully ambushed and killed by the Rus', this was the only minor encounter that occurred before the Byzantine army reached Dorostolon. Once the Byzantines reached the fortress, the events were similar to what happened at Tarsos, in that the emperor first ordered his men to build a fortified camp to get ready for the siege but then found the Rus' outside the defensive walls to meet the Byzantines in battle. After John made sure to leave a small contingent to guard the siege equip-ment and the supplies of the baggage train, he then led his men to face the Rus'. The ancient sources claim the Rus' army numbered as many as 60,000 men. This is definitely an exaggerated figure, though the Rus' forces did almost certainly outnumber the roughly 30,000 Byzantine soldiers.[91]

The Rus' infantrymen were drawn up in close formation again with their shields and armed with spears, though the ranks were deeper and the front extended much further than at the previous encounter outside Preslav due to the greater amount of the warriors on the battlefield, under the command of the Grand Prince. Upon seeing the densely packed lines of Rus' foot soldiers, the Byzantine emperor decided where to place his troops, including the lethal cataphracts:

> *After the emperor deployed the Romans in the van and placed [cataphracts] on both wings, and assigned the archers and sling-ers to the rear and ordered them to keep up steady fire, he led out the army.*[92]

Whereas, normally, the late Byzantine *kataphraktoi* were stationed in the centre of the army formation, John changed the common heavy cavalry tactics slightly by placing the cataphracts on both wings instead. On the other hand, the Byzantine emperor also ordered his ranged warriors to barrage the Rus' front with missiles in order to soften it up before the impact of the cataphract cavalry charge, just as at the Battle of Tarsos.

The first battle outside of Dorostolon began early in the afternoon when both sides formed up to face each other and the Rus' initiated the combat by charging straight at the Byzantine forces, ferociously screaming and shouting war cries in the process. The Byzantine soldiers not only managed to withstand the rushing mass of Rus' footmen, but also succeeded in driving their way through the enemy infantry lines in one or two locations along the front. However, in each instance, the Rus' were also able to regroup and halt the Byzantine advance with their shield walls. After over an hour of brutal combat, the troops of both sides were forced to fall back due to exhaustion, especially for the cataphracts in their heavy armour, so the warriors had a short break before the fighting vigorously began anew. The battle continued for most of the day as neither side was able to gain the upper hand. The Byzantines did manage to force the Rus' to give ground, but at the same time the imperial forces were also unable to break the enemy infantrymen and defeat them.[93] According to Leo the Deacon, it was when evening was quickly approaching that Emperor John gave the order for a decisive strike:

> *Until late afternoon victory appeared to be in the balance, as the course of battle swayed this way and that. The sun was already setting, when the emperor threw the cavalry against them in force, and bolstered the men's spirits, shouting that, since they were Romans, they should display their prowess by means of their deeds. So they pressed forward with an extraordinary assault and the trumpeters sounded the call to battle, and a shout arose from the Romans in a body. And the [Rus'] were not able to withstand their attack, and turned to flight and rushed to the fortifications, losing many of their men in this battle.[94]*

With the Byzantine infantrymen attacking the Rus' from the centre, while the cataphracts charged from both sides on the wings, the Rus' foot soldiers could not take the onslaught and were finally broken and routed.[95] The first major encounter in the field outside Dorostolon was a Byzantine victory with numerous Rus' slain, though many Rus' had also survived and escaped to the safety of the stronghold. With the Rus' back behind the fortified walls, the Byzantine siege of Dorostolon officially began.

For most of the next day, as the siege was underway, the Rus' remained inside the fortress successfully repelling the attackers. It was not until late in the day that Rus' horsemen actually left Dorostolon to attack the Byzantines, though the far-superior imperial cavalrymen were able to drive the Rus' back into the stronghold, as stated by Leo the Deacon:

> *The Romans quickly protected themselves with armour and mounted their horses, and after snatching up lances (they use very long ones in battle), they rode out against them with a vigorous and mighty charge. And since [the Rus'] did not even know how to guide their horses with reins, they were cut down by the Romans, and turned to flight and shut themselves up inside the walls.*[96]

The next day, the Byzantine forces surrounded the fortress, though Emperor John kept his men at bay for the most part in the hopes that if he slightly relented with the intensity of the siege, it might draw the Rus' outside of Dorostolon again so that the Byzantine army could crush them once again on the battlefield. The plan did not work right away, but that did not matter because the Byzantines were given a huge morale boost on the third day of the siege when the fleet arrived to blockade Dorostolon from the Danube River. Not only were the Rus' completely encircled and trapped, but the fleet also brought further reinforcements and supplies, including the devastating napalm-like weapon known as 'Greek fire'.[97]

Following the arrival of the Byzantine naval forces, the surrounded Rus' decided to face their attackers on the field another time in order to try and break the siege:

> *The next day the [Rus'] slipped out of the town and arrayed them-selves on the plain, protecting themselves with shields that reached to their feet and chainmail breastplates; and the Romans also emerged from their camp completely sheathed in armour.*[98]

In the next major encounter, the two armies fought to a stalemate again for most of the day until the Byzantine cataphracts were able to break and ultimately defeat the Rus' infantrymen once again. In his account of the battle, Leo the Deacon emphasized how much the late Byzantine *kataphraktoi* relied on their lethal maces in a description of the martial prowess of one individual cavalryman:

> *Theodore Lalakon, a man who was hard to withstand and invincible*
> *in the might and strength of his body, killed great numbers of the*
> *enemy with an iron mace; for he wielded it with such force in his*
> *arm that he would crush at the same time the helmet and the skull*
> *protected by it.*[99]

The Rus' who managed to survive the second major encounter with the cataphracts did make it back to Dorostolon; however, the Byzantines finished setting up the siege engines shortly after, so the defenders were forced to endure a continuous bombardment from then on.[100]

The Rus' attempted several times to leave the defences and destroy the siege engines, though it was futile, for they were always forced back into the fortress. The Rus' were taking heavy casualties from the missile fire of the siege engines, and in one of their sorties outside of the fortress gates they managed to kill the commander of a unit guarding the war machines; therefore, they decided to try and defeat the Byzantines in another pitched battle. With no more luck than in the previous encounters, the Rus' were, yet again, overwhelmed and defeated. The Byzantine army, with its infantry phalanx in the centre, supported by the cavalry on the wings, including the cataphracts, and the ranged troops in the rear, drove them back into Dorostolon once more. This time the victory was even better for the Byzantines though, for one of the emperor's imperial guardsmen, Anemas, managed to kill Svyatoslav's best general, Ikmor, in the combat.[101]

During the night following the battle, Grand Prince Svyatoslav and the other Rus' military commanders held a council to discuss their next actions. Many of the Rus' nobles were well aware of the fact that they were not winning the conflict; thus, they desired to end it:

> *Some advised that they should embark on their boats in the middle*
> *of the night and steal away by any means whatsoever; for they were*
> *not able to contend with [cataphracts], and besides they had lost their*
> *best warriors, who had encouraged the army and sharpened their*
> *mettle. Others counselled, on the contrary, that they should come to*
> *terms with the Romans, and receive pledges in return, and thus save*
> *the remaining army.*[102]

The Rus' were clearly terrified of the Byzantine cataphracts, though Svyatoslav and many of the warriors were unwilling to retreat or surrender. Therefore, later that same night, a group of 2,000 Rus' stealthily left Dorostolon to desperately seek food supplies along the banks of the Danube River. In the end, not only did the Rus' succeed in their mission, but they also managed to surprise and kill some unarmoured Byzantine cavalrymen who were gathering wood and watering their horses. The incident gave a much-needed boost in morale to the Rus' warriors in the stronghold, while it also infuriated Emperor John who almost executed the military officers in charge of the guard on the naval side of the siege.[103]

Following up their success the night before, in the late afternoon of the next day, on Friday, 24 July, the Rus' foot soldiers formed up on the field outside of Dorostolon in their densely packed infantry formation, armed with shields and spears. However, the Rus' tried to adapt and counter the assaults of the cataphracts and the other Byzantine cavalry on the flanks by placing foot archers on their wings. Emperor John used the same formation he had utilized before, with the cataphracts stationed behind the other Byzantine cavalrymen on the wings and the infantry phalanx in the centre, along with the ranged soldiers placed in the rear. The Byzantine Emperor then led his troops with his imperial guardsmen held in reserve behind the ranged warriors and the infantry phalanx. Even though the formations remained relatively the same, this battle was different, in that it was fought closer to the fortress than any of the other previous encounters, on a stretch of the field between woods and marshland, making the battlefield much more compact.[104] Leo the Deacon has provided an account of the initial combat:

> *Once the battle broke out, the [Rus'] stoutly attacked the Romans, harassing them with javelins and wounding their horses with arrows, and hurling their riders to the ground. At this point Anemas, who had distinguished himself the previous day by killing Ikmor, saw Svyatoslav charging the Romans in a frenzied rage and encouraging his regiments; and he spurred on his horse (for he was accustomed to doing this, and had previously killed many [Rus'] in this way), and giving the horse free rein, he rode up to him and struck him on the collarbone with his sword, and knocked him flat, but did not kill him; for he was protected by his coat of mail and the shield with which he was equipped, out of fear of the Roman spears. And although Anemas was surrounded by the [Rus'] army, and his horse was brought down by numerous spear thrusts, he killed many of the [Rus'], but then was himself killed, a man surpassed by no one his age in brave feats in battle.[105]*

The Rus' were managing to slay formidable warriors like Anemas and other Byzantine cataphracts, regardless of their heavy armour, mostly

by using the age-old tactic of targeting their horses. The infantry bowmen on the wings were also making a positive impact in the battle for
the Rus' as well. John could see that his men were both exhausted and
dehydrated, yet the violent encounter was far from over. Therefore,
the Byzantine emperor ordered the military support staff to provide
the troops with a mixture of water and wine, without disrupting the
combat taking place on the front.[106]

Eventually, Emperor John realized that he must fall back to the
more wide-open plains in order for his cataphracts to meet their true
potential on the battlefield. Therefore, the Byzantine forces made a
tactical retreat but they were severely hard-pressed by the vigorous
attacks of the Rus' at the same time. When it looked to the emperor like
his lines might break, John then entered the combat himself with his
heavily armed, elite mounted bodyguard. At first, the action instantly
rallied the Byzantine troops, but then the emperor and his elite cataphract guardsmen made an even greater impact in the battle when
they smashed into the Rus' lines. As the attack was made, a thunder-
storm began over the battlefield, which, fortunately for the Byzantines,
caused fierce winds to blow rain and dust into the faces of the Rus' warriors.[107] The coup de grace of the encounter then occurred when one of
the Byzantine commanders led his men into a devastating assault on
the flank of the Rus' army:

> When fierce fighting broke out, the [Rus'] could not withstand the
> assault of the cavalry, and were surrounded by the magistros *Bardas*,
> whose surname was Skleros (for he made the encircling movement
> with his accompanying host), and turned to flight, and were tram-
> pled right up to the city wall and fell ignobly.[108]

Once the battle was over, possibly as many as 15,000 Rus' lay dead on
the field, while the Byzantines only suffered 350 casualties.[109]

After the last major battle of Dorostolon, Svyatoslav and the Rus'
were forced to finally surrender. In exchange for the stronghold, along
with the plunder and captives the Rus' seized during the entire conflict, the Byzantines allowed the Rus' to cross the Danube River and
return home. After securing the fortress, along with the rest of eastern
Bulgaria, which was claimed by the Byzantines as a new province, the
victorious emperor then led his men back to Constantinople where a triumph was celebrated.[110] The Byzantine cataphracts were a pivotal part
of the overall success of the Bulgarian campaign against the Rus', just as
they were in the conflicts with the Hamdanid Arabs in Cilicia and Syria

during the reign of Nikephoros Phokas. However, over the next hundred years, they played an increasingly smaller role in the Byzantine
military. It is possible that the heavily armoured cavalrymen may have
continued to still be a part of the Byzantine forces of Emperor John, and
the later emperor, Basil II (r. 976–1025), against the Fatimids in Palestine
and Syria throughout the 970s and 990s. Yet, from the beginning of the
eleventh century there is much less evidence of the existence of the
Byzantine cataphracts; in fact, the term *kataphraktoi* completely fell out
of use in the medieval written record during that century.[111]
    A major reason for the gradual decline of the late Byzantine cata-
phracts from the end of the tenth to the early eleventh century was due
to a change in the type of warfare that was fought during the period.
When the Byzantine military was focused on its Arab enemies in the
east, the heavily armoured horsemen were very useful against infantry on the wide, level ground that was common in the region and was
ideal for cavalry warfare. However, in 1001, Byzantine Emperor Basil
II made peace with the Fatimid ruler, al-Hakim (r. 996–1021). With no
more great threats from the east, the focus of the Byzantine military
shifted to the west, to the Balkans were the terrain was predominantly
uneven and filled, with wooded areas, characteristics of ground very
unsuitable for cavalry warfare. Furthermore, in many border regions of
the Byzantine Empire, from Bulgaria to Antioch, the combat shifted to
a much more mobile focus, involving raids and skirmishes rather than
large, pitched battles. Evidence of this shift is located in the words of
Nikephoros Ouranos in his military treatise, *Taktika,* written c.1000.[112]
For instance, if the Byzantine mounted troops were carrying out a raid
for plunder or captives, the medieval writer recommended that the
cataphracts should be left behind:

> *He must leave the entire infantry force and the baggage train of the*
> *infantry to proceed in good order behind him and he must not leave*
> *any cavalrymen behind for the protection of the infantry save only*
> *the* kataphraktoi.[113]

On top of that statement, Ouranos even suggested that many of the
cataphracts should remove their armour so that they could claim their
share of the booty with the rest of the cavalry:

> *Forty or fifty of the* kataphraktoi *should be set apart, who will leave*
> *their heavy armour and that of their horses with the baggage train*
> *and head out with the other light horsemen.*[114]

But aside from the change in enemies, strategy and tactics, another obvious reason for the eventual fall of the Byzantine *kataphraktoi* (and certainly the reason for the disappearance of the more heavily armoured version, the *klibanophoroi*) was the same problem that the ancient Romans had probably had with the heavy horsemen: both their expensive cost to put them on the battlefield and the amount of training it took to make the mounted warriors effective in combat.[115] The final reason for the decline of the cataphracts, especially the part-time cavalrymen from the *themata*, was the growing trend throughout the period of the soldier-farmer owners of the *strateia* paying the fine instead of serving in the military. Not only did this increasingly popular practice drastically decrease the amount of thematic forces available to the Byzantine military, but so too did the largest landowners, who managed to gradually obtain the farmlands of many other minor landowners over time. Because of these two trends of the eleventh century, the Byzantine military became more and more reliant upon the Tagmata troops of the professional army and foreign mercenaries.[116] Then, after 1071 when the Byzantine Empire suffered the disastrous defeat at the Battle of Manzikert, the Eastern Romans were so devastated financially that the heavily armoured *klibanophoroi* were completely gone from their armies from then on.[117]

Byzantine armoured riders upon armoured mounts still existed after Manzikert, but they were almost exclusively in the elite imperial Tagmata units. Byzantine royalty and their horses were also still extensively protected as well. For instance, when three Norman knights attacked the Byzantine emperor Alexios I Komnenos (r. 1081–1118) with their lances at the Battle of Dyrrachium in 1081, he emerged from the incident completely unscathed, most likely because of the layers of heavy armour the emperor wore.[118] Even after the disaster at Manzikert, the economy of the Byzantine Empire improved in the twelfth century, allowing the military to supply its troops with more higher quality arms and armour than at the end of the eleventh century. Additionally, the improved finances of the empire led Emperor Manuel Komnenos (r. 1143–1180) to try to reintroduce numerous heavily armoured cavalrymen into the Byzantine armies once more. The new cataphract type of troops, however, were much more of an imitation of Western European knights than the earlier *kataphraktoi*, as shown in features such as the replacement of the old *skoutaria* with the new kite-style shields and the adoption of saddles with higher pommels and cantles that were better for lancers. However, Manuel's attempt to reestablish the prominence of the cataphracts ultimately failed, for the Byzantine type of knights fared poorly against the empire's main enemy of the period, the Turks.

In 1176, the empire was dealt another serious blow that severely weakened it when the Turks crushed the Byzantines at the Battle of Myriokephalon. Although devastated from the defeat, it was not until the havoc and destruction of the Fourth Crusade and the sack of Constantinople in 1204 that the late Byzantine cataphract truly died. From that point on, the Byzantine Empire never recovered, and even though it officially lasted until 1453, the damage caused by the Latin crusaders was so great that the sophisticated lamellar armour, which was so prized by the late Byzantine *kataphraktoi*, completely disappeared.[119] Thus, as the once great empire of the Eastern Romans became a shadow of its former self, the last heavily armoured cavalry-men called cataphracts faded from existence.

NOTES

Introduction

1. Peter Wilcox, *Rome's Enemies (3): Parthians and Sassanid Persians* (Oxford: Osprey Publishing, 1986.), p.16; Gareth C. Sampson, *The Defeat of Rome in the East: Crassus, the Parthians, and the Disastrous Battle of Carrhae, 53 BC* (Philadelphia: Casemate, 2008), pp. 114–15.
2. Plutarch, *Crassus*, 18.3.
3. Plutarch, *Crassus*, 23.6–7.
4. Plutarch, *Crassus*, 24.1.
5. Philip Sidnell, *Warhorse: Cavalry in Ancient Warfare* (London: Hambledon Continuum, 2006), pp. 86, 143–4, 148; Peter Wilcox, *Parthians and Sassanid Persians*, p. 10.
6. Edward N. Luttwak, *The Grand Strategy of the Byzantine Empire* (Cambridge: Harvard University Press, 2009), p. 277.
7. Mariusz Mielczarek, *Cataphracti and Clibanarii: Studies on the Heavy Armoured Cavalry of the Ancient World* (Officya Naukowa, 1993), pp. 44–50; Peter Wilcox, *Parthians and Sassanid Persians*, p. 10.
8. Heliodorus, Aet*hiopica*, 9.14–18.
9. Julian the Emperor, *Panegyric in Honour of the Emperor Constantinus*, Oration 1, 37C–38A.
10. Leo VI, *The Taktika*, 6.9–39.
11. Leo VI, *The Taktika*, 6.40–55.
12. Leo VI, *The Taktika*, 6.56–68.

Chapter 1: Origins of the Cataphracts

1. Ann Hyland, *The Horse in the Ancient World* (Westport: Praeger Publishers, 2003), p. 3–4.
2. Christoph Baumer, *The History of Central Asia: The Age of the Steppe Warrior* (London: I.B. Tauris, 2012), pp. 83–4.
3. Sidnell, *Warhorse*, pp. 1–2.
4. Baumer, *Age of the Steppe Warrior*, p. 84.
5. Sidnell, *Warhorse*, p. 2.
6. Baumer, *Age of the Steppe Warrior*, p. 84.
7. Ann Hyland, *The Horse in the Ancient World*, pp. 8–9.
8. Sidnell, *Warhorse*, pp. 5–6.

9. Baumer, *Age of the Steppe Warrior*, p. 84.
10. Sidnell, *Warhorse*, p. 14.
11. Baumer, *Age of the Steppe Warrior* , pp. 84–85.
12. Baumer, *Age of the Steppe Warrior* , p. 85.
13. Sidnell, *Warhorse*, p. 14.
14. Sidnell, *Warhorse*, pp. 7, 12–13.
15. Sidnell, *Warhorse*, p.13.
16. Arthur Cotterell, *Chariot: From Chariot to Tank, the Astounding Rise and Fall of the World's First War Machine* (New York: The Overlook Press, 2004), p. 83.
17. Mark Healy, *The Ancient Assyrians* (Oxford: Osprey Publishing, 1991), pp. 3–5.
18. Healy, *The Ancient Assyrians*, p. 20; Sidnell, *Warhorse*, p. 7.
19. Healy, *The Ancient Assyrians*, p. 20.
20. Sidnell, *Warhorse*, p. 14–15; Baumer, *Age of the Steppe Warrior*, p. 85.
21. Sidnell, *Warhorse*, p.15.
22. Healy, *The Ancient Assyrians*, pp. 20–21.
23. Healy, *The Ancient Assyrians*, pp. 3, 21.
24. Baumer, *Age of the Steppe Warrior*, pp. 224–6.
25. Baumer, *Age of the Steppe Warrior*, p. 226.
26. Baumer, *Age of the Steppe Warrior*, p. 227; E.V. Cernenko, *Scythians 700–300 B.C.* (Oxford: Osprey Publishing, 1983), pp. 5, 7.
27. Cernenko, *Scythians*, p. 7.
28. Baumer, *Age of the Steppe Warrior*, p. 227.
29. Baumer, *Age of the Steppe Warrior*, pp. 228.
30. Baumer, *Age of the Steppe Warrior*, pp. 232–3.
31. Cernenko, *Scythians*, p. 7.
32. Cernenko, *Scythians*, pp. 7–8, 36.
33. Cernenko, *Scythians*, pp. 7–8, 11.
34. Cernenko, *Scythians*, pp. 8, 17, 35–6.
35. Baumer, *Age of the Steppe Warrior*, pp. 174, 199; D. T. Potts, 'Cataphractus and kamāndār: Some Thoughts on the Dynamic Evolution of Heavy Cavalry and Mounted Archers in Iran and Central Asia', *Bulletin of the Asia Institute*, New Series, Vol. 21 (2007), pp. 152, 155.
36. *Age of the Steppe Warrior*, pp. 199–200.
37. Potts, 'Cataphractus and kamāndār', p. 152.
38. Herodotus, *The Histories*, 1.215.
39. Richard Brzezinski and Mariusz Mielczarek, *The Sarmatians 600 BC–AD 450* (Oxford: Osprey Publishing, 2002), p. 16.
40. Sidnell, *Warhorse*, pp. 87–8.
41. *The Age of the Steppe Warrior*, p. 197.
42. *The Age of the Steppe Warrior*, pp. 199–203.
43. Nick Sekunda, *The Persian Army 560–330 BC* (Oxford: Osprey Publishing, 1992), p. 22.

44. Sekunda, *The Persian Army*, pp. 22–3, 25.
45. Nick Sekunda, *The Persian Army*, p. 54; Hyland, *The Horse in the Ancient World*, p. 30; Sidnell, *Warhorse*, p. 86.
46. Arrian, *Anabasis of Alexander*, 7.13.1.
47. Hyland, *The Horse in the Ancient World*, p. 30.
48. Philip Sidnell, *Warhorse*, p. 86.
49. Sekunda, *The Persian Army*, p. 25.
50. Sekunda, *The Persian Army*, p. 25.
51. Xenophon, *On Horsemanship*, 12.
52. Xenophon, *On Horsemanship*, 12.
53. Xenophon, *On Horsemanship*, 12.
54. Sekunda, *The Persian Army*, pp. 26–9.
55. Sidnell, *Warhorse*, pp. 89, 93–5.
56. Arrian, *Anabasis of Alexander*, 1.15.
57. Sidnell, *Warhorse*, pp. 80–85.
58. Sidnell, *Warhorse*, pp. 96–8.
59. Sidnell, *Warhorse*, pp. 99–102.
60. Quintus Curtius Rufus, *History of Alexander,* 3.11.
61. Sidnell, *Warhorse*, pp. 103–4.
62. Arrian, *Anabasis of Alexander*, 2.11.
63. Sidnell, *Warhorse*, pp. 105–6.
64. Diodorus Siculus, *Universal History*, 17.53.
65. Quintus Curtius Rufus, *History of Alexander,* 4.9.
66. Quintus Curtius Rufus, *History of Alexander,* 4.9.
67. Sidnell, *Warhorse,* pp. 105–8.
68. Sidnell, *Warhorse,* pp. 108–9, based on the accounts of Arrian and Quintus Curtius Rufus.
69. Sidnell, *Warhorse*, pp. 110–11.
70. Arrian, *Anabasis of Alexander*, 3.13.
71. Sidnell, *Warhorse*, pp. 111–12.
72. Sidnell, *Warhorse*, pp. 112–13.
73. Sidnell, *Warhorse*, pp. 113–114.
74. Vesta Sarkhosh Curtis, 'The Iranian Revival in the Parthian Period', in *The Age of the Parthians: The Idea of Iran Volume II*, edited by Vesta Sarkhosh Curtis and Sarah Stewart (London: I.B. Tauris, 2007), p. 7.

Chapter 2: The First Cataphracts

1. John D. Grainger, *The Rise of the Seleukid Empire (323–223 BC): Seleukos I to Seleukos III* (Barnsley: Pen & Sword, 2014), p. 200.
2. John D. Grainger, *The Seleukid Empire of Antiochus III (223–187 BC)* (Barnsley: Pen & Sword, 2015), pp. 55, 62, 66.
3. Grainger, *Seleukid Empire of Antiochus III*, pp. 67–9.
4. Grainger, *Seleukid Empire of Antiochus III*, pp. 70–2.
5. Grainger, *Seleukid Empire of Antiochus III*, p. 71.

6. Grainger, *Seleukid Empire of Antiochus III* , pp. 101–2, 106–7; Bezalel Bar-Kochva, *The Seleucid Army: Organization and Tactics in the Great Campaigns* (Cambridge: Cambridge University Press, 1976), p. 146.
7. Bar-Kochva, *Seleucid Army*, p.146.
8. Grainger, *Seleukid Empire of Antiochus III*, p. 109–10; Bar-Kochva, *Seleucid Army*, p. 150–152.
9. Polybius, *Histories*, 16.18.
10. Mielczarek, *Cataphracti and Clibanarii*, p. 68.
11. Grainger, *Seleukid Empire of Antiochus III*, p. 110.
12. Bezalel Bar-Kochva, *Seleucid Army*, p. 153.
13. Grainger, *Seleukid Empire of Antiochus III*, p. 110.
14. Polybius, *Histories*, 16.18.
15. Grainger, *Seleukid Empire of Antiochus III*, pp. 110, 112–14; Bar-Kochva, *Seleucid Army*, p. 156.
16. Grainger, *Seleukid Empire of Antiochus III* , p. 115.
17. Livy, *The History of Rome*, 35.48.3.
18. Plutarch, *Moralia*, 197C.
19. Grainger, *Seleukid Empire of Antiochus III* , pp. 180–181; Bar-Kochva, *Seleucid Army*, pp. 165–7.
20. Livy, *History of Rome*, 37.40.
21. Livy, *History of Rome*, 37.40.
22. Livy, *History of Rome*, 37.42.7.
23. Appian, *The Syrian Wars*, 34.
24. Grainger, *Seleukid Empire of Antiochus III*, pp. 181–2; Bar-Kochva, *Seleucid Army*, pp. 170.
25. Grainger, *Seleukid Empire of Antiochus III*, p. 182.
26. Livy, *History of Rome*, 37.42.1–2.
27. Appian, *Syrian Wars*, 33.
28. Appian, *Syrian Wars*, 34.
29. Grainger, *Seleukid Empire of Antiochus III*, p. 182.
30. Sidnell, *Warhorse*, p. 143; Nick Sekunda, *The Seleucid and Ptolemaic Reformed Armies, 168–145 BC (v. 1): The Seleucid Army* (Montvert, 1994), p. 21.
31. Mielczarek, *Cataphracti and Clibanarii*, pp. 69–71; Sekunda, *Seleucid Army*, p. 21.
32. Sidnell, *Warhorse*, pp. 143–4; Mielczarek, *Cataphracti and Clibanarii*, p. 72; Wilcox, *Parthians and Sassanid Persians* , p. 10; Sekunda, *Seleucid Army*, p. 21.
33. In *Warhorse* (pp. 143–4), Sidnell makes the argument that in Livy's description of the Battle of Magnesia in 190 BC, when he writes about the cataphracts and states, 'On the right…3,000 cavalry in breastplates – *cataphracti* is the name for them…On the left… 3,000 *cataphracti* and 1,000 other cavalry, the royal squadron, with lighter protection for riders and their mounts but in their other equipment not unlike the *cataphracti*'

(Livy, *History of Rome*, 37.40), the ancient writer is implying that the cataphracts were equipped with further armour.

34. Sidnell, *Warhorse*, pp. 143–4; Wilcox, *Parthians and Sassanid Persians*, p.10; Sekunda, *Seleucid Army*, p. 76.
35. Sekunda, *Seleucid Army*, p. 21.
36. Bar-Kochva, *Seleucid Army*, p. 74; Mielczarek, *Cataphracti and Clibanarii*, p. 69.
37. Nick Sekunda, *Seleucid Army*, p. 21.
38. Polybius, *Histories*, 31.3.
39. Sekunda, *Seleucid Army*, pp. 12, 21.
40. Wilcox, *Parthians and Sassanid Persians*, p. 14.
41. M. Chahin, *The Kingdom of Armenia: A History* (Richmond: Curzon Press, 2001), p. 197–198.
42. Asclepiodotus, *Tactica*, 1.3.
43. Chahin, *Kingdom of Armenia*, pp. 182–3, 188–90, 193.
44. Chahin, *Kingdom of Armenia*, pp. 197–9.
45. Strabo, *Geography*, 11.4.4.
46. Valerii P. Nikonorov, 'Cataphracti, Catafractarii and Clibanarii: Another Look at the Old Problem of their Identifications', in *Voennaia arkheologiia: Oruzhie i voennoe delo v istoricheskoi i sotsial.noi perspektive* (Military Archaeology: Weaponry and Warfare in the Historical and Social Perspective), St. Petersburg (1998), p. 131.
47. Sidnell, *Warhorse*, p. 217; Chahin, *Kingdom of Armenia*, p. 201.
48. Plutarch, *Moralia*, 203A.
49. Sidnell, *Warhorse*, p. 217.
50. Plutarch, *Life of Lucullus*, 26.6.
51. Chahin, *Kingdom of Armenia*, p. 201.
52. Plutarch, *Lucullus*, 27.6.
53. Plutarch, *Lucullus*, 28.2–4.
54. Eutropius, *Breviarium*, 9.1.
55. Festus, *Breviarium*, 15.3.
56. Plutarch, *Lucullus,* 37.3.
57. Rose Mary Sheldon, *Rome's Wars in Parthia: Blood in the Sand* (London: Vallentine Mitchell, 2010), p. 18.

Chapter 3: The Parthian Cataphracts

1. Sampson, *Defeat of Rome*, p. 107.
2. Plutarch, *Crassus*, 24.3–4.
3. Sampson, *Defeat of Rome*, pp. 128–9.
4. Plutarch, *Crassus*, 25.4–8.
5. Cassius Dio, *Roman History*, 40.22.2–3.
6. Sampson, *Defeat of Rome*, p. 130.
7. Sampson, *Defeat of Rome*, p. 132–3.
8. Plutarch, *Crassus*, 27.1–2.

9. Sampson, *Defeat of Rome*, pp. 134–5.
10. Sampson, *Defeat of Rome*, p. 145.
11. Wilcox, *Parthians and Sassanid Persians*, p. 10; Mielczarek, *Cataphracti and Clibanarii*, pp. 57–9; Sidnell, *Warhorse*, p. 238.
12. Wilcox, *Parthians and Sassanid Persians*, p. 10; Mielczarek, *Cataphracti and Clibanarii*, p. 61; Sidnell, *Warhorse*, p. 238.
13. Cassius Dio, *Roman History*, 40.24.1.
14. Cassius Dio, *Roman History*, 40.15.2.
15. Wilcox, *Parthians and Sassanid Persians*, p. 10; Mielczarek, *Cataphracti and Clibanarii*, p. 59.
16. Mielczarek, *Cataphracti and Clibanarii*, pp. 53–6.
17. Sheldon, *Rome's Wars in Parthia*, pp. 55, 57.
18. Sheldon, *Rome's Wars in Parthia*, pp. 57–58.
19. Sheldon, *Rome's Wars in Parthia*, p. 58.
20. Richard Alston, *Rome's Revolution: Death of the Republic and Birth of the Empire* (Oxford: Oxford University Press, 2015), pp. 184–5.
21. Sheldon, *Rome's Wars in Parthia*, p. 58.
22. Sheldon, *Rome's Wars in Parthia*, p. 59–60.
23. Cassius Dio, *Roman History*, 49.20.1–2.
24. Sheldon, *Blood in the Sand*, p. 60.
25. Sheldon, *Rome's Wars in Parthia*, p. 65.
26. Sheldon, *Rome's Wars in Parthia*, pp. 65–6; Alston, *Rome's Revolution*, p. 186.
27. Sheldon, *Rome's Wars in Parthia*, p. 67; Alston, *Rome's Revolution*, p. 186.
28. Cassius Dio, *Roman History*, 49.26.2.
29. Sheldon, *Rome's Wars in Parthia*, pp. 67, 69–73.
30. Sheldon, *Rome's Wars in Parthia*, pp. 73–4.
31. Wilcox, *Parthians and Sassanid Persians*, p. 23.
32. Propertius, *The Elegies*, 3.12.12.
33. Wilcox, *Parthians and Sassanid Persians*. p. 23.
34. Sheldon, *Rome's Wars in Parthia*, p. 125–6.
35. Sheldon, *Rome's Wars in Parthia*, pp. 129, 132–3, 135, 137–8.
36. Sheldon, *Rome's Wars in Parthia*, pp. 138–40.
37. Sheldon, *Rome's Wars in Parthia*, pp. 140–43.
38. Mielczarek, *Cataphracti and Clibanarii*, p. 73.
39. Nazarius, *Panegyric of Constantine*, 24.6–24.
40. Sheldon, *Rome's Wars in Parthia*, pp. 155–6.
41. Sheldon, *Rome's Wars in Parthia*, pp. 157, 159–60.
42. Sheldon, *Rome's Wars in Parthia*, pp. 160–61.
43. Wilcox, *Parthians and Sassanid Persians*, pp. 23–4.
44. Sheldon, *Rome's Wars in Parthia*, pp. 171–2.
45. Sheldon, *Rome's Wars in Parthia*, pp. 172–4.
46. Herodian, *History of the Roman Empire*, pp. 4.14.3.

47. Sheldon, *Rome's Wars in Parthia*, p. 174.
48. Herodian, *History of the Roman Empire*, p. 4.15.2–3.
49. Sheldon, *Rome's Wars in Parthia*, p. 174.
50. Sheldon, *Rome's Wars in Parthia*, pp. 174–5.
51. Sheldon, *Rome's Wars in Parthia*, pp. 175–7.

Chapter 4: Cataphracts of the Minor Kingdoms

1. Baumer, *Age of the Steppe Warrior*, pp. 253–4.
2. Brzezinski and Mielczarek, *Sarmatians*, pp. 16–17.
3. Brzezinski and Mielczarek, *Sarmatians*, p. 21.
4. Strabo, *Geography*, 7.3.17.
5. Brzezinski and Mielczarek, *Sarmatians*, pp. 20–21.
6. Brzezinski and Mielczarek, *Sarmatians*, pp. 17, 21–2.
7. Brzezinski and Mielczarek, *Sarmatians*, p. 22.
8. Brzezinski and Mielczarek, *Sarmatians*, p. 37.
9. Brzezinski and Mielczarek, *Sarmatians*, pp. 23–4.
10. The term *'contus sarmaticus'* was even used in non-Sarmatian contexts by Roman writers, such as in the poems of Silus Italicus, *Punica* 15.684–5 and Statius, *Achilleid* 2.132–4.
11. Brzezinski and Mielczarek, *Sarmatians*, p. 24. The differences between the Sarmatian lancers and the cataphracts is specifically stressed by Mielczarek in *Cataphracti and Clibanarii*, pp. 95–102, and (with Brzezinski) *Sarmatians*, pp. 16–19.
12. Brzezinski and Mielczarek, *Sarmatians*, p. 17.
13. Tacitus, *The History*, 1.79.
14. Sidnell, *Warhorse*, p. 263.
15. Sidnell, *Warhorse*, pp. 271–2.
16. Cassius Dio, *Roman History*, 72.16.
17. Brzezinski and Mielczarek, *Sarmatians* , pp. 40–41.
18. Wilcox, *Parthians and Sassanid Persians*, pp. 43–4.
19. Mielczarek, *Cataphracti and Clibanarii*, p. 86.
20. Mariusz Mielczarek, *Cataphracti and Clibanarii*, p. 87.
21. Kaveh Farrokh, *Sassanian Elite Cavalry, AD 224-642* (Oxford: Osprey Publishing, 2005), p. 46.
22. Farrokh, *Sassanian Elite Cavalry*, p. 46.
23. Sidnell, *Warhorse* , pp. 275–6.
24. Sidnell, *Warhorse*, pp. 276–7.
25. Zosimus, *New History*, 1.45.
26. Festus, *Breviarium*, 24.1.
27. Sidnell, *Warhorse*, pp. 277–8.
28. Sidnell, *Warhorse*, p. 278.
29. Sidnell, *Warhorse*, p. 278.

Chapter 5: The Sassanian Persian Cataphracts and *Clibanarii*

1. Touraj Daryaee, *Sasanian Iran (224–651 CE): Portrait of a Late Antique Empire* (Costa Mesa: Mazda Publishers Inc, 2008), pp. 13–14, 19–20; Wilcox, *Parthians and Sassanid Persians*, p. 36.
2. Wilcox, *Parthians and Sassanid Persians*, p. 34.
3. Nikonorov, 'Cataphracti, Catafractarii and Clibanarii', in *Military Archaeology* (1998), p. 132.
4. Nikonorov, 'Cataphracti, Catafractarii and Clibanarii', in *Military Archaeology* (1998), p. 132.
5. Ammianus Marcellinus, *Rerum Gestarum*, 16.10.8.
6. In his article, 'Cataphracti, Catafractarii and Clibanarii', Nikonorov has provided concise summaries of the scholarly work written on the subject, including experts such as Eadie, Gamber, Hoffmann, Rostovtzeff, Speidel, Michalak, Mielczarek, etc.
7. Farrokh, *Sassanian Elite Cavalry*, pp. 9–11, 61.
8. Farrokh, *Sassanian Elite Cavalry*, pp. 9–10.
9. Farrokh, *Sassanian Elite Cavalry*, pp. 10–11; Wilcox, *Parthians and Sassanid Persians*, pp. 33–4, 44, 47; Mielczarek, *Cataphracti and Clibanarii*, pp. 65–6.
10. Farrokh, *Sassanian Elite Cavalry*, pp. 16–17; Mielczarek, *Cataphracti and Clibanarii*, pp. 65–7.
11. Farrokh, *Sassanian Elite Cavalry*, pp. 16, 35.
12. Farrokh, *Sassanian Elite Cavalry*, pp. 15–16; Mielczarek, *Cataphracti and Clibanarii*, p. 67.
13. Farrokh, *Sassanian Elite Cavalry*, pp. 18–19; Wilcox, *Parthians and Sassanid Persians*, pp. 34, 44, 47.
14. Farrokh, *Sassanian Elite Cavalry*, pp. 13–15.
15. Farrokh, *Sassanian Elite Cavalry*, p. 14.
16. Wilcox, *Parthians and Sassanid Persians*, pp. 35, 44, 47; Mielczarek, *Cataphracti and Clibanarii*, p. 67.
17. Farrokh, *Sassanian Elite Cavalry*, pp. 11–12.
18. Farrokh, *Sassanian Elite Cavalry*, p. 12.
19. Farrokh, *Sassanian Elite Cavalry*, pp. 12–13.
20. Farrokh, *Sassanian Elite Cavalry*, pp. 12–14.
21. Farrokh, *Sassanian Elite Cavalry*, pp. 13, 18; Mielczarek, *Cataphracti and Clibanarii*, p. 67.
22. Farrokh, *Sassanian Elite Cavalry*, pp. 17–18.
23. Scriptores Historiae Augustae, *Alexander Severus*, 56.5.
24. Wilcox, *Parthians and Sassanid Persians*, p. 36.
25. Farrokh, *Sassanian Elite Cavalry*, pp. 44–5.
26. Farrokh, *Sassanian Elite Cavalry*, pp. 44, 46.
27. Ammianus Marcellinus, *Rerum Gestarum*, 18.8.7.
28. Ammianus Marcellinus, *Rerum Gestarum*, 19.7.4.
29. Touraj Daryaee, *Sasanian Iran*, pp. 47, 49.

30. Ammianus Marcellinus, *Rerum Gestarum*, 20.7.2.
31. Farrokh, *Sassanian Elite Cavalry*, p. 47.
32. Farrokh, *Sassanian Elite Cavalry*, pp. 47–8.
33. Farrokh, *Sassanian Elite Cavalry*, pp. 48, 50.
34. Wilcox, *Parthians and Sassanid Persians*, p. 38.
35. Ammianus Marcellinus, *Rerum Gestarum*, 24.6.8.
36. Wilcox, *Parthians and Sassanid Persians*, p. 38.
37. Ammianus Marcellinus, *Rerum Gestarum*, 25.1.12–13.
38. Farrokh, *Sassanian Elite Cavalry*, pp. 48–9; Wilcox, *Parthians and Sassanid Persians*, p. 38.
39. Farrokh, *Sassanian Elite Cavalry*, p. 49.
40. Farrokh, *Sassanian Elite Cavalry*, p. 50.
41. Ammianus Marcellinus, *Rerum Gestarum*, 25.3.4
42. Farrokh, *Sassanian Elite Cavalry*, p. 50.
43. Ammianus Marcellinus, *Rerum Gestarum*, 25.6.2
44. Farrokh, *Sassanian Elite Cavalry*, p. 50.
45. Ammianus Marcellinus, *Rerum Gestarum*, 29.1.1
46. Farrokh, *Sassanian Elite Cavalry*, p. 52–53; Wilcox, *Parthians and Sassanid Persians*, pp. 38–9.
47. Farrokh, *Sassanian Elite Cavalry*, p. 50–51.
48. Farrokh, *Sassanian Elite Cavalry*, p. 50–51.
49. Farrokh, *Sassanian Elite Cavalry*, p. 51–52.
50. Farrokh, *Sassanian Elite Cavalry*, p. 53.
51. Maurice, *Strategikon*, 11.1.
52. Maurice, *Strategikon*, 11.1.
53. Maurice, *Strategikon*, 11.1.
54. Farrokh, *Sassanian Elite Cavalry*, p. 54.
55. Farrokh, *Sassanian Elite Cavalry*, pp. 53–4.
56. Farrokh, *Sassanian Elite Cavalry*, pp. 55–6.
57. Farrokh, *Sassanian Elite Cavalry*, pp. 57.

Chapter 6: Imperial Roman *Cataphracti, Cataphractarii* and *Clibanarii*

1. *CIL* XI, 5632.
2. Mielczarek, *Cataphracti and Clibanarii*, p.73.
3. Flavius Josephus, *The Wars of the Jews*, 3.253.
4. Sidnell, *Warhorse*, pp. 268–9.
5. Sidnell, *Warhorse*, pp. 262, 269.
6. Aelian, *Tactics,* pp. 2.12–13.
7. Arrian, *Ars Tactica*, 4.1.
8. Philip Sidnell, *Warhorse*, pp. 268–9.
9. Simon MacDowall, *Late Roman Cavalryman AD 236–565* (Oxford: Osprey Publishing, 1995), pp. 18, 52; Sidnell, *Warhorse*, p. 268.
10. Mielczarek, *Cataphracti and Clibanarii*, p. 81.

11. MacDowall, *Late Roman Cavalryman AD 236–565*, pp. 18, 52, 54; Mielczarek, *Cataphracti and Clibanarii*, pp. 80, 82.
12. Mielczarek, *Cataphracti and Clibanarii*, p. 75.
13. Herodian, *History of the Roman Empire*, 8.1.3.
14. Mielczarek, *Cataphracti and Clibanarii*, p. 75; John W. Eadie, 'The Development of Roman Mailed Cavalry', in *The Journal of Roman Studies*, 57 (1967), p. 168.
15. Nikonorov, 'Cataphracti, Catafractarii and Clibanarii', in *Military Archaeology* (1998), pp. 132, 137.
16. Mielczarek, *Cataphracti and Clibanarii*, pp. 75–6.
17. Scriptores Historiae Augustae, *Divus Claudius*, 16.2–3.
18. Scriptores Historiae Augustae, *Divus Aurelianus*, 11.4.
19. Sidnell, *Warhorse*, p. 280.
20. Scriptores Historiae Augustae, *Divus Aurelianus*, 34.4.
21. Nikonorov, 'Cataphracti, Catafractarii and Clibanarii', in *Military Archaeology* (1998), p. 132.
22. Nikonorov, 'Cataphracti, Catafractarii and Clibanarii', in *Military Archaeology* (1998), pp. 132, 137.
23. MacDowall, *Late Roman Cavalryman*, p. 19.
24. MacDowall, *Late Roman Cavalryman*, pp. 18–19. See also, *Ambianenses: CIL* XIII, 3493, 3495; *Pictavenses: CIL* III, 14406a.
25. Eadie, 'Development of Roman Mailed Cavalry', in *JRS* 57 (1967), p.168. The three stelae are *CIL* XIII, 3493, 3495, 6238.
26. Nikonorov, 'Cataphracti, Catafractarii and Clibanarii', in *Military Archaeology* (1998), pp. 132, 136–7.
27. Nikonorov, 'Cataphracti, Catafractarii and Clibanarii', in *Military Archaeology* (1998), p. 132.
28. Nikonorov, 'Cataphracti, Catafractarii and Clibanarii', in *Military Archaeology* (1998), p.137; MacDowall, *Late Roman Cavalryman*, pp. 19–20.
29. MacDowall, *Late Roman Cavalryman*, pp. 19, 54; Mielczarek, *Cataphracti and Clibanarii*, p. 81.
30. Stephen Mitchell, *A History of the Later Roman Empire AD 284–641: The Transformation of the Ancient World* (Oxford: Blackwell Publishing, 2007), p. 62.
31. Nazarius, *Panegyric of Constantine*, 22.3–24.6.
32. Julian the Emperor, *The Heroic Deeds of the Emperor Constantius, or on Kingship, Oration II*, 57B-C.
33. Libanius, *Funeral Oration upon the Emperor Julian*, pp. 186–7.
34. Mitchell, *Later Roman Empire*, p. 70.
35. Julian the Emperor, *Panegyric in Honour of the Emperor Constantius, Oration I*, 37A.
36. Mitchell, *Later Roman Empire*, p. 70.
37. Eadie, 'Development of Roman Mailed Cavalry', *JRS* 57 (1967), p. 172.
38. David Nicolle, *Romano-Byzantine Armies, 4th–9th Centuries* (Oxford: Osprey Publishing, 1992), p. 39.

39. Libanius, *Funeral Oration upon the Emperor Julian,* p. 134.
40. Ammianus Marcellinus, *Rerum Gestarum,* 16.2.5–6.
41. Nikonorov, 'Cataphracti, Catafractarii and Clibanarii', in *Military Archaeology* (1998), p. 137.
42. Ammianus Marcellinus, *Rerum Gestarum,* 16.12.7.
43. Sidnell, *Warhorse,* pp. 283–4; Mitchell, *Later Roman Empire,* pp. 74–5.
44. Ammianus Marcellinus, *Rerum Gestarum,* 16.12.22.
45. Sidnell, *Warhorse,* p. 284.
46. Sidnell, *Warhorse,* p. 284.
47. Ammianus Marcellinus, *Rerum Gestarum,* 16.12.38.
48. Sidnell, *Warhorse,* pp. 284–5.
49. Ammianus Marcellinus, *Rerum Gestarum,* 16.12.63.
50. Ammianus Marcellinus, *Rerum Gestarum,* 28.5.6–7.
51. Nikonorov, 'Cataphracti, Catafractarii and Clibanarii', in *Military Archaeology* (1998), p. 132.
52. Mielczarek, *Cataphracti and Clibanarii,* p. 77; Eadie, 'Development of Roman Mailed Cavalry', in *JRS* 57 (1967), pp. 169, 171.
53. Mielczarek, *Cataphracti and Clibanarii,* p. 78; Eadie, 'Development of Roman Mailed Cavalry', *JRS* 57 (1967), p. 168.
54. Mielczarek, *Cataphracti and Clibanarii,* pp. 78–9.
55. Mielczarek, *Cataphracti and Clibanarii,* p. 79.
56. Claudius Claudianus, *In Rufinum,* 2.353–365.
57. Claudius Claudianus, *Panegyricus de Sexto Consulatu Honorii Augusti,* 1.564–577.
58. Nicolle, *Romano-Byzantine Armies,* p. 39–40.
59. Vegetius, *De Re Militari,* 3.
60. Vegetius, *De Re Militari,* 3.24.
61. Vegetius, *De Re Militari,* 3.23.
62. Macdowall, *Adrianople AD 378: The Goths Crush Rome's Legions* (Westport: Praeger Publishers, 2005), p. 21.
63. Stephen Mitchell, *Later Roman Empire,* pp. 94, 115–16.

Chapter 7: The Byzantine *Kataphraktoi* and *Clibanarii*

1. Timothy E. Gregory, *A History of Byzantium* (Malden: Wiley-Blackwell, 2010), p. 61–63.
2. Eric McGeer, *Sowing the Dragon's Teeth: Byzantine Warfare in the Tenth Century* (Washington, D.C.: Dumbarton Oaks, 1995), p. 211.
3. Nicolle, *Romano-Byzantine Armies,* p. 6–7.
4. John Haldon, *The Byzantine Wars: Battles and Campaigns of the Byzantine Era* (Stroud: Tempus, 2001), p. 24.
5. Nicolle, *Romano-Byzantine Armies,* p. 40.
6. Haldon, *Byzantine Wars,* pp. 42, 53.
7. Maurice, *Strategikon,* 1.2.

8. Maurice, *Strategikon*, 1.2.
9. Maurice, *Strategikon*, 1.2.
10. Maurice, *Strategikon*, 1.2.
11. Luttwak, *Grand Strategy of the Byzantine Empire*, p. 278.
12. Haldon, *Byzantine Wars*, pp. 26–27.
13. Maurice, *Strategikon*, 1.2.
14. Maurice, *Strategikon*, 1.2.
15. Luttwak, *Grand Strategy of the Byzantine Empire*, pp. 277–8.
16. Mark-Anthony Karantabias, 'The Crucial Development of Heavy Cavalry under Herakleios and His Usage of Steppe Nomad Tactics', in *Hirundo: The McGill Journal of Classical Studies* 4 (2005–2006), pp. 30–32.
17. Karantabias, 'Crucial Development of Heavy Cavalry under Herakleios', in *Hirundo* 4 (2005–2006), p. 30.
18. Farrokh, *Sassanian Elite Cavalry*, p. 56.
19. Karantabias, 'Crucial Development of Heavy Cavalry under Herakleios', in *Hirundo* 4 (2005–2006), pp. 30–31.
20. Karantabias, 'Crucial Development of Heavy Cavalry under Herakleios', in *Hirundo* 4 (2005–2006), pp. 32, 34–5.
21. Theophanes, Chronicle, 318.25–28.
22. Karantabias, 'Crucial Development of Heavy Cavalry under Herakleios', in *Hirundo* 4 (2005–2006), pp. 35–6.
23. Karantabias, 'Crucial Development of Heavy Cavalry under Herakleios', in *Hirundo* 4 (2005–2006), pp. 37–9.
24. Gregory, *A History of Byzantium* (Malden: Wiley-Blackwell, 2010), pp. 176, 182.
25. Nikonorov, 'Cataphracti, Catafractarii and Clibanarii', in *Military Archaeology* (1998), p. 137.
26. Nicolle, *Romano-Byzantine Armies*, pp. 45–6.
27. Ian Heath, *Byzantine Armies 886–1118* (Oxford: Osprey Publishing, 1979), p. 18.
28. Nikonorov, 'Cataphracti, Catafractarii and Clibanarii', in *Military Archaeology* (1998), p. 137.
29. Timothy Dawson, *Byzantine Cavalryman C. 900–1204* (Oxford: Osprey Publishing, 2009), pp. 34–6.
30. Nikephoros Phokas, *Praecepta Militaria*, 3.34–37.
31. Dawson, *Byzantine Cavalryman*, pp. 34–6, 61.
32. Heath, *Byzantine Armies*, p. 35.
33. Dawson, *Byzantine Cavalryman*, pp. 37–8.
34. Nikephoros Phokas, *Praecepta Militaria*, 3.26–33.
35. Dawson, *Byzantine Cavalryman*, pp. 37–8.
36. Dawson, *Byzantine Cavalryman*, p. 38.
37. Dawson, *Byzantine Cavalryman*, pp. 34, 38, 61.
38. Dawson, *Byzantine Cavalryman*, p. 38.
39. Heath, *Byzantine Armies*, p. 36.

40. McGeer, *Sowing the Dragon's Teeth*, p. 217; Raffaele D'Amato, *Byzantine Imperial Guardsmen 913–1025: The Tághmata and Imperial Guard* (Oxford: Osprey Publishing, 2012), p. 15.
41. Dawson, *Byzantine Cavalryman*, pp. 42–4; Heath, *Byzantine Armies*, p. 36.
42. Nikephoros Phokas, *Praecepta Militaria*, 3.37–45.
43. Dawson, *Byzantine Cavalryman*, pp. 42–4; Heath, *Byzantine Armies*, p. 36.
44. Nikephoros Phokas, *Praecepta Militaria*, 3.45–46.
45. Dawson, *Byzantine Cavalryman*, p. 36.
46. Heath, *Byzantine Armies*, p. 8.
47. D'Amato, *Byzantine Imperial Guardsmen*, p. 46.
48. Dawson, *Byzantine Cavalryman*, pp. 34–6; Heath, *Byzantine Armies*, p. 8.
49. Heath, *Byzantine Armies*, p. 10, pp. 34–5.
50. Nikephoros Phokas, *Praecepta Militaria*, 3.46–53.
51. Heath, *Byzantine Armies*, pp. 10, 34–35.
52. Nikephoros Phokas, *Praecepta Militaria*, 3.65–73.
53. Dawson, *Byzantine Cavalryman*, pp. 37, 52.
54. Nikephoros Phokas, *Praecepta Militaria*, 3.54–65.
55. D'Amato, *Byzantine Imperial Guardsmen*, p. 51.
56. Dawson, *Byzantine Cavalryman*, pp. 42–4.
57. Dawson, *Byzantine Cavalryman*, pp. 17–20; Heath, *Byzantine Armies*, pp. 17–18.
58. Dawson, *Byzantine Cavalryman*, pp. 17–18.
59. Heath, *Byzantine Armies*, p. 5.
60. Dawson, *Byzantine Cavalryman*, pp. 17–18.
61. Heath, *Byzantine Armies*, p. 18.
62. Heath, *Byzantine Armies*, p. 20.
63. Nikephoros Phokas, *Praecepta Militaria*, 3.73–84.
64. Dawson, *Byzantine Cavalryman*, p. 19.
65. Nikephoros Phokas, *Praecepta Militaria*, 2.111–124.
66. Dawson, *Byzantine Cavalryman*, pp. 53–4.
67. Nikephoros Ouranos, *Taktika*, 61.204–214.
68. Nikephoros Phokas, *Praecepta Militaria*, 3.1–25.
69. Nikephoros Phokas, *Praecepta Militaria*, 2.124–139.
70. Gregory, *A History of Byzantium*, pp. 255–6.
71. McGeer, *Sowing the Dragon's Teeth*, p. 226.
72. McGeer, *Sowing the Dragon's Teeth*, pp. 179, 201, 214.
73. al-Mutanabbi, *to Sayf al-Dawla*.
74. McGeer, *Sowing the Dragon's Teeth*, pp. 222, 308.
75. McGeer, *Sowing the Dragon's Teeth*, pp. 226, 228, 312.
76. McGeer, *Sowing the Dragon's Teeth*, pp. 197, 228.
77. Haldon, *Byzantine Wars*, p. 96.
78. McGeer, *Sowing the Dragon's Teeth*, pp. 231–2, 314.
79. Nikonorov, 'Cataphracti, Catafractarii and Clibanarii', in *Military Archaeology*, p. 137.

80. Leo the Deacon, *The History*, 4.3.
81. McGeer, *Sowing the Dragon's Teeth*, p. 228.
82. Haldon, *Byzantine Wars*, pp. 96–7.
83. Leo the Deacon, *The History*, 5.2.
84. Haldon, *Byzantine Wars*, p. 97.
85. Haldon, *Byzantine Wars*, p. 97–9.
86. Haldon, *Byzantine Wars*, p. 99.
87. McGeer, *Sowing the Dragon's Teeth*, p. 316.
88. Leo the Deacon, *The History*, 8.4.
89. Haldon, *Byzantine Wars*, p. 99.
90. Haldon, *Byzantine Wars*, p. 99.
91. Leo the Deacon, *The History*, 8.9.
92. Haldon, *The Byzantine Wars*, 100.
93. Leo the Deacon, *The History*, 8.10.
94. Haldon, *The Byzantine Wars*, 100.
95. Leo the Deacon, *The History,* 9.1.
96. Haldon, *Byzantine Wars*, pp. 100–101.
97. Leo the Deacon, *The History*, 9.2.
98. Leo the Deacon, *The History,* 9.2.
99. Haldon, *Byzantine Wars*, p. 101.
100. Haldon, *Byzantine Wars*, p. 101.
101. Leo the Deacon, *The History*, p. 9.7.
102. Haldon, *Byzantine Wars*, pp. 101–2.
103. Haldon, *Byzantine Wars*, p. 103.
104. Leo the Deacon, *The History*, 9.8.
105. Haldon, *Byzantine Wars*, p. 103.
106. Haldon, *Byzantine Wars*, p. 103–4.
107. Leo the Deacon, *The History*, 9.10.
108. Haldon, *Byzantine Wars*, p. 104.
109. Haldon, *Byzantine Wars*, pp. 104–5.
110. McGeer, *Sowing the Dragon's Teeth*, pp. 316–7.
111. McGeer, *Sowing the Dragon's Teeth*, p. 317.
112. Nikephoros Ouranos, *Taktika*, 63.21–24.
113. Nikephoros Ouranos, *Taktika*, 63.29–32.
114. McGeer, *Sowing the Dragon's Teeth*, p. 317.
115. Dawson, *Byzantine Cavalryman*, p. 18; Heath, *Byzantine Armies*, p. 21.
116. Heath, *Byzantine Armies*, p. 36.
117. Dawson, *Byzantine Cavalryman*, p. 54.
118. Dawson, *Byzantine Cavalryman*, p. 12, 16; McGeer, *Sowing the Dragon's Teeth*, p. 318.

BIBLIOGRAPHY

Primary Sources

al-Mutanabbi, *to Sayf al-Dawla*
Ammianus Marcellinus, *Rerum Gestarum*
Appian, *The Syrian Wars*
Arrian, *Anabasis of Alexander*
Arrian, *Ars Tactica*
Cassius Dio, *Roman History*
Claudius Claudianus, *Panegyricus de sexto consulatu Honorii Augusti*
Claudius Claudianus, *In Rufinum*
Diodorus Siculus, *Universal History*
Eutropius, *Breviarium*
Festus, *Breviarium*
Heliodorus, *Aethiopica*
Herodian, *History of the Roman Empire*
Herodotus, *The Histories*
Josephus, *The Wars of the Jews*
Julian the Emperor, *Panegyric in Honor of the Emperor Constantinus, Oration I*
Leo the Deacon, *The History*
Libanius, *Funeral Oration upon the Emperor Julian*
Livy, *The History of Rome*
Maurice, *Strategikon*
Nazarius, *Panegyric of Constantine*
Nikephoros Ouranos, *Taktika*
Nikephoros Phokas, *Praecepta Militaria*
Plutarch, *Life of Crassus*
Plutarch, *Life of Lucullus*
Plutarch, *Moralia*
Polybius, *Histories*
Propertius, *The Elegies*
Quintus Curtius Rufus, *History of Alexander*
Scriptores Historiae Augustae, *Alexander Severus*
Scriptores Historiae Augustae, *Divus Aurelianus*
Scriptores Historiae Augustae, *Divus Claudius*
Strabo, *Geography*
Theophanes, *Chronicle*

Vegetius, *Epitome of Military Science*
Xenophon, *On Horsemanship*
Zosimus, *New History*

Secondary Sources

Alston, Richard, *Rome's Revolution: Death of the Republic and Birth of the Empire* (Oxford: Oxford University Press, 2015).
Bar-Kochva, Bezalel, *The Seleucid Army: Organization and Tactics in the Great Campaigns* (Cambridge: Cambridge University Press, 1976).
Baumer, Christoph, *The History of Central Asia: The Age of the Steppe Warrior* (London: I. B. Tauris, 2012).
Brzezinski, Richard, and Mariusz Mielczarek, *The Sarmatians 600 BC–AD 450* (Oxford: Osprey Publishing, 2002).
Cernenko, E.V., *Scythians 700–300 B.C.* (Oxford: Osprey Publishing, 1983).
Chahin, M., *The Kingdom of Armenia: A History* (Richmond: Curzon Press, 2001).
Cotterell, Arthur, *Chariot: From Chariot to Tank, the Astounding Rise and Fall of the World's First War Machine* (New York: The Overlook Press, 2004).
Curtis, Vesta Sarkhosh, and Sarah Stewart, (eds.), *The Age of the Parthians: The Idea of Iran Volume II* (London: I.B. Tauris, 2007).
D'Amato, Raffaele, *Byzantine Imperial Guardsmen 913–1025: The Tághmata and Imperial Guard* (Oxford: Osprey Publishing, 2012).
Daryaee, Touraj, *Sasanian Iran (224–651 CE): Portrait of a Late Antique Empire* (Costa Mesa: Mazda Publishers, Inc., 2008).
Dawson, Timothy, *Byzantine Cavalryman c. 900–1204* (Oxford: Osprey Publishing, 2009).
Eadie, John W., 'The Development of Roman Mailed Cavalry', in *The Journal of Roman Studies*, 57 (1967), pp. 161–73.
Farrokh, Kaveh, *Sassanian Elite Cavalry, AD 224–642* (Oxford: Osprey Publishing, 2005).
Gamber, Ortwin, 'Kataphrakten, Clibanarier, Normannenreiter', in *Jahrbuch der kunsthistorischen Sammlungen in Wien* (1968), pp. 7–44.
Grainger, John D., *The Rise of the Seleukid Empire (323–223 BC): Seleukos I to Seleukos III* (Barnsley: Pen & Sword, 2014).
Grainger, John D, *The Seleukid Empire of Antiochus III (223–187 BC)* (Barnsley: Pen & Sword, 2015).
Gregory, Timothy E., *A History of Byzantium* (Malden: Wiley-Blackwell, 2010).
Haldon, John, *The Byzantine Wars: Battles and Campaigns of the Byzantine Era* (Stroud: Tempus, 2001).
Healy, Mark, *The Ancient Assyrians* (Oxford: Osprey Publishing, 1991).
Heath, Ian, *Byzantine Armies 886–1118* (Oxford: Osprey Publishing, 1979).
Hoffmann, D, 'Das spätrömische Bewegungsheer und die "Notitia Dignitatum"', in *Epigraphische Studien 7.1 und 7.2* (Düsseldorf, 1969–1970).
Hyland, Ann, *The Horse in the Ancient World* (Westport: Praeger Publishers, 2003).

Karantabias, Mark-Anthony, 'The Crucial Development of Heavy Cavalry under Herakleios and His Usage of Steppe Nomad Tactics', in *Hirundo: The McGill Journal of Classical Studies* 4 (2005–2006), pp. 28–41.

Luttwak, Edward N, *The Grand Strategy of the Byzantine Empire* (Cambridge: Harvard University Press, 2009).

MacDowall, Simon, *Adrianople AD 378: The Goths Crush Rome's Legions* (Westport: Praeger Publishers, 2005).

MacDowall, Simon, *Late Roman Cavalryman AD 236–565* (Oxford: Osprey Publishing, 1995).

McGeer, Eric, *Sowing the Dragon's Teeth: Byzantine Warfare in the Tenth Century* (Washington, D.C.: Dumbarton Oaks, 1995).

Michalak, M., 'The Origins and Development of Sassanian Heavy Cavalry', in *Folia Orientalia* 24 (1987), pp. 73–86.

Mielczarek, Mariusz, *Cataphracti and Clibanarii: Studies on the Heavy Armoured Cavalry of the Ancient World* (Łódź: Officya Naukowa, 1993).

Mitchell, Stephen, *A History of the Later Roman Empire AD 284–641: The Transformation of the Ancient World* (Oxford: Blackwell Publishing, 2007).

Nicolle, David, *Romano-Byzantine Armies, 4th–9th Centuries* (Oxford: Osprey Publishing, 1992).

Nikonorov, Valerii P., 'Cataphracti, Catafractarii and Clibanarii: Another Look at the old problem of their Identifications', in *Military Archaeology: Weaponry and Warfare in the Historical and Social Perspective* (1998), pp. 131–8.

Potts, D. T., 'Cataphractus and kamāndār: Some Thoughts on the Dynamic Evolution of Heavy Cavalry and Mounted Archers in Iran and Central Asia', in *Bulletin of the Asia Institute* New Series, Vol. 21 (2007), pp. 149–58.

Rea, John R., 'A Cavalryman's Career, A.D. 384(?)–401', in *Zeitschrift für Papyrologie und Epigraphik* Bd. 56 (1984), pp. 79–88.

Sampson, Gareth C., *The Defeat of Rome in the East: Crassus, the Parthians, and the Disastrous Battle of Carrhae, 53 BC* (Philadelphia: Casemate, 2008).

Sekunda, Nick, *The Persian Army 560–330 BC* (Oxford: Osprey Publishing, 1992).

Sekunda, Nick, *The Seleucid and Ptolemaic Reformed Armies, 168–145 BC (v. 1): The Seleucid Army* (Montvert, 1994).

Sheldon, Rose Mary, *Rome's Wars in Parthia: Blood in the Sand* (London: Vallentine Mitchell, 2010).

Sidnell, Philip, *Warhorse: Cavalry in Ancient Warfare* (London: Hambledon Continuum, 2006).

Speidel, M.P., 'Catafractarii, Clibanarii and the Rise of the Later Roman Mailed Cavalry: A Gravestone from Claudiopolis in Bythinia'. *Epigraphica Anatolica*, 4 (1984), pp. 151–6.

Wilcox, Peter, *Rome's Enemies (3): Parthians and Sassanid Persians* (Oxford: Osprey Publishing, 1986).

INDEX